PSYCHOLOGICAL NEEDS AND POLITICAL BEHAVIOR

PSYCHOLOGICAL NEEDS AND POLITICAL BEHAVIOR

A THEORY OF PERSONALITY AND POLITICAL EFFICACY

Stanley Allen Renshon

City University of New York, Lehman College

Fp

THE FREE PRESS
A Division of Macmillan Publishing Co., Inc.
NEW YORK

Collier Macmillan Publishers
LONDON

The Free Press
A Division of Macmillan Publishing Co., Inc.
866 Third Avenue, New York, N.Y. 10022

Collier–Macmillan Canada Ltd.

Library of Congress Catalog Card Number: 73-11735

Printed in the United States of America

printing number
1 2 3 4 5 6 7 8 9 10

Library of Congress Cataloging in Publication Data

Renshon, Stanley Allen.
Psychological needs and political behavior.

Bibliography: p.
1. Political psychology. 2. Personality.
3. Political participation--United States. I. Title.
[DNLM: 1. Personality. 2. Politics. 3. Social behavior. JA74.5 R421p 1974]
JA74.5.R45 320'.01'9 73-11735
ISBN 0-02-926320-4

For Nancy, who showed me it was all possible

CONTENTS

PREFACE

In the several years that have passed since I began this project, my thinking has changed considerably. What started in my mind as a rather narrowly stated problem, has progressively expanded in both scope and context. My thinking on the problem continues to evolve, and I am faced with presenting a book that appears to suggest closure, when in fact there is the continuing desire to write, rewrite, expand, and interpret.

I began this study by asking myself why some people participate in political life, while others, who appear to be no less directly affected by the government, do not take part. As I examined the problem it became clear to me that the beginnings of an adequate answer would have to involve several disciplines, and that the context of my original question would have to be considerably broadened.

This book is meant to address itself to the analysis of a series of propositions about the motivation for, and the implications of, participation in American political life. As such, I hope it will be a useful addition to the understanding of this part of the political world. But I would also like to place this work in a somewhat larger context; namely, the relationship between applied empirical research and American democracy.

Most social scientists recognize the distinction between making a value judgment and the study of particular phenomena. The accumulation of understanding and knowledge depends in part on the presentation of propositions about reality which are subject to replication and open to invalidation. There are however, the related questions: (1) of what use is this information and (2) to what use will it be put.

The accumulation of knowledge can be justified from a variety of positions. My own reason for selecting this particular problem and not some other is the desire to increase the viability of democratic systems by increasing our understanding of the psychological processes and implications of these systems in action. Related to the question of usefulness is the question of the use that the information will be put to, and it is at this point that the relationship between applied empirical research and public policy becomes clearer.

Public policy implies a selection of particular courses of action from a number of possibilities. These decisions must be based on accurate information about the likely consequences of particular forms of action. It is here that empirical social science can provide some help. If we want to know what the consequences of limiting or enlarging citizen participation in the political system are, social science research can help to provide some data on the relationships between participation and orientations to political authority, or a number of related questions. Such information, however, is only a part of the policy-making process, for the information is not useful without a goal or series of goals toward which the policy is aimed. In this sense, empirical theory and political values are symbiotic, not mutually exclusive. Although values may influence the selection of a particular topic and the information gained may help to further a particular value, the use of social science techniques hopefully allows the researcher to have values and yet guard against the possibility of systematic bias in the design, analysis, and interpretation of the data. Systematic bias may have the desired result of "proving" a particular contention, but, since this bias is based on wish rather than reality, it suffers as a guide to action. Desire (wish) does play a role in the policy process. However, the question of what the relationships are among the motivation, nature, and satisfaction derived from participation is a related but different one from the question of how we can increase participation. In part, then, I would like to place this work within the "policy sciences" framework developed several decades ago by one of the most original social science thinkers of our time: Harold D. Lasswell.

Finally, I would like to state that this work on the origins, development, and political implications of the need for personal control is part of a strong and growing interest in the psychology of democratic man. I believe that this is an extremely important area of research and one in which political psychologists can make a concrete contribution. There needs to be a great deal of additional work on the theory of democratic personality characteristics and, even more importantly, further study of the factors that facilitate or retard the development of these characteristics. I am not the first to believe that personal control is an important component of the democratic character. What I sincerely hope this study contributes to in this area is the beginning of understanding, based on empirical research, of some of the factors that facilitate the development of personal control. I do not for a moment believe that this characteristic is *the* defining characteristic of democratic people, but I do think that without it the democratic person cannot develop. Obviously, much research is needed. In that sense, this book, rather than being a completed product, is only a beginning.

SAR

ACKNOWLEDGMENTS

Looking back over the years of work on this project I can only marvel at the great number of people who gave generously of their time and talents and who, in a most direct way, made this book possible. The interviewers, especially Miss Jane Tierney, were both dependable and excellent. Miss Lyn Carole did an unusually fine job of typing and editing the first draft, along with raising a number of interesting and important questions. Mrs. Sylvia Katz has done an equally excellent job retyping the subsequent drafts of this manuscript with great cheer and efficiency.

A number of people read parts or all of this manuscript in various forms. They are of course not directly responsible for any errors of commission and omission on my part. They are, however, responsible in many instances for extremely useful comments, which have really helped me. I would like to express my thanks to Alexander George, Jeanne Knutson, George Marcus, Karl Deutsch, and Willard Kiem. Neal Cutler read the whole manuscript and proved to be an invaluable source of ideas and information, as well as a helpful prodder when the going was slow. Both the book and the author owe much to him.

Finally, a number of people who did not read the manuscript helped me in extended conversations about the ideas that I had. My discussions with David Schwartz expanded my interests and horizons in the area of psychology and politics, as have my discussions with Steve Elkin and Noel Kaplowitz. A special word of thanks is due to Kenneth Gergen, chairman of the Psychology Department, Swarthmore College, where I was a visiting lecturer in the spring of 1972. His wide knowledge of the variety of psychological approaches to social phenomena served as both a stimulant and a model.

A great deal of the work on this manuscript was facilitated by a grant from the National Institute of Mental

Health, which supported the author as a Postdoctoral Fellow in psychology and politics at Yale University during the 1972–1973 academic year. I wish to express my thanks for this valuable support.

Lastly, and most importantly, my wife Nancy has helped in so many ways that I truthfully feel that without her this book could not have been written. As an organizer she is without equal, but more importantly her ability to help me over the rough spots, both emotional and intellectual, was invaluable. Her encouragement, patience, and persistence were instrumental at so many points along the way that I have lost count. This book is dedicated to you, Nancy.

SAR

PSYCHOLOGICAL NEEDS AND POLITICAL BEHAVIOR

Chapter One

THE NEED FOR PERSONAL CONTROL:

AN INTRODUCTION AND OVERVIEW

This book has two major, related themes. The first is that there is within each of us a desire to have some control over the people, events, and processes that impact upon and shape our lives. The second is that there are important political consequences that flow from this desire. Subsequent chapters of this book are meant to introduce, explicate, analyze, and draw out the political importance of these dual themes.

The first theme revolves around what I have called the need for personal control.[1] Briefly stated, it is my contention that each person has within him a basic need to gain control over his physical and psychological life-space. A person's life-space can be as varied as human experience, but generally refers to those aspects of the environment that are perceived by the individual to be important in the ongoing pursuit of his goals, values, or needs. Very often this will include neither politics nor the political system. By political system I refer to the people, institutions, and processes that are perceived to have the power and/or authority to make decisions which are binding on both the individual and the other components of the social system. Why is it, we might ask, that the political system is not perceived as salient by its citizens?

Several reasons are possible for the decreased salience of

[1] The term "personal control" was first utilized in an article by P. Gurin *et al.*, "Internal-External Control in the Motivational Dynamics of Negro Youth," *Journal of Social Issues*, 55, 1969, *passim*. However, nowhere do they refer to *the need for personal control* which would have linked political attitudes with basic personality orientations.

politics. First, an individual may not see that the outputs of the political system have any impact on the way he lives his life. This in turn may be the case because the political system has neither the ability nor the inclination to become involved in those areas. An example of the first would be a political system in which neither the administrative nor communications resources to implement intervention were available. On the other hand, the norms of the political system (one aspect of political culture) might circumscribe the areas of activity for political decision makers. It is also possible that the individual sees the link between the political system and his life as taking place in areas that are not of immediate concern to him, thereby decreasing the importance of politics.

Yet, if all of these are explanations of the nonsalience of politics, they also point to the conditions under which politics and the political system do become important. Governments waiting to modernize seek to bring previously autonomous groups under centralized authority. Other more "modern" countries find that the solution of the increasingly complex social and economic problems of mass societies require government intervention in areas that previously were defined as "private sectors." The end result is that the number and scope of the areas which are regulated by the political system is steadily increasing, with the corresponding increase in the possibility that the areas being regulated will be perceived as important to the individual. In the United States, for example, the circumstances of our arrival into the world and our departure from it are subject to a variety of political regulations. All of these considerations would appear to suggest the increasing importance of the political sphere as a control relevant, or important part, of the individual's life-space.

When politics is perceived to be a control-relevant aspect of the individual's psychological life-space, the link is forged between psychological needs and political life. This book is an attempt to trace this relationship between human psychological needs and political life, by focusing on one specific need, the need for personal control. There is of course the danger that by focusing on one need—its origins, development, and political implications—some will gain the mistaken impression that I mean to convey that it is the only or most relevant explanation of political orientations and political actions. I do not subscribe to unicausal explanations of any social phenomena, including political life. Rather with full knowledge that I have excluded other important needs, I have chosen to focus on one in order to detail the fit between human needs and political life and to follow the origins, development and political implications of this need in both a theoretical and empirical way.

In addition, rather than focus on one facet of the relationship between the need for personal control and political life, I have attempted to trace the relationship through a number of diverse, but related, areas of analysis. The result is that this book deals in part with political theory, in part with psychological theory, in part with political socialization, in part with political attitudes, and in part with political behavior. For some this will prove to be too many parts. Yet my central concern is to trace an important concept from its origins to its implications. In order to carry out this self-assigned task, it seems reasonable to touch upon a number of areas, all of which are connected by their relations to the need for personal control.

Two major methods are utilized in this book to investigate the need for personal control and its political implications. The first is a systematic and critical analysis of a variety of relevant literatures. These include a variety of personality theories, socialization theories, and literatures dealing with specific political traits, such as political efficacy and political alienation. The second is a presentation of some empirical data obtained from a study designed to examine some of the dimensions and implications of the need for personal control.

Several words should be said about the data. The sample (N = 300) consists of a randomly selected group of university undergraduates, interviewed several times. The author is only too painfully aware of the limitations of the sample. No claim is made for its representativeness. *It is felt that the most important thrust of this research lies in the relationships uncovered is indicators of important future research possibilities.* Therefore, throughout the presentation of the empirical data *we will be concerned with uncovering relationships, rather than generalizing our results to populations.* We emphasize these remarks, because as Jeanne Knutson has perceptively written, "Too often reviews have been written, which, ignoring the value of the relationships uncovered, could be summarized under the heading of 'But are students people?' "[2] It is hoped that the ideas and relationships uncovered in this book will serve to stimulate additional research in this area. This work is not meant to be a final definitive statement, nor is it meant to be a brief introduction. Rather it is hoped that the work contained herein will provide a firm and valuable base from which to build more complex models of the linkages between a variety of human needs and their complex outplay in political life. Lastly, this book is meant to detail the ways in which politically important attitudes (in this case, political efficacy) can profitably be linked with personality theory, and as such provide another perspective on the growing realization of the utility of psychological explanations in political analysis.[3]

[2] Jeanne Knutson, *The Human Basis of the Polity* (Chicago: Aldine-Atherton, 1973), p. 174.

[3] For a recent and eloquent statement along these lines, see Fred Greenstein, "Political Psychology: A Pluralistic Universe," in J. Knutson (ed.), *Handbook of Political Psychology* (San Francisco: Jossey-Bass, 1973).

Chapter Two deals with the relationship between political theory and political participation, focusing on the questions of the nature and extent of political participation in a given political system and the meaning given to these findings. The chapter then goes on to analyze two traditional explanations of political participation, political utility (the search for political rewards), and civic obligation (the perception that the good-citizen role requires certain levels of participation). Certain problems are analyzed for both these explanations, including some data which suggests that many people define the good-citizen role without any reference to political behavior.

Of course, there is a third traditional explanation of political participation, and that is political efficacy, or the feeling of effectiveness and capacity in the political sphere.[4] Chapter Three deals with the traditional concept of political efficacy, including its conceptualization, reliability, operationalization, and motivational dynamics. In this chapter, after reviewing a number of considerations, we suggest that efficacy itself, under specified conditions, can be intrinsically motivating. The chapter suggests, therefore, that in order to build a viable theory of political efficacy, it is first necessary to establish the psychological basis which underlies the feelings of political efficacy and then to examine the conditions under which efficacy may be intrinsically motivating.

Chapter Four formally presents the concept of a need for personal control. A formal definition is introduced and explicated in terms of the nature and scope of the need for personal control. Of course to propose a need is one matter, and to provide evidence to support its existence is another. This chapter surveys a variety of areas of psychological research and theory to provide support for the hypothesis that there is within each of us a need to have control over rele-

[4] David Easton and Jack Dennis, "The Child's Acquisition of Regime Norms: Political Efficacy," *The American Political Science Review*, 61, 1967, p. 25.

vant aspects of our life-space. In this chapter, comparative (animal) psychology, psychoanalytic theory, neo-Freudian theory, developmental psychology, and "third force" psychological theories are examined and suggested to provide support for the existence of the need for personal control. To suggest the existence of a need for personal control is only a first step, however, for important questions remain to be answered about the origins and development of this need.

Chapter Five begins the processes of detailing the origins and nature of the development of the need for personal control. In this chapter we suggest that the need for personal control arises out of the existential condition of newborn human life, namely, dependency. It is with reference to such physiological needs as food and water that the need for personal control develops. We suggest that, out of the early experience of trying to satisfy these biological and other needs, the child develops basic beliefs about the nature of the world.

These beliefs are suggested to be five in number: (1) beliefs about the nature of physical reality, (2) beliefs about the potential for individual action in the world (personal control), (3) beliefs involving evaluations of the world (that is, whether it is hostile or friendly), (4) beliefs about the other persons who occupy the life-space of the individual (that is, whether people are basically good and can be trusted), and (5) beliefs about the self (that is, whether the self has a positive or negative valence). These basic beliefs are then explicated and examined in the context of a general theory of psychological needs and human development, with specific applicability to the analysis of political life.

While Chapter Five is concerned with a general theory of psychological needs and basic beliefs as a suitable model for the explanation of a variety of political behaviors, Chapter Six is concerned with specifically positing and explicating the relationship between the need for personal control and the political system. In this chapter we suggest that political efficacy may be defined as the belief that one has sufficient personal control over political processes to satisfy the need for personal control. Thus, we suggest that the need for personal control is a necessary but insufficient component of political efficacy, and that political efficacy is, therefore, an attitudinal manifestation of a basic personality orientation. It is only when the political system becomes control relevant, however, that the need for personal control is transposed to political life.

In this chapter we discuss three kinds of political salience; political-reward salience, political-punishment salience, and political-obligation salience. After this discussion we go on to suggest the kinds of behaviors one might hypothesize, given the need for personal control and a high degree of political salience, including greater rates of political participation. Lastly, this chapter sets out some of the implications of the need for personal control for democratic theory in general and more specifically for the whole argument over participatory democracy.

With these considerations as background, Chapter Seven goes on to present a detailed suggestion for the reconceptualization of the political-efficacy concept based on the important consideration of the need for personal control. We suggest that such a reconceptualization might take place along the lines suggested by Julian Rotter in his work on the perceived internal-versus-external sources of rewards for individual behavior. Rotter suggests that those who do not view their rewards in life as contingent upon their own behavior (that is, those with a need for personal control but a lack of need satisfaction) may attribute their outcomes to either luck, fate, the designs of powerful others, or to great complexity. This chapter develops each of these four possibilities with specific reference to the political system.

Chapter Eight presents the research design used to analyze various dimensions and implications of the need for personal control. Attention is focused both on the data collection and the nature of the questions asked. The major variable with which we are concerned is the degree of personal control, and as Chapter Seven suggests, the work, and more specifically the scale, developed by Julian Rotter is introduced and explicated. In addition, the other dimensions of social and political life to be explored in subsequent chapters are introduced.

Chapter Nine is the first of three chapters dealing with socialization and personal control. In this chapter we attempt to trace some general considerations in examining the socialization experience in relation to personal control. More specifically, this chapter examines the impact of culture on the acquisition and definition of personal control. We then go on to systematically explore the impact of the larger socioeconomic context within which socialization for personal control takes place. The impact of wealth, family norms, and job status are specifically analyzed in relation to their impact upon the acquisition of personal control.

With these general considerations as background, we then go on to present and analyze some data dealing specifically with the impact of family authority relationships and the acquisition of personal control. Specifically, we examine the impact of who makes the family rules, the consistency of rule application, and the degree of autonomy allowed while growing up on the acquisition of personal control. The hypotheses explored in Chapter Ten include:

1. The greater the autonomy allowed while growing up, the greater the personal control.

2. The more "democratic" the family decision-making structure, the greater the personal control.

3. The greater the consistency of rule enforcement, the greater the personal control.

Chapter Eleven deals with the emotional dimension of family life and its impact on personal control. In this chapter we analyze the impact of parental trust, parental empathy, and the nature of family composition. Specifically, we explore the following hypotheses:

1. The greater the trust in parents, the greater the personal control.
2. The greater the perceived parental empathy, the greater the personal control.
3. The later the sequential arrival into the family, the greater the personal control.

In addition, Chapter Eleven presents a multivariate analysis of the relative impact of all of the dimensions of family life that we have been considering, including the direct transmission of basic personal orientations from parents to their children. Our data suggests the importance of the family in the socialization process, but in a way somewhat different from conventional explanations.

Chapter Twelve turns from a focus on the conceptualization and development of the need for personal control to a consideration of its psychodynamics. In this chapter we explore some of the relations between personal control, the self, and the political system. A number of areas are examined, including interpersonal trust, life satisfaction, faith in government, and evaluations of the political system. Some of the hypotheses explored in this chapter include:

1. The greater the personal control, the greater the degree of interpersonal trust.
2. The greater the level of personal control, the greater the degree of life satisfaction.
3. The greater the level of personal control, the greater the political trust.

4. The greater the degree of personal control, the greater the perceived effectiveness.

5. The greater the degree of personal control, the more rewarding the outputs of the political system will be perceived.

Chapter Thirteen continues our inquiry into the political correlates of personal control. Specifically, we examine the relation between personal control and political alienation, political time orientations, governmental accessibility, and governmental effectiveness. Specifically, the hypotheses we explore in this chapter include:

1. The greater the degree of personal control, the less the political alienation.

2. The greater the personal control, the less the desire of immediate political rewards.

3. The greater the degree of personal control, the more accessible the government will be perceived to be.

4. The greater the degree of personal control, the more effective the government will be rated.

Of course as social scientists have been pointing out for a long time, there is or can be a great difference between attitudes and behaviors. Chapter Fourteen is designed to deal specifically with the impact of the need for personal control on the extent and nature of political participation. To this end we collected data on participation in numerous political activities, including both the traditional (working for a candidate, writing letters) and less traditional activities (mass-demonstrations, sit-ins, and political violence). In addition to this recall data, our survey was conducted around two concrete political events, to provide an additional check on the results. A need theory of political efficacy and political participation would hypothesize that given a need for personal control and a degree of political salience, greater, and not lesser, amounts of political participation would result. Our findings appear to provide some support for the hypothesis and additional support for the importance of the need for personal control. In addition, a number of variables are utilized in a multivariate model to assess the relative importance of a number of the variables we have been discussing in the explanation of political participation.

Chapter Fifteen takes up an important question; one with the most profound implications for the stability and persistence of the political system. Namely, how does an individual select the mode of political participation. More specifically, is there anything we can say about the circumstances in which one selects to participate in political violence or more traditional behaviors? In order to obtain some insight into this problem we asked each respondent to rate the effectiveness of a group of political behaviors ranging from voting to political assassination. We then utilized some of the political attitudes discussed, and also incorporated the basic belief of personal control, to try to determine which circumstances were associated with either the selection or rejection of political violence as an effective method to obtain personal control. Our results suggest that unmet needs have an important and deleterious impact on political behavior and political systems.

At this point we will have come full circle, having introduced and traced the need for personal control in a variety of frameworks and under a variety of conditions. Chapter Sixteen sums up our theories and findings and goes on to suggest the political relevance of the need for personal control with specific reference to democratic theory.

With this overview in mind, let us begin our task and set the stage for the analysis to follow by examining political theory and political participation.

Chapter Two

POLITICAL THEORY AND POLITICAL PARTICIPATION

Political participation has been an area of concern for both political theorists and practitioners for some time. Interest in this area has been closely related to political theory in general and more recently to democratic political theory in particular.

The relationship between political theory and political participation has its roots in the attempt to answer three questions of perennial interest in political life: (1) how much and what kind of citizen participation is desirable, (2) what in fact is the nature and extent of citizen participation in any given political system, and (3) what are the consequences for the political system, given the answers to questions (1) and (2).

The attempt to analyze how much and what kind of citizen participation is most desirable has traditionally been an integral part of political philosophy. Political theorists within this tradition have been involved in the politics of possibilities, or the attempt "to state the necessary or sufficient conditions for obtaining ends which for one reason or another are deemed good or desirable."[1] Sometimes this search has led political theorists to different positions on the complex problem of the optimal relation between citizenship and political participation. Plato, for example, separated the concept of citizenship from the opportunity for participation in political decision-making. As Wolin notes: "Plato did not deny that each member of the community, no matter how humble his contribution, had a right to share the benefits of the community; what he did deny was that his contribution could be erected into a claim

[1] Sheldon Wolin, *Politics and Vision* (Boston: Little, Brown, 1960), p. 13.

to share in the decision-making."[2] Aristotle, on the other hand, starting from a different set of assumptions about human nature and capacities, was led to a different position on the relationship between citizenship and political participation. He rejected Plato's distinction between the politically active elites of the polity and the politically passive citizens. Aristotle's definition of a citizen was one who took part in the legislative and judicial deliberations of the polity.[3]

While the desirability of citizen participation was, and for some may still be, an issue for political theorists, later scholars concerned with democratic institutions and representative government have begun with the assumption that some form of citizen participation is desirable. Indeed, citizen participation has been incorporated as one of the defining characteristics of political democracy. Thus, Ranney and Kendall have defined one of the four basic principles of democracy as political equality, or "an equal chance of each member of the community to participate in the total decision-making process of the whole community."[4] Along the same lines, Neubauer has suggested that "by definition, political democracy in Nation or State requires some minimal level of citizen participation in political decision-making."[5]

While contemporary democratic theorists no longer appear to debate the inherent desirability of some citizen participation, a debate has developed over the meaning of the findings associated with the attempt to answer the

[2] *Ibid.*, p. 57.

[3] Richard McKeon (ed.), *The Basic Works of Aristotle* (New York: Oxford U. Press, 1941), *passim.*

[4] Austin Ranney and Willmore Kendall, *Democracy and the American Party System* (New York: Harcourt, Brace & World, 1956), Chapter 2.

[5] Deane Neubauer, "Some Conditions of Democracy," *American Political Science Review*, 61, 1967, pp. 1002–1009.

second question; namely, what is the nature of political participation in the United States. The emergence in the last 20 years of the sophisticated descriptive capacities of survey research has allowed an unprecedented amount of information to be gathered about the behavioral and attitudinal orientations of the citizenry in this and other countries. Research findings have repeatedly confirmed the lack of information,[6] interest,[7] and activity[8] that characterizes many citizens. Similar research in other democratic countries suggest that the same is true cross-nationally.[9] Summing up the research findings in the area, one political scientist notes:

> About one-third of the American adult population can be characterized as politically apathetic or passive. . . . another 60% play largely spectator roles in the political process; they watch, they cheer, they vote, but they do not do battle. . . . probably only one or two percent can be called gladiators.[10]

While the results of this research may be clear, the implications for the political system (question 3) are a matter of serious debate by political scientists. Milbrath, for example, suggests that "there is doubt that society as a whole would benefit if intense interest and active involvement became widespread through the population."[11] Other po-

[6] Bernard Berelson *et al.*, Voting (Chicago: University of Chicago Press, 1954).

[7] Seymour Lipset, *Political Man* (Garden City, N.Y.: Doubleday, 1960), *passim.*

[8] Julian Woodward and Elmo Roper, "Political Activity of American Citizens," *American Political Science Review*, 44, 1950, pp. 972–975.

[9] Stein Rokkan, "Cross-National Studies of Political Participation," *International Social Science Journal*, 12, 1960, pp. 7–14.

[10] Lester Milbrath, *Political Participation* (Chicago: Rand McNally, 1965), p. 21.

[11] *Ibid.*, p. 147.

litical scientists have suggested that widespread citizen participation may not be necessary because "elites may anticipate possible demands and activities and act in response to what they anticipate. They act responsively not because citizens are actively making demands, but in order to keep them from becoming active."[12] Perhaps the clearest expression of this position comes from Professor Lane Davis, who suggests that in contemporary democracy, popular rule means only the periodic election of elites who make political decisions, and "although popular participation may often go well beyond this minimum, this is strictly speaking, a matter of indifference to the theory."[13]

Other political theorists have not been quite so sanguine about the low levels of citizen participation. E. E. Schattschneider has warned that narrow ranges of political participation in determining political choices may undermine the long-term stability of the political system.[14] Other theorists have suggested that low levels of citizen participation do not originate in satisfaction with the political system, but rather with a deep sense of despair about the possibility for producing any changes. According to this view, low participation is the sign of a diseased rather than a healthy polity.[15]

It is important to note that both interpretations of the meaning of the empirical findings rest on unstated and untested assumptions about the functions of political participation. What is at issue here is not only the rate of

[12] Gabriel Almond and Sidney Verba, *The Civic Culture* (Princeton: Princeton University Press, 1963), p. 487.

[13] Lane Davis, "The Cost of Realism: Contemporary Restatements of Democracy," *Western Political Science Quarterly*, 17, 1964, pp. 43–44.

[14] E. E. Schattschneider, *The Semi-Sovereign People* (New York: Holt, Rinehart & Winston, 1960), *passim*.

[15] Jack Walker, "A Critique of the Elitist Theory of Democracy," *American Political Science Review*, 60, 1966, pp. 285–295.

participation, but the meanings of political participation to the citizen. *The assumption that low, or for that matter high, levels of political participation indicate citizen satisfaction rests on assumptions both about the efficacy of the behavior and its ability to satisfy the original motivation to participate in political activities.* Yet the link or links between the motivation to participate in politics, the modes of participation chosen, and the resulting level of satisfaction remains largely unchartered territory. We are thus in a curious position of not knowing why and under what circumstances certain types of participation are selected, and the relation between the selection of the participation mode, the satisfaction derived from it, and the implications of these considerations for the political system.

Traditional explanations of the origins of participation have not been lacking. Generally these explanations have focused on three major explanatory concepts: (1) political utility, (2) civic obligation, and (3) political efficacy. The first two are traditionally put forward as explanations for the motivation to participate in politics, while the third is put forward not so much as an explanation as it is as a correlate of participation. Each of these concepts has played a large role in the explanation of the motivation to participate in politics, yet an analysis of each suggests that, as general explanations for political participation, each has considerable problems.

POLITICAL UTILITY

If Easton is correct in describing the political system as being concerned with the authoritative allocation of values,[16] then clearly one motivation to participate in politics is to obtain some of these values. This assumption is the

16 David Easton, A *Framework for Political Analysis* (Englewood Cliffs, N.J.: Prentice-Hall, 1965), p. 50.

basis for what might be called the "exchange theory of political participation." The idea of exchange comes to political science via two routes—economic-utility theory and behaviorist psychology.

Briefly stated, utility theory in economics is based on the assumption that

> an individual gains utility (or satisfaction) from the consumption of goods and services (or rewards). . . . Total utility is the total amounts of satisfaction obtained from obtaining various quantities of rewards. . . . the more of a reward obtained per unit of time, the greater the utility (or satisfaction) any individual will receive up to a certain point.[17]

The focus of economic-utility theory is to explain an individual's participation in the market place. Recently, however, it has been utilized to explain an individual's participation in the political process. Here, as in economics, the assumption is that "political actors seek utility in the same way that economic actors do, and that they attempt, therefore, to make exchange decisions . . . to get more rewards than they currently do."[18] Just as economic-utility theory requires certain assumptions about the market context within which exchange takes place, in the same manner does its application to the political system require certain assumptions. According to Curry and Wade, these assumptions are that (1) preferences to maximize individual rewards and to minimize individual costs are given and fixed for each actor, (2) each actor prefers the systems constitution to any alternative set of rules, and he accepts the system's allocation of rewards and costs; and (3) resources controlled by individuals and the government are

[17] R. L. Curry and L. L. Wade, A *Theory of Political Exchange* (Englewood Cliffs, N.J.: Prentice-Hall, 1966), pp. 5–6.

[18] *Ibid.*, p. 9.

fixed in quantity, quality, and distribution.[19] We shall comment on these assumptions shortly.

Somewhat less economics-oriented, is the exchange theory derived from the work of B. F. Skinner, but most clearly associated with the work of Homans.[20] Homans, in an attempt to explain human behavior, has put forward five laws which when taken together constitute the basic framework within which exchange takes place in social life. These laws have been called "fundamental social process" and are as follows:[21]

1. If in the past the occurrence of a particular stimulus or set of stimuli has been the occasion on which a man's activity has been rewarded, then the more similar the present stimulus to the past one, the more likely he is to emit that activity, or some similar activity in response to the present stimulus.
2. The more often a person's activity has been rewarded, the more likely he is to perform the activity.
3. The more valuable the reward of an activity is to a person, the more likely he is to perform that activity.
4. The more often in the recent past a person has received a particular reward, the less valuable any further reward becomes to him.
5. When the person's activity does not receive the reward he expects, or receives punishment, he will be angry, and in anger, the results of aggressive behavior are rewarding.

A review of these principles has led one political scientist to the conclusion that

19 *Ibid.*, p. 35.

20 George Homans, *Social Behavior, Its Elementary Forms* (New York: Harcourt, Brace & World, 1969). Homans notes his intellectual debt to Skinner in both his Preface and on p. 18.

21 *Ibid.*, pp. 51–82.

> Exchange theory in our view provides a powerful means for explaining *all* activities (behaviors), including those we call sentiments. It explains behavior that is oriented towards ends that can only be achieved through interaction with other persons and that seeks to adapt means to further the achievement of these ends.[22]

Viewed from the perspective of exchange theory, one might posit that an exchange theory of political participation would assume that the decision to take part in politics is motivated by the desire to obtain rewards.

Clearly, the idea of reward is crucial to the utilization of exchange theory in either social or political life. We have suggested that in economics the concept of reward includes any goods or services that brought about satisfaction (utility). As Curry and Wade note, it is only as a convention that economists deal with resources in monetary terms. When applying the concept of reward to political action, they note that

> we can express the same idea in terms of any type of marginal evaluations placed on anything that people are interested in, regardless of the index of valuation used. It makes no difference whether the index is money, social approval, power, respect or any other individual or social value.[23]

For Homans the concept of reward is synonymous with reinforcers. A reinforcer appears to be any stimulus that either increases the likelihood of given response (positive reinforcer) or decreases its likelihood (negative reinforcer).[24]

[22] Sidney Waldman, *Foundations of Political Action: An Exchange Theory of Politics* (Boston: Little, Brown, 1973), p. 1.

[23] Curry and Wade, *op. cit.*, p. 10.

[24] Homans, *op. cit.*, p. 24.

Homans notes that the discontinuation of a negative reinforcer may itself be a positive reinforcer, just as the discontinuation of a positive reinforcer may be a negative reinforcer. In his application of Homan's theory to political behavior, Waldman suggests that reward is the satisfaction of anything that a man needs, wants, or values.[25]

Having looked at some basic elements in the exchange paradigm, we are now in a position to point out several problems. Some of these are specific to the economically oriented paradigm and some to both paradigms.

The assumption that men seek to maximize rewards is an assumption that contains several difficulties. One difficulty has been noted by Simon who contends that some men may be "satisficers" rather than "maximizers."[26] That is, certain people may be content with only incremental gains, while others will be satisfied with only the most they can obtain in a given situation. Moreover, the same can be said for the rewards themselves. Is it the case that all rewards must be maximized? Are there some rewards that an individual is willing to have less of than others? Thus, an individual may desire a variety of possible rewards, some of which he wants to maximize and others of which he may be willing just to satisfy. Finally, there may be particular contexts where an individual who has previously been a "satisficer" becomes a maximizer of the same reward. The congressman who wants to run for higher public office may not be satisfied with a one-vote margin of victory.

These remarks suggest that Curry and Wade's first assumption about the fixed nature of maximization may have to be modified. The same is true of their second assumption. The suggestion that individuals accept the system's

[25] Waldman, *op. cit.*, p. 3.

[26] Herbert Simon, *Models of Man* (New York: Wiley & Sons, 1957), p. 247.

allocation of rewards and costs, while useful for their model, appears to be contrary to the political experiences of this country in the last eight years.[27]

Along the same lines, a further problem is raised by the low rates of political participation by the citizenry. Certainly, there is no theoretical reason to assume that the desire to obtain rewards from the political system is limited to the small percentage of active participants at all levels of society that engage in systematic political activity.[28] Thus, while it may be true that people participate in politics in order to gain rewards, the real problem, as Barber points out, "is to understand why people do political rather than other things."[29] We might add that the other side of that problem is to understand why people do not do political rather than other things.

The concept of reward itself presents crucial problems to exchange explanations of political behavior. The idea that people take part in the political system to obtain some rewards seems intuitively accurate. After all, the political system is the place where millions in contracts can be awarded, new hospitals built, and new housing put up, not to mention the esteem and power rewards to political leadership. Yet, herein lies the problem, for even if it is true that the motivation to participate is the likelihood of reward, one is still left with the problem of specifying the reward. Recent empirical and theoretical work has established varied motives for participation. Wilson and Banfield have reported that some groups apparently vote in order to obtain immediate material rewards, such as hospitals, increased

[27] The increased participation of a variety of minority groups, from women to gay liberations members, not to mention the more traditional racial and ethnic groups, suggests not everyone is satisfied with the present distributional arrangements.

[28] Milbrath, *op. cit.*, p. 19.

[29] James Barber, *Citizen Politics* (Chicago: Markham, 1969), p. 17.

veteran's pension, and so forth.[30] Keniston[31] and Fishman[32] have noted that student activists participate out of ideological conviction rather than the desire for material benefits, and Lane[33] has suggested that a variety of unconscious needs, such as relief of intrapsychic tension, are often satisfied by political participation.

In short, people appear to participate in politics for a variety of reasons, each of which might be subsumed under the concept of reward. Yet, assembling these varied motives under the reward rubric does not extend our understanding of political participation. The level of generality that would place these motives together obscures, in our view, important differences relevant to the understanding of the motivation to participate and the selection of participation modes.

Finally, aside from all the problems mentioned above, there remains the problem of measurement. If we adapt the definition of reward used by Homans, we are forced to see how much behavior over a specified period of time is elicited by the stimulus before it can be called a reinforcer. Such a definition allows for post hoc explanation but not for prediction. If a prediction is made about a person's behavior based on our perception of his needs, desires or values and it proves erroneous, one is always capable of suggesting that we did not really understand his values. We are thus in a position where empirical results could cause substitution of particular values, desires or needs, but not an abandonment of the theory.

In order to make an accurate prediction about a person's

30 James Wilson and Edward Banfield, "Political Ethos Revisited," *American Political Science Review*, 65, 1971, p. 1055.

31 Kenneth Keniston, "The Sources of Student Dissent," *Journal of Social Issues*, 4, 1967, pp. 108–137.

32 J. Fishman and F. Solomon, "Youth and Social Action," *Journal of Social Issues*, 2, 1964, pp. 1–2.

33 Robert Lane, *Political Life* (New York: Free Press, 1959), especially Chapter 9.

exchange behavior we need to know the level of need at time one, the extent to which the satisfaction of that need is valued, and the amount of time since the last satisfaction of that desire. It does not profit us to suggest that

> in-so-far as we can establish that a person needs a particular reward or set of rewards and *in-so-far as we are willing to grant that there are no substitutes for this reward* (that is, no other rewards that can satisfy the want or need for this particular reward) we can estimate what the value of the reward will be.[34] (Emphasis added.)

We have already touched on the problem establishing the nature of a person's need for a particular reward. The assumption of nonsubstitutability is also somewhat problematic. The assumption that a need can be satisfied in one and only one way runs contrary to a great deal of theory and a great deal more fact. At the level of physiological needs for example, it is true that all humans need food, but the kind of food, frequency of ingestion, and social rituals surrounding its use are quite varied. In the political arena the desire for self-esteem might be met variously by joining a local political party, running for public office, or even assassination of a government official.

CIVIC OBLIGATION

Even in the absence of direct or immediate material rewards, people take part in politics because they feel they ought to. In many societies, the enactment of the good-citizen role requires at least minimal participation in the political system. Campbell has noted that in American society "wide currency . . . is given the idea that an individ-

[34] Waldman, *op. cit.*, pp. 10–11.

ual has a civic responsibility to vote."[35] Not surprisingly,[36] Campbell has found that a high sense of citizen duty is moderately related to the likelihood of voting in a national election;[37] but if, as Campbell's data suggests, national elections are the high point of, and in many cases the only indication of, participation for most citizens, then we would expect that in the absence of other motivating forces, civic duty alone would sustain only minimal levels of political participation.

Recent empirical work provides some evidence for this assertion. For example Levenson, in his reanalysis of the Michigan survey of high-school seniors and their parents, found that high civic obligation by itself was only slightly correlated with political activity.[38] Levenson also found in reanalyzing national election data from 1952, 1956, and 1960 that those people who had a high sense of civic obligation and high feelings of political efficacy were most likely to vote, but that correlations between civic duty alone and voting were generally low.[39]

It would appear then, that in the absence of other forces, the power of civic obligation to motivate political behavior is somewhat limited. Clearly, civic obligation by itself is not intrinsically motivating. We are still left, however, with the question of why this should be the case. One possibility is that the origin of civic obligation is external to the individual and does not arise from any human need. Rather it is

[35] Campbell *et al.*, *The American Voter* (New York: Wiley & Sons, 1960), p. 58.

[36] Not surprisingly, since all four of the items in the SRC civic duty *specifically* mention voting. One wonders if it is a generalized sense of citizen duty or attitudes about a specific political behavior that is being tapped by this scale.

[37] Campbell, *op. cit.*, p. 59.

[38] G. Levenson, "The Behavioral Relevance of the Obligation to Participate," paper presented to the American Political Science Association Meeting, Chicago, 1971, p. 22.

[39] *Ibid.*, p. 24.

an obligation imposed on the individual by society, a moral obligation rather than a psychological imperative.

The mechanism through which the sense of civic obligation is instilled is usually traced to the schools. Thus, as Key notes:

> The characteristic national values and outlooks permeate the entire school curriculum from the kinds of problems posed in arithmetic to the formal instruction in civics. . . . Whatever the content and whatever the approach, the school system functions as a powerful molder of politically relevant attitudes and as a means of induction into citizenship.[40]

Recent findings in a five-nation study[41] as well as data from this country[42] link increased civic duty with increased education, thus providing some support for Key's hypothesis.

But exactly what is it that is learned in school? A look at some recent empirical studies suggests that the answer is far from obvious and may be surprising.

Beginning in the 1930s, a number of researchers have noted a bias toward unreality and political passivity[43] in civics curricula and textbooks. In separate studies, Merriam[44] and Pierce[45] analyzed American history textbooks used in primary and secondary schools and noted that in many instances the good citizen was essentially a passive citizen. They noted that passive civic virtues, such as respect for the flag, pride in national history, and the founding

[40] V. O. Key, *Public Opinion and American Democracy* (New York: Alfred A. Knopf, 1961), p. 325–326.

[41] Almond and Verba, *op. cit.*, p. 133.

[42] Campbell, *op. cit.*, p. 59.

[43] Charles Andrain, *Children and Civic Awareness* (Columbus, Ohio: Charles E. Merrill, 1971), p. 22.

[44] Charles Merriam, *The Making of Citizens* (Chicago: University of Chicago Press, 1930), pp. 211–246.

[45] Bessie Pierce, *Civic Attitudes in American School Textbooks* (Chicago: University of Chicago Press, 1930), pp. 113–126.

fathers were stressed, often at the expense of more active democratic orientations. Over 30 years later, in a study of contemporary textbooks, one perceptive scholar notes that little has changed:

> In their treatment of good citizenship in a democracy, these three texts take a rather passive view towards the citizen. What qualities does the good citizen display? He votes. He pays taxes willingly. He serves on juries. He loves the flag. He keeps informed about the actions of government policy. He understands American principles. He respects the rights, property, and opinions of other people. He obeys and respects the law. Other than voting, the minimum form of participation, *all of these virtues are quite passive.*[46] (Emphasis added.)

Apparently, the acquisition of these norms takes place quite early. A recent study by Jennings and Langton found that, by high school, civics courses had little or no effect on a number of politically relevant attitudes, including perceptions of the good-citizen role.[47] One particularly interesting result of this study is that, for the Black subsample, an increase in the number of civics courses appeared to increase the tendency to define the good citizen in terms of loyalty, rather than activity,[48] although the tendency was not particularly large (beta coefficient = – .10).

The passive nature of the definition of the good citizen has important implications for our understanding of the motivations for political activity. If it is true that many citizens define civic responsibility in terms of passive orientations to the political system, it is not surprising that civic

[46] Andrian, *op. cit.*, p. 24.

[47] Kenneth Langton and M. Kent Jennings, "Political Socialization and the High School Civics Curriculum," *The American Political Science Review*, 63, 1968, p. 415.

[48] *Ibid.*, p. 417.

responsibility *alone* does not lead to political action. Of course, whether or not people do define civic obligation passively is an empirical question.

Fortunately for our purposes, some data on this question is available. In a nationwide survey undertaken in 1965 by the Survey Research Center, respondents were asked the following open-ended question:

> People have different ideas about what being a good citizen means. We're interested in what you think. Tell me how you would describe a good citizen in this country—that is, what things about a good citizen are most important in showing that he is a good citizen.[49]

In all, 39 categories, spanning the range from voting to doing nothing, were recorded with the average respondent giving two or three codable answers. However, no more than four responses were coded for each respondent. Each respondent was categorized. Subjects who *did not* at any time mention participation as a criterion for defining good citizenship were placed in category one, while those who mentioned *any* form of participation in their responses were placed in category two. The results appear in Table 1.

TABLE 1. PARTICIPATORY VS. NONPARTICIPATORY DEFINITIONS OF THE GOOD CITIZEN

	Number	*Percent*
Passive (category 1)	825	42%
Active (category 2)	1,102	58%
Total	1,927	100%

[49] G. Levenson, *op. cit.*

The results suggest that a substantial minority do indeed define civic responsibility in a passive manner. The results are even more interesting when one remembers that to gain entry into category two, one need only have mentioned participation *once* out of the four possible coded responses. Clearly, large numbers of adults in the second category could have a high degree of civic duty, participate in politics little if at all, and still think of themselves as good citizens. Indeed, this may be one reason why a high degree of civic obligation alone will not lead to high rates of political participation.

In the next chapter we will go on to take a detailed look at the third major explanatory concept, political efficacy.

Chapter Three

POLITICAL EFFICACY:

CONTENT AND MEASUREMENT

The third major concept to be examined as an explanation for political participation, political efficacy, is *never mentioned as a motivation to participate;* rather it is put forward as a *condition* of participation. That is, it is never suggested that people participate in politics *in order to be efficacious,* but rather that one is more likely to participate in politics *if one is efficacious.*

As we proceed in our examination of the psychological origins of political efficacy, we will suggest that under certain conditions, efficacy itself *can be intrinsically motivating.* Before that point is reached, however, it will be necessary to consider the traditional conceptualization and role of political efficacy in the explanation of political behavior.

Political efficacy has been defined as "a disposition towards politics, a feeling of effectiveness and capacity in the political sphere.[1] Similarly, Campbell has defined it as, "the feeling that individual political action does have or can have an impact upon the political process—that is, that it is worthwhile to perform one's civic duties."[2] It is not suggested that the motivation for participation in politics is the feeling of political efficacy itself; but rather that political efficacy is an attitude set which makes participation (for other reasons) more likely. In Campbell's definition of political efficacy, noted above, these other reasons apparently include the discharge of civic responsibilities, but for the most part, these reasons are left unspecified.

1 David Easton and Jack Dennis, "The Child's Acquisition of Regime Norms: Political Efficacy," *The American Political Science Review,* 61, 1967, p. 25.

2 Angus Campbell, Gerald Gurin, and Warren Miller, *The Voter Decides* (Evanston, Ill.: Row, Peterson, 1954), p. 187.

However, even looked at as a facilitating rather than a motivating force, the documentation of the linkage between efficacy and participation has been impressive. Along these lines, Almond and Verba have found evidence to support the proposition that "if any individual believes that he has influence, he is likely to use it."[3] Barber has noted that "there is good evidence that a sense of political efficacy . . . encourages voting participation in the United States,"[4] while Campbell has noted that "the rate of voting turnout was found to increase uniformly with the strength of an individual's sense of political efficacy."[5] These findings linking political participation and feelings of political efficacy have been confirmed in separate studies by Berelson,[6] Almond and Verba,[7] and Dahl.[8] Although the empirical evidence to support the linkage between feelings of political efficacy and certain types of political participation is extensive, the concept of political efficacy and its measurement are not without their problems. In the following sections we will discuss some of these problems, focusing on four areas; conceptualization, reliability, operationalization, and motivation.

CONCEPTUALIZATION

As one social scientist has noted, "Studies of voting behavior carried out by Campbell and his associates at the Survey Research Center of the University of Michigan since the

[3] Gabriel Almond and Sidney Verba, *The Civic Culture* (Princeton: Princeton University Press, 1963), p. 139.

[4] James Barber, *Citizen Politics* (Chicago: Markham, 1969), p. 139.

[5] Campbell, *op. cit.*, p. 104.

[6] Bernard Berelson *et al.*, *Voting* (Chicago: University of Chicago Press, 1954).

[7] Almond and Verba, *op. cit.*, Chapter 6.

[8] Robert Dahl, *Who Governs?* (New Haven: Yale University Press, 1961).

early fifties have shaped much of the subsequent inquiry into political efficacy and its correlates."[9] This relationship has been a source of great effectiveness, but at the same time it has lead to several problems of considerable importance. When the concept was first introduced into political science nearly two decades ago by Campbell, surprisingly little attention was given to its conceptual development. Campbell simply supplied a definition and then devoted only one other paragraph to a theoretical discussion of the concept.[10] It is only fair to note that Campbell introduced this variable on an experimental basis, with the intention of stimulating interest in the concept.[11] To be sure, there has been a great deal of interest, but the interest has been in the predictive, not the theoretical aspects of the concept. Thus, one scholar has noted that

> for the most part, political scientists have accepted the concept and the measurement wholeheartedly. The concept is taken as unidimensional and a scale composed of the four items as the measure of the concept. To be sure, one occasionally hears discontented mutterings from colleagues [but] such mutterings have yet to find their way into published print.[12]

The point stressed here is that since the concept was introduced over a decade ago by Campbell and his associates, there has been little development of the political efficacy concept, and therefore no empirical research that

[9] Robert Hess, "The Acquisition of Feelings of Political Efficacy in Pre-Adults," in G. Abcarian and J. Soule (eds.), *Social Psychology and Political Behavior* (Columbus, Ohio: Charles E. Merrill, 1971), p. 64.

[10] Campbell *et al., op. cit.*, p. 188.

[11] *Ibid.*, p. 187.

[12] George Balch, "Multiple Indicators in Survey Research: The Concept Sense of Political Efficacy," paper presented to the American Political Science Association Meeting, Chicago, 1971.

could flow from such development. Advances in personality theory, social psychology, child development, and developmental psychology in the last decade have had little impact on the political efficacy concept; at least, little that is evident in the literature. One of the reasons for this is quite straightforward; *there is not now, nor has there ever been, a systematic social-psychological theory of political efficacy.*

One of the consequences of this lack of theory is a certain degree of conceptual confusion. This, in turn, has led to a series of studies that focus on the bivariate relationship of political efficacy and another variable, with little conceptual, operational, or methodological continuity. Thus, work may be found on efficacy and trust,[13] efficacy and cynicism,[14] and efficacy and intelligence.[15] Most of this work is excellently done, but each study starts from a different conceptual framework and employs different operational measures. The same is true of the alienation literature, some of which operationalizes alienation as powerlessness/inefficacy[16] and some of which does not.[17] While such studies individually are well done and often interesting, they do not permit us to fit these findings into a larger theoretical framework.

Another problem relates to conceptual dimensionality. Campbell has argued for the unidimensionality of his scale, yet other research has suggested that the concept is multidimensional. Almond and Verba have suggested the importance of strategies of influence—that is, of whether a person

[13] John Fraser, "The Mistrustful-Efficacious Hypothesis and Political Participation," *Journal of Politics*, 32, 1970, pp. 288–304.

[14] Schley Lyons, "The Political Socialization of Ghetto Children: Efficacy and Cynicism," *Journal of Politics*, 32, 1970, pp. 288–304.

[15] Elliot White, "Intelligence and the Sense of Political Efficacy in Children," *Journal of Politics*, 30, 1968, pp. 710–731.

[16] Melvin Seeman, "Powerlessness and Knowledge: A Comparative Study of Alienation and Learning," *Sociometry*, 30, 1967, pp. 105–123.

[17] D. Schwartz, *Political Alienation and Political Behavior* (Chicago: Aldine Atherton, 1973), *passim*.

would find it efficacious to work alone or in a group.[18] Along the same lines, Schwartz has suggested that a person may feel individually inefficacious, yet feel that there is a group that represents his views that is efficacious.[19] Lane, in addition, has suggested that one must distinguish a person's perceptions of the efficacy of particular political behavior, such as voting and other forms of legitimate (and one might add illegitimate) political actions.[20] Each of these points is well taken, but does not by itself suggest the lines along which a *general theory of political efficacy* might proceed.

RELIABILITY

Since there is no theory of political efficacy, there have been few attempts until recently to explore the acquisition of political efficacy. Two recent studies, however, have focused on the child and political efficacy, at least indirectly.[21] In neither case was political efficacy the main concern of the study, and in both studies certain assumptions were raised which introduced questions of reliability.

Drawing from the psychoanalytic tradition, these studies sought to demonstrate the importance of childhood experiences on the development of political attitudes. Underlying these and similar studies, of course, is the assumption that most children do indeed have political attitudes and definite opinions about politics. Work by Vaillancourt[22]

18 G. Almond and S. Verba, *op. cit.*, Chapter 8.

19 Schwartz, *op. cit.*, Chapter 2.

20 Robert Lane, *Political Life* (New York: Free Press, 1959), Chapter 11.

21 R. Hess and J. Torney, *The Development of Political Attitudes in Children* (New York: Doubleday, 1967); David Easton and Jack Dennis, *Children in the Political System: Origins of Political Legitimacy* (New York: McGraw-Hill, 1969).

22 Pauline Vaillancourt, *The Political Socialization of Young People: A Panel Survey of Youngsters in the San Francisco Bay Area* (unpublished Ph.D. dissertation, Berkeley, University of California, 1970).

suggests this assumption may have to be modified. She notes two major problems with these and similar studies: (1) a failure to explain variations in the dependent variable with traditional independent variables and (2) the tendency for children's attitudes to become crystallized after filling out the questionnaire, which may indicate the lack of a stable attitude.[23]

The first problem was encountered by Easton and Dennis in their attempt to predict cognitions and affects toward the president and policemen. Using ten independent variables they can explain only 7 percent of the variance.[24] The authors suggest looking for new and different predictor variables,[25] but Vaillancourt feels that the real problem may be that "the results are due to the high percentage of youngsters in a number of different demographic groups that had no stable attitudes at all on the dependent variables.[26] Niemi, in his review of the Easton and Dennis study, also suggests that their limited findings may be due in part to the low stability of children's responses.[27]

A second problem in these studies was noted by Torney. After examining questionnaires of a national sample study, she wrote, "it appears that answering questions about an attitude object does increase the crystallization of that attitude."[28] Given the general agreement in the psychological

[23] *Ibid.*, Chapter 2.

[24] Easton and Dennis, *op. cit.*, p. 370

[25] *Ibid.*, p. 378.

[26] Pauline Vaillancourt, "The Stability of Children's Political Orientations: A Panel Study," paper presented to the American Political Science Association, Los Angeles, 1970, p. 9.

[27] Richard Niemi, "Review of Children in the Political System," *American Political Science Review*, 64, 1970, pp. 181–191.

[28] Judith V. Torney, "Structural Dimensions of Children's Political Attitude-concept Systems: A Study of Developmental and Measurement Aspects," unpublished Ph.D. dissertation, Chicago, University of Chicago, 1965, p. 133.

literature that "the concept of attitude is typically reserved for the more enduring, persistent organization of predispositions,"[29] the possibility exists that responses that did not exist prior to the administration of the questionnaire should not be considered attitudes at all. Converse has suggested that similar reliability problems exist for studies among adults, because survey research often creates attitudes by asking subjects to consider subjects about which they have no attitudes.[30]

In a recent empirical examination of the reliability of the political efficacy scale in a national study, Welch and Clark found other problems. Their findings suggest that, "individual feelings of political efficacy are not stable over time and temporal changes that do occur are not readily explanable by the usual predictors of political efficacy."[31] According to the authors, "these findings raise questions about the 'deep seated' nature of political efficacy in the personality structure of an individual and about the measurement of the attitude."[32] It is probable however that the suggested relationship between personality and political efficacy need not be abandoned, especially if political efficacy is not conceptualized as part of "the deep seated personality structure." We will suggest that it is not the attitude of political efficacy that is part of the personality structure, but rather the need for personal control. As to problems with the measurement of the political efficacy concept, we will turn to that in the following section and again in Chapter Seven.

29 See, for example, Milton Rokeach, *The Open and Closed Mind* (New York: Basic Books, 1960), Chapter 2.

30 Philip E. Converse, "The Nature of Belief Systems in Mass Publics," in David Apter (ed.) *Ideology and Discontent* (New York: Free Press, 1965), Chapter 6.

31 S. Welch and C. Clark, "Political Efficacy as an Underlying Political Orientation: The Problem of Attitudinal Instability," unpublished manuscript, 1973, p. 20.

32 *Ibid.*

OPERATIONALIZATION

Operationalization is, of course, closely linked to theoretical conceptualization and is one of the last major problem areas to be examined in connection with recent studies of political efficacy. Many of these studies, including the Easton and Dennis study, relied upon the scale first developed by Campbell nearly two decades ago. Generally, this scale includes the following items:

1. I don't think that public officials care much what people like me think.
2. The way people vote is the main thing that decides how things are run in this country.
3. Voting is the only way that people like me can have a say about how the government runs things.
4. People like me don't have much say about how the government runs things.
5. Sometimes politics and government seems so complicated that a person like me can't really understand what is going on.

Items 1, 3, 4, and 5 are coded as efficacious if the answer is "disagree," while item 2 is scored as efficacious if the answer is "agree." In practice, item 2 is usually dropped from the analysis because of scalability problems.[33] Several points should be noted: first, questions two and three suggest some range of behaviors that must be engaged in to feel efficacious, yet the other behaviors are not specified. Secondly, it is certainly possible that one could answer question three in the affirmative and still consider oneself to be efficacious. Moreover, it seems possible that given prevailing American norms about the efficacy of voting, a person who answers

[33] John Robinson *et al.*, *Measures of Political Attitudes* (Ann Arbor: Institute for Social Research, 1968), p. 459.

"agree" to *either* question (items 2 or 3) may be efficacious. Some confirmation of this possibility is suggested by a look at the national distribution of responses to item 3:[34]

ITEM 3: Voting is the only way that people like me can have a say about how the government runs things.

	1952	*1956*	*1960*	*1964*	*1966*
Agree	81%	73%	73%	73%	69%
Disagree	17%	25%	25%	26%	26%

The high percentage of "agree" responses suggests the possibility that a democratic norm centering around the emphasis on voting as the most important element in democratic participation is being tapped by this item. This focus on voting as a civic norm is also evident in the "civic duty scale," also developed by Campbell,[35] in which all four items specifically mention voting, and which highly correlates with the political efficacy scale. It is also interesting to note that 12 percent decline in the number of "agree" responses to item 3, indicating perhaps that other behaviors are perceived to have a substantial impact on the political system. This suggests that there are important links between individual feelings of political efficacy and the perceived efficacy of specific behaviors; however, at present, these links remain unexplored.

MOTIVATION

One of the important unanswered questions in the field of political behavior has to do with the explanation of the often-reported finding that the more efficacious are more

[34] *Ibid.*, p. 635.

[35] *Ibid.*, p. 461.

likely to participate in politics, or at least in such behaviors as voting, wearing campaign buttons, or contributing money.[36] At first glance, there appears to be little problem with this finding, and by now it is quite familiar. But why is it that the efficacious participate more frequently? An explanation of the literature suggests that the answer is far from obvious. Indeed, the question has never been directly confronted!

The most frequent response is not so much an explanation of the finding as it is an implication from the finding. That is, the implication is that since the more efficacious *do* participate more, they participate *because* they are efficacious. Such reasoning raises a number of important problems, especially when viewed from the perspective of the current conceptualization of political efficacy.

If Easton and Dennis' conceptualization of political efficacy as "a feeling of effectiveness and capacity in the political sphere" is used, for example, then the assumption must be that people participate in areas where they have effectiveness. This suggests that people *choose* arenas of action based on their feelings that they can be effective there. Applied to political systems, it would suggest that politics becomes salient to people *as a result* of their feelings that they can be effective, rather than *as a result of the impact of political systems upon their lives.*

Moreover, the suggestion that people participate *because* they feel efficacious hints that there is something about efficacy itself that is rewarding. One possibility is that such feelings are rewarding because they increase the self-esteem of the efficacious individual. Such a model would suggest that men are motivated to political activity to heighten their self-esteem. Yet for many people politics is perceived as a complex formidable arena, where the chances for in-

[36] See, for example, the review in Lester Milbrath, *Political Participation* (Chicago: Rand McNally, 1965), *passim.*

creases in self-esteem in the form of positions of political leadership are small.

Another possibility is implied in the definition of political efficacy put forward by Campbell: "that political action does have an impact upon the political process, that is, that it is worthwhile to perform one's civic duties."[37] The implication here is that efficacy is rewarding because it allows one to perform one's civic duties. Yet, we have already presented some data which suggest that a large minority of the population defines civic duty without reference to any type of political activity. This suggests that for many people the link between political efficacy and political participation as a condition for the satisfaction of civic obligation motivation is not crucial.

Clearly, increases in self-esteem or performance of one's civic duties do not seem sufficiently powerful to motivate many people to participate in politics. Are we therefore to assume that the suggestions about motivation implied in some current conceptualizations of political efficacy are completely erroneous? I should like to suggest that the answer to this question be phrased in the negative. *Political efficacy is by itself, under certain conditions, intrinsically motivating.* The task before us, therefore, in order to build a viable theory of political efficacy, is first to establish the psychological basis which underlies the feelings of political efficacy, and then examine the conditions under which political efficacy may be intrinsically motivating. In other words, a viable theory of political efficacy must examine psychogenesis, as well as psychodynamics.

[37] Campbell, *op. cit.*, p. 187.

Chapter Four

THE NEED FOR PERSONAL CONTROL:

SOME EVIDENCE

The basic theme of this chapter is that there is within each of us a basic need to have control over the forces and experiences that impact upon and shape our lives. When these forces and experiences include the political system the link is forged between the need for personal control and political life. The major purpose of this chapter is to introduce the concept of the need for personal control and to explore various branches of psychological research to review the evidence for this proposed need.

Before examining the evidence, however, several observations about the need for personal control should be made. First, by basic need I mean that the need is a basic psychological organizer of people's motivation and orientation to the world. The implication of this is that theoretically predictable consequences flow from this hypothesis. For example, if this basic need is unmet, we would hypothesize renewed efforts to gain personal control. If such efforts were to prove unrewarding we might hypothesize psychological consequences in the form of either apathy (withdrawal) or anger. This is not to suggest that all people have the same level of this need: rather it suggests that whatever the level of individual need, certain observable psychological and behavioral consequences would follow from its frustration.

Second, personal control has both a degree and a scope dimension. The degree of personal control refers to the person's belief in his ability to shape and effect the forces and experiences that impact upon and shape his life. This in turn is based on two related and important abilities. First, the ability to acquire and successfully utilize a variety of skills and pathways to reach personal goals, and second, the ability to engage in successful reality testing. The first point seems quite obvious: in order to effect the forces that impact upon one's life, certain skills are necessary. The exact nature of the skills required will vary with the goals of the person and problems peculiar to reaching those goals. For example, to become president of the United States one must acquire certain intellectual, interpersonal, and other skills. Moreover, one must learn to integrate the utilization of the skills in ways appropriate to the particular problems of the context (for example, being the first Catholic to run or the first black).

The second aspect of the degree dimension of personal control, that is, reality testing, is no less important. We suggested above that personal control was the belief in one's ability to shape his life-space. The word belief requires some consideration. Inherent in the concept of belief is the potential that one could hold that belief in spite of obvious evidence that one's personal control is low or nonexistent. This places us in somewhat of a quandary, for if we concentrate on the person's subjective beliefs about his personal control we run the risk that they will grossly distort his "objective" level of control. On the other hand, if we attempt to "objectively" assess the actual degree of personal control, we run the risk of neglecting the person's subjective beliefs, which, if he believes them and acts upon them, does constitute social facts. The principle of adequate reality testing allows us to come to grips with this problem. The degree of personal control that a person believes himself to have is the basic starting point for personal control assessment. Yet, it should be clear that gross distortions of the level of personal control will be behaviorally and psychologically self-defeating. The person who distorts either his capacities or their impact on the particular goals he desires gets no closer to those goals. Thus, unless the individual takes notice of the potentially self-correcting feedback, he must suffer the consequences of being frustrated in his attempts. Another alternative is to change goals, to lower one's aspirations. This may be an alternative for some, but it still leaves the problem of reaching the new goal and of the ability of the new goal to satisfy the original motivation.

As we stated above, not all people have the same level of need for personal control. Although we would expect the need to be within certain parameters, there would still be room for individual variation. If we were to undertake a national survey of adults in the United States with an accurate instrument that measured the need for personal control on a scale from 1 (a low need) to 10 (a high need), we might find that most of the people vary between 6 and 8, yet there would also be a few people for whom the need would either be very high (perhaps 9 or 10), or very low (perhaps 2 or 3). Obviously the level of need will be associated with the degree of control needed. A person with low needs for personal control will be satisfied with less, while an individual with high levels of need for personal control will require greater amounts of control in order to be satisfied. Thus, a person who lowers his goal of obtaining a certain amount of personal control could only do so as long as that degree of control was commensurate with the strength or level of his need. Of course, at this stage of research there is no way to assess the level of this need nor its distribution within the social system. We are dealing here with a much more general statement—that there is a need for personal control.

Lastly, I suggested that personal control has a scope dimension, which refers to the extent of the life-space area that the individual seeks to affect. This may vary from a limited, narrow scope involving only one specially defined area, or it may be more expansive, involving multiple areas. There is, of course, a relationship between the scope of personal control and the degree of personal control possible. Other things being equal, the greater the desired scope of personal control, the less the degree of personal control.

That is, if we accept that an individual has finite capacities and skills and that each sector of control requires a certain degree of skills, skill capacity, and utilization, then it follows that the potentials for personal control are limited by capacity. A related hypothesis says that the greater the skill acquisition and utilization capacity, the greater the potential scope of personal control. The areas of life that become control relevant are not always chosen by the individual. That is, a person might select certain areas as control relevant based on his perception that he has a good chance (given his skills and capacities) to obtain personal control, yet there are other instances where the area becomes control relevant because of the nature of the social structure. For example, in a highly politicized society where the political elites make a number of decisions affecting the citizen, politics might become a control-relevant sphere regardless of the individual's skills or capacities in the area. These considerations will be considered in the context of a theory of personality, personal control, and political socialization in the next chapter. However, at this point we return to the original consideration of this chapter, namely the search through various branches of psychological research to provide evidence of the need for personal control. Our purpose here is not to detail each theory or set of findings but to trace the concept of a need for personal control from a variety of perspectives.[1]

ANIMAL STUDIES

There is sometimes the suggestion that man is an animal, and that therefore the study of other animals might shed light on human behavior. Without becoming involved in the nature of man, and in what way or ways, if any, he dif-

[1] The following discussion owes much to a similar discussion in Robert White, "Motivation Reconsidered: The Concept of Competence," *Psychological Review*, 66, 1959, pp. 297–333.

fers from other animals, we do find some evidence of a drive resembling personal control in lower animals.

As early as 1925, Dashiell found that rats would cross an electrified grid to explore new territory on the other side of their environment with no apparent reinforcement, under conditions of hunger and thirst satiation.[2] Montgomery reported an experiment in which rats with their organic needs satiated selected the longer arm of the Y maze which led them into new territory suitable for exploration,[3] while Butler reported the same phenomenon in a series of experiments with monkeys.[4] These and other experiments led Zimbardo and Miller to conclude that "the opportunity to explore a novel environment *or to effect a stimulus change in the environment is the reinforcing agent.*"[5] (Emphasis added.)

Further evidence of the control drive in animals comes from experiments by Harlow and his associates with rhesus monkeys.[6] They have demonstrated that monkeys will attempt to learn to solve puzzles with no apparent extrinsic reward; indeed, the research found that the introduction of an external incentive caused a deterioration in the manipulative behavior. The authors interpret their results to show a manipulatory drive which they consider to be a source of intrinsic motivation. Later research by Harlow, Blazek,

[2] J. F. Dashiell, "A Quantitative Demonstration of Animal Drive," *Journal of Comparative Psychology*, 5, 1925, pp. 205–208.

[3] K. G. Montgomery, "The Role of Exploratory Drive in Learning," *Journal of Comparative Physiological Psychology*, 47, 1954, pp. 60–64.

[4] R. A. Butler, "Exploratory and Related Behavior: A New Trend in Animal Research," *Journal of Individual Psychology*, 14, 1958, pp. 111–120.

[5] P. G. Zimbardo and N. E. Miller, "Facilitation of Exploration by Hunger in Rats," *Journal of Comparative Psychology*, 51, 1958, pp. 43–46.

[6] H. F. Harlow *et al.*, "Learning Motivated by a Manipulation Drive," *Journal of Experimental Psychology*, 40, 1950, pp. 228–234.

and McClearn demonstrated that manipulatory motivation is exhibited by infant monkeys before the age at which it could have been learned as being instrumental to drive reduction.[7]

Lastly, in a later series of experiments involving wild strains of mice in complex environments, Kavanau found that

> confined animals are likely to seize upon and repeatedly exercise virtually any opportunities to modify [and alter their relationship with] their surroundings. In addition, they have a strong tendency to counteract non-volitional and "unexpected" deviations from the status quo. . . . The results . . . suggest the complex interplay of tendencies to modify features of the environment, to avoid conditions imposed compulsorily, and to select preferred levels of illumination.[8]

It appears then that there is some support for the proposition that animals do exhibit evidence of a drive that is very similar to the need for personal control.

PSYCHOANALYTIC THEORY[9]

Freud, the father of psychoanalytic theory, had little directly to say about a need for personal control. Yet, an inspection of his writings reveals that parts of his theory, either directly or indirectly touch on the concept of a need for personal control.

[7] H. F. Harlow *et al.*, "Manipulatory Motivation in the Infant Rhesus Monkey," *Journal of Comparative Physiological Psychology*, 49, 1956, pp. 444–448.

[8] J. L. Kavanau, "Behavior of Captive White-footed Mice," *Science*, 155, 1967, pp. 1623–1639.

[9] The discussion that follows is based on the following works: S. Freud, *An Outline of Psychoanalysis* (New York: Norton, 1945); S. Freud, *New Introductory Lectures in Psychoanalysis* (London: Hogarth Press, 1955).

Freudian motivation theory is based on the assumption that instincts are the sole energy sources for human behavior. While Freud never enumerated specific instincts, he did suggest that eventually all instincts would be subsumed under two major classifications: the life instincts (Eros) and the death instincts (Thanatos). Freud spent much of his time dealing with the former category, under which he included such drives as hunger, thirst, and sex.

Freud's analysis of the structure of personality suggests that the id is the repository of the instincts, as well as the reservoir of psychic energy, which in the case of the life instincts is called libido. The relations between the id and libido were seen to be governed by the pleasure principle. According to Freud, the id experiences increases in energy as an uncomfortable state of tension that it seeks to reduce. Whether the source of this increased energy is external (excessive stimulation) or internal (need for food or water), the reaction of the id is the same: it seeks to immediately discharge the tension and return to equilibrium.

The emphasis on a tension-reduction model led Freud to a conservative position on human action in general and the concept of personal control in particular. For example, in a famous discussion of a child seeking to control and master the anxiety produced by his mother leaving him, Freud noted that one function of compulsive, repetitive play is the attempt by the child to reduce anxiety in one sphere (temporary loss of mother) through mastery in another sphere (play).[10] The tension reduction explanation of this episode has been contested by Schachtel [11] and others.[12] Schachtel suggested that

[10] S. Freud, *Beyond the Pleasure Principle* (London: Hogarth Press, 1955), pp. 14–18.

[11] E. G. Schachtel, *Metamorphosis* (New York: Basic Books, 1959).

[12] See, for example: Charlotte Buhler, "The Reality Principle," *American Journal of Psychotherapy*, 8, 1954, pp. 626–647; and N. O. Brown, *Life Against Death* (New York: Random House, 1959).

> much of what impressed Freud as repetitive compulsion in the child's need to repeat a story or a play activity over and over again turns out to be neither the result of a desire to return to an earlier state nor the effect of the principle of inertia, but an essential requirement for the gradual exploration of the environment . . . and the child's relation to it . . . *the enjoyment in doing that which one already masters.*[13] (Emphasis added.)

Whether one accepts Freud's or Schachtel's explanation of this episode, the important point is that Freud recognized a need for control, even if only as a compensatory device. Furthermore, he realized that control of an environment or situation reduced anxiety. This in turn suggests that lack of control is in itself anxiety producing. These insights into the interface between control and anxiety reduction have been the basis of several provocative formulations in the literature of personality and politics. For example, in his analysis of Woodrow Wilson's compulsiveness, George notes that "orderliness and stubbornness . . . are derived in part from a desire for more power or dominance which is said to be related to a more basic need for security."[14]

A close examination of Freud's writing suggests that the concept of personal control is also implied, but unexplicated, in his analysis of personality development. It has already been noted that the id is the repository of human motivating forces (life instincts), which are governed by the pleasure principle; yet according to Freud, the id represents subjective experience and *has no knowledge of objective reality*. The implications of this state for personality growth were for Freud momentous.

[13] Schachtel, *op. cit.*, p. 265.

[14] Alexander George, "Some Uses of Dynamic Psychology in Political Biography: Case Materials on Woodrow Wilson," in F. Greenstein and M. Lerner (eds.), *A Source Book for the Study of Personality and Politics* (Chicago: Markham, 1971), p. 85.

One process through which the id seeks to reduce tension is by forming an image of the object.[15] Thus, a hungry child might form the image of food in an attempt to decrease the tension brought about by hunger. Clearly, such attempts are doomed to failure and it is out of this failure that the ego develops. The ego becomes differentiated from the id because the organism requires realistic transactions with its environment in order to secure satisfaction of the id's needs. The necessity of the ego to find realistic objects for the gratification of the id is what Freud called the reality principle.

We would suggest that, viewed in Freudian terms, id gratification assumes some minimal level of mastery or personal control. This begins as soon as the child's self-assertion (by crying) results in a need-gratification response from an environmental object (being fed by mother). If, as Freud suggested, the ego develops in response to the need to gratify the needs of the id, then clearly the growth of mastery or personal control would be a crucial dimension of ego development. This would be especially true in complex, differentiated environments that characterize human social systems. Although Freud never examined this idea directly, at least one of Freud's followers was interested in personal control.

Alfred Adler, although a charter member and later president of the Vienna Psychoanalytic Society, differed with Freud over the motivation of human behavior. While Freud believed man's behavior to be motivated by instincts, Adler located human motivation largely in the social matrix. Accordingly, Adler suggested that man was motivated primarily by social urges, chief among which was "striving for superiority." Adler, like Freud, is difficult to associate with particular positions, because an analysis of his various writings reveals changes in emphasis and labeling. Adler's striving

[15] This process is called the primary process by Freud.

for superiority developed from an emphasis on the aggressive impulse which he later called the will to power. This striving for superiority did not mean for Adler social prestige or high peer esteem, Adler noted:

> I begin to see clearly in every psychological phenomena the striving for superiority. It runs parallel to physical growth and is an intrinsic necessity of life itself. . . . All our functions follow its direction. They strive for conquest, security.[16]

In other words, Adler saw the attempt to master one's environment and to achieve ever-higher degrees of control as the motivating forces in human behavior. According to Adler, this need is innate, and while it may manifest itself in a variety of ways, all social behavior can ultimately be traced back to this need.

The consequences of the frustration of this need are most fully developed in the work of Karen Horney. Horney's basic concept is basic anxiety, which she defined as "the feeling of being isolated and helpless in a potentially hostile world."[17] In discussing children, she noted that a hostile world may include one in which there is too much domination by parents, erratic parental behavior, or too little responsibility.[18] All these elements in some way suggest an inability of the child to control his fate, or exert some control over his environment. Horney developed at some length the strategies that children adopt to reduce feelings of helplessness,[19] including at least one which is

[16] Alfred Adler, "Individual Psychology," in C. Murchison (ed.), *Psychologies of 1930* (Worcester, Mass.: Clark University Press, 1930), p. 398.

[17] Karen Horney, *Our Inner Conflicts* (New York: Norton, 1945), p. 41.

[18] *Ibid.*, p. 41.

[19] Karen Horney, *Neurotic Personality of Our Times* (New York: Norton, 1937), *passim.*

very similar to the authoritarian submission component noted in the authoritarian personality studies.[20]

This review of some of the original psychoanalytic theorists has suggested at least some, and in most cases, much concern with personal control or mastery. We now turn our attention to some post-Freudian thinkers to see if their revisions of psychoanalytic theory have suggested the need to revise our theory of a need for personal control.

NEO-FREUDIAN THEORY

It has been suggested that at least one of Freud's major disciples was concerned with the nature of a control need, and the same is true for other post-Freudian thinkers. With the passage of time, it became increasingly clear that Freud's two instincts, Eros and Thanatos, were insufficient by themselves to explain the variety of human behavior. The psychoanalyst Hendrict proposed one solution, in the form of a third instinct—the "instinct to master" a segment of the environment.[21] Other analysts in the mode of Fenichel neglected Hendrict's formulation, since Freud had conceived of instincts as having somatic sources external to the ego; but at the same time, Fenichel noted that "mastery is a general aim of every organism, but not of a specific instinct."[22]

Later psychoanalytic work stressed the autonomous nature of the ego and its development and attenuated the relation between the instinctual urges of the id and the development of the ego. This trend is most clearly associated with the

[20] Theodore Adorno *et al., The Authoritarian Personality* (New York: Harper, 1950).

[21] I. Hendrict, "The Discussion of the Instinct to Master," *Psychoanalytic Quarterly*, 12, 1943, pp. 311–329.

[22] Fenichel, *The Psychoanalytic Theory of Neurosis* (New York: Norton, 1945).

work of Hartman,[23] Kardiner,[24] Mittlemann[25] and Erikson.[26] For each of these scholars, the need for control was an important concept. For example, Kardiner noted that childhood ego growth is associated with the discovery of the relationship between an executed movement and the accompanying and subsequent sensations.[27] Mittlemann regarded motility, which manifests itself in locomotion and manipulation behavior, as "an urge in its own right,"[28] while for Erikson, the mastery of certain modalities at each of his eight stages of development is a crucial part of his theory. Erikson noted that even children's games are related to mastery: "The playing child advances forward to new stages of real mastery."[29] This brief survey suggests that, even though some of Freud's ideas were revised, the concept of a need for personal control is still an important part of Neo-Freudian theory.

DEVELOPMENTAL PSYCHOLOGY

Turning from an examination of psychoanalytic theories to developmental models, one finds less systematic attention paid to theories of motivation. For example, Piaget's six-stage model of human intellectual development is not formally concerned with motivation; yet his keen observations on infant motility are highly suggestive[30] about the need for

23 Harry Hartman, "Comments on the Psychoanalytic Theory of the Ego," *Psychoanalytic Study of the Child*, 34, 1943, pp. 9–36.

24 A. Kardiner and H. Spiegal, *War, Stress and Neurotic Illness* (New York: Hoeber, 1947).

25 B. Mittlemann, "Motility in Infants, Children, and Adults," *Psychoanalytic Study of the Child*, 9, 1954, pp. 142–177.

26 Erik Erikson, *Childhood and Society* (New York: Norton, 1952).

27 Kardiner and Spiegal, *op. cit.*, p. 10.

28 Mittlemann, *op. cit.*, p. 143.

29 Erikson, *op. cit.*, p. 222.

30 Jean Piaget, *The Origins of Intelligence in Children* (New York: International University Press, 1952).

personal control. Piaget has noted that as early as the fourth month, the play of his children "centered on a result produced in the external environment . . . rediscovering the movement which by chance exercised an advantageous action upon things."[31] By the end of nine months, Piaget noted that the presentation of a new stimulus elicits four types of responses: (1) visual exploration, (2) tactile exploration, (3) slow movement of the object in space, and (4) use of the child's repertory of action upon the object, "each in turn with a sort of prudence, as though studying the effect produced."[32] For example, one day,

> Laurent, by chance strikes the chain while sucking his fingers. He grasps it and slowly displaces it while looking at the rattles. He then begins to swing it very gently, which produces a slight movement of the hanging rattles and an as yet faint sound inside them. Laurent then definitely increases by degree his own movements. He shakes the chain more and more vigorously and laughs uproariously at the result obtained.[33]

If Piaget's observations are correct, it would appear that Laurent seems to be systematically testing his impact on his environment and experiencing some intrinsic reward for being the locus of causality. In this sense, Piaget's observations parallel the findings we discussed in the area of comparative psychology. It is possible to argue that Piaget's observations suggest multiple strands of motivation, but, as White pointed out,

> it is equally possible to discern a theme of mastery, power or control, perhaps even a bit of primitive self-

[31] *Ibid.*, p. 151.
[32] *Ibid.*, p. 255.
[33] *Ibid.*, p. 185.

> assertion, in the child's concentration upon those aspects of the environment which respond in some way to his own activity.[34]

Moreover, an examination of Piaget's observations suggest that the child is more likely to manipulate for extended periods of time those objects in the environment upon which he finds he has some effect; consequently, he will receive more intrinsic rewards. We shall return to this observation again when we discuss personal control and political participation.

HUMANISTIC PSYCHOLOGY

Lastly, we turn our attention to the humanistic, or "third force," psychology associated with the work of Rogers,[35] Goldstein,[36] Angyal,[37] and Maslow.[38] Although many differences separate these theorists, they are united in their rejection of both orthodox Freudian theory and stimulus-response paradigms. Each theorist has stressed self-actualization as a master motivating tendency. This is variously defined as the desire for self fulfillment, the attempt to actualize what is potential, or, as Maslow put it, "to become everything that one is capable of becoming."[39] The concept of self-actualization striving is closely associated with the need for control. Angyal's discussion makes this relation clear.

Angyal noted that life is a process of self-expansion, in

[34] Robert White, *op. cit.*, p. 318.

[35] Carl Rogers, *On Becoming a Person* (Boston: Houghton Mifflin, 1961).

[36] Kurt Goldstein, *The Organism* (New York: American Press, 1939).

[37] A. Angyal, *Foundations for a Science of Personality* (New York: Commonwealth Fund, 1941).

[38] A. Maslow, *Motivation and Personality* (New York: Harper, 1954).

[39] A. Maslow, "A Theory of Human Motivation," *Psychological Review*, 50, 1943, pp. 370–396.

which the living system expands at the expense of its surroundings through the process of assimilation. The living system engages in assimilation in order to bring greater parts of its environment under increasing control. Angyal also suggested that there is a tendency toward organism autonomy, which results in an increase in the preponderance of internal over external sources of force on the organism. In short, the human being "has a characteristic tendency towards self-determination, that is, a tendency to resist external influences and to subordinate the heteronomous forces of the physical and social environment to its own sphere of influence."[40]

Clearly, control of competence is the foundation on which Angyal's "autonomy," Rogers' "becoming," and Goldstein's "self-actualization" are built. In a sense all of these theories are built around the need to achieve control and competence in individually specified areas.

That control is at least a necessary component of self-actualization is brought out in a more sophisticated way by the work of Maslow.[41] Maslow has posited the existence of a need hierarchy in the following order of ascendance: (1) physiological needs, (2) safety needs, (3) love needs, (4) esteem needs, and (5) self-actualization needs.

Physiological needs refer to the need of the body for food, sleep, or water. Safety needs are next in the need hierarchy and refer to the need to be physically secure as well as the need to be psychologically secure. When these needs have been met the love needs emerge, which refer to the desire for human warmth, affection, and inclusion by others. The next need to emerge is that of self-esteem, which refers to the desire for feelings of self-worth originating in the interplay between personal competence and social norms that govern the area and nature of the competence. Lastly, when all of these needs

40 A. Angyal, *op. cit.*, p. 30.

41 A. Maslow, *Motivation and Personality, passim.*

have been fulfilled, the need for self-actualization emerges. Once people have met their more basic needs, they can concentrate on realizing their full potential. Thus, Maslow's need hierarchy suggests that the need to have control over aspects of an individual's world is a basic need and the foundation upon which later need satisfaction and personal growth are erected.

PERSONAL CONTROL AND PSYCHOLOGICAL THEORY

Our review of various fields of psychology has suggested that the concept of a need for personal control is an important part of psychological theory and research. In such widely diverse fields as experimental psychology, psychoanalytic psychology, ego psychology, and humanistic psychology, the evidence appears strong that there is within each of us a need to exert some amount of control over relevant aspects of our life-space. This need we have called the need for personal control.

If the weight of our review of psychological theory and research is sufficient to establish the possibility of a need for personal control, then it becomes possible to put forward a theory of personal control and then go on to specify the link, or links, between personal control and political behavior. It is to these twin tasks that we now turn our attention.

Chapter Five

PERSONALITY AND POLITICAL SOCIALIZATION: THE ORIGINS AND DEVELOPMENT OF PERSONAL CONTROL

Our survey of the findings in psychological research providing some support for the existence of a need for personal control supplies a foundation for a theory of personal control and political behavior. Important questions remain to be answered, however, about the origins, development, and subsequent political linkages of this need. This chapter presents a theory of personal control within the general framework of personality development. While our attention will be focused on the need for personal control, this theory does have important implications for political socialization theory and research.

THE ORIGINS OF PERSONAL CONTROL

There has for some time been a controversy in psychology over the nature of the origins of needs. Some, following the work of Freud, have viewed needs as arising out of a deficit, while others have seen the deficit model as too limiting for the variety of human experience. Yet it appears to us a base that the need for personal control is a deficit need arising out of the nature of the child and its relation to the environment.

Unlike other species, the human child is brought into the world totally unprepared to take care of itself. Also unlike many other species, the period of such dependency is relatively long. This prolonged dependency is indeed one of the few cultural universals that anthropologists have been able to find[1] and has profound implications for human development in general and the need for personal control in particular.

The child arrives in the world with hunger and thirst needs but with no knowledge of how to satisfy them. At a minimum, unsatisfied hunger and thirst needs create physiological discomfort, and the child has no way to communicate these needs. Typically, the child begins to thrust and cry, until an alert parent (traditionally the mother) interprets the cries correctly and feeds the child. From the child's point of view, there is no connection between his crying and the arrival of food. This means that the child is experiencing *two*, not one, unpleasant experiences. First, there is the discomfort of the unmet needs, and second, there is the fear (anxiety) that these needs might not be met again in the future. Out of these twin discomforts, the need for personal control is born.

The typical child is hungry seven or eight times a day,[2] which means that the same discomfort-crying-feeding ritual is played out more than a hundred times in the first two weeks of life. Gradually, the child begins to connect his crying with the appearance of food. This is, of course, the beginning of associative learning, but more importantly, it is the child's first experience of being the locus of causality, the initiator of the action that successfully meets biological needs.

At this point, unknown to the child, he is approaching one of life's frequent choice points, although he, in effect, has little choice. At some point the parents have to decide on demand feeding or a feeding schedule. When the child has learned to associate crying with food he has gone some distance towards mastering the first problem—hunger satis-

[1] M. Wolfenstein and M. Mead (eds.), *Child-Rearing in Six Cultures* (Chicago: University of Chicago Press, 1966).

[2] Paul Mussin *et al.*, *Child Development and Personality* (New York: Harper and Row, 1969), p. 184.

faction—and if the parents decide on demand feeding, in which he is fed whenever he cries, the child will build up a basis of successful reinforcement that should help to dispel anxiety about future feeding situations.

On the other hand, the use of a schedule means that the child is fed at regular intervals regardless of his immediate needs, and indeed there is some evidence to suggest that children will modify their behavior in accordance to such external demands as feeding schedules.[3] Yet, in this situation there is no consummation of the union between self-initiated action and successful outcomes. The child learns not that he is the locus of causality but that compliance to external demands brings with it rewards. He is learning to trust in others but not in himself.

We *do not* mean to suggest that the feeding situation is *the single crucial* encounter for the development of personal control, but it is the earliest social encounter and one of the first chances for the child to master discomfort through his own efforts. And we do not wish to discount, even at this early stage, individual differences in temperament and spontaneous motor activity. Research has suggested that children are born with different tendencies toward activity, and there is some evidence that early activity levels are precursors of future behavior.[4] These observations suggest, but do not exhaust, the possibilities for the beginnings of personal control.

The concept of compensation alerts us to the fact that failure to control one's food availability in the feeding process need not irreparably damage the acquisition of personal control. There is ample research to demonstrate that children are more likely to repeat a *variety of actions* if these

[3] D. P. Marquis, "Learning in the Neonate: The Modification of Behavior Under Three Feeding Schedules," *Journal of Experimental Psychology*, 29, 1949, pp. 263–287.

[4] S. Escalona and G. M. Heider, *Prediction and Outcome* (New York: Basic Books, 1959).

actions bring some response, especially from a parent.[5] In many cases, the knowledge that certain action has a related result is enough to increase the probability of a repeated action. Piaget has noted that as early as the fourth month, children will engage in play "centered on a result produced in the external environment" which can be described as an exploration of actions that by chance produced a serendipitous effect upon things.[6] What this means is that the child enjoys many opportunities to develop his ability to control his environment, and inability in one area of potential control may not lead to inability in others.

Generally, however, we would expect that those areas involved with biological satisfaction or rudimentary social needs, such as separation anxiety, would be the most important areas of mastery control. We find ourselves in substantial agreement with Erikson, who suggested that if the child is to develop a meaningful sense of personal control, or to use Erikson's term, autonomy,

> it is necessary that he experience *over and over again* that he is a person who is permitted to make choices. He has the right to choose, for example, whether to approach a visitor or to lean against his mother's knee, whether to accept offered food or reject it. At the same time, he must learn some of the boundaries of self-determination . . . that there are walls he cannot climb . . . objects out of reach, and above all, commands enforced by powerful adults.[7] (Emphasis added.)

[5] Mussin *et al., op. cit.*, Chapter 6.

[6] J. Piaget, *The Origins of Intelligence in Children* (New York: International University Press, 1952), p. 15.

[7] E. Erikson, "A Healthy Personality for Every Child: A Fact Finding Report: A Digest," in J. Seidman (ed.), *The Adolescent: A Book of Readings* (New York: Holt, Rinehart & Winston, 1953), p. 108.

Our brief review of the ontological origins of personal control has suggested some of the ways in which a basic personal need is shaped by the social context and human interactions that surround it. We have suggested that the child's need for personal control grows out of and is shaped by interactions with primary figures associated with the satisfaction of biological necessities. Even at this early stage of development, the basic components of cognitive, affective, and behavioral orientations to environment are already present. In the complex interchange between the child's biological needs, and the frequency and nature of their satisfaction basic-core beliefs about the nature of the world are being developed. These core beliefs are not in themselves political, but I would argue that they have important political implications.

What the child is beginning to learn is a basic belief in controllability of the world in general and his ability to control it in particular. This belief has the most profound implication for political life. Pye, for example, in his discussion of the inability of the Burmese adult to develop stable political identities, traces the origins of this problem to childhood. He notes that the Burmese child is

> brought up to feel that he has no control over the ways in which he is treated by others. . . . Thus from the time of his earliest experiences, the child exists in a world in which there is no rational relationship, no recognizable connection between his powers of action and choice and the things that he most desperately wants. From the beginning the Burmese child comes to feel unconsciously that the world is a fickle place. [He] thus learns the most profound lesson of his life.[8]

[8] Lucian Pye, *Politics, Personality and Nation-Building* (New Haven: Yale University Press, 1962), p. 182.

Our discussion to this point, then, suggests that basic human needs are shaped by social experience and that the acquisition of core beliefs about the nature of the world are acquired via social learning. Having examined the origins of personal control in some detail, we are now able to make a more general statement about the relationship between personality development, personal control, and political socialization.

PSYCHOLOGICAL NEEDS AND BASIC BELIEFS

Our discussion of the nature of the personal-control need stressed three related ideas: (1) that the child arrives in the world with physiological needs, but no independent ability to satisfy them, (2) that the need for personal control originates in the attempt to satisfy these physiological needs, and (3) that in the course of attempting to satisfy these needs, the child develops basic beliefs about the controllability of the world in general and his ability to exert control in particular.

Stated in a more general way we wish to suggest, (1) that the child acquires a set of basic beliefs about the world at a very early age, (2) that these beliefs are acquired in the attempt to satisfy certain basic human needs, and (3) that these basic beliefs are the foundation upon which later political learning is built. It is upon these three contentions that we suggest a theory of political socialization might profitably proceed, and we will examine each in turn, beginning with a theory of human needs and personality development.

Needs

Political scientists interested in personality theory have had their choice of utilizing either Freudian or trait theories of personality. In effect, however, most of the work in personality and politics has utilized the latter, with less than overwhelming success.[9] There is, however, another alternative and that is the utilization of a "third force" approach; more specifically Abraham Maslow's theory of a need hierarchy. We discussed this theory briefly in Chapter Four, but we will elaborate further here. The needs in order of ascendance are; (1) physiological, (2) safety, (3) love, (4) self-esteem, and (5) self-actualization.

Physiological needs refer to the need of the body for food, sleep, or water. These needs, if unfulfilled, become the basic organizing mechanism of human activity. While it may be true that man does not live by bread alone, caloric deprivation appears to lead to a decreased interest in the surrounding environment and an increased interest, one might say preoccupation, with food.[10] Physiological deprivation is not without its implications for political behavior. As Hoffer noted:

> To be engaged in a desperate struggle for food and shelter is to be wholly free from a sense of futility. The goals are concrete and immediate. Every meal is a fulfillment; to go to sleep on a full stomach is a triumph. . . . Where people toil from sunrise to sunset for a bare living they nurse no grievances and dream no dreams.[11]

Even more directly political is the description of Angelica Balabanoff of the effect of abject poverty on the political con-

[9] In a forthcoming work I will analyze and compare the various approaches in the personality-and-politics field. See Stanley Renshon, *Personality Theories and Political Analysis* (New York: Free Press, forthcoming).

[10] See the discussion of the Minnesota experiments in J. Davies, *Human Nature and Politics* (New York: Wiley & Sons, 1963), pp. 11–15.

[11] Eric Hoffer, *The True Believer* (New York: Harper & Row, 1951), pp. 26–27.

cerns of radicals in Moscow during the early days of the Communist revolution. Balabanoff writes that, "she saw men and women who had lived all of their lives for ideas, who had voluntarily renounced material advantages, liberty, happiness, and family affection for the realization of their ideals, completely absorbed by the problems of hunger and cold."[12]

The second set of needs to emerge according to Maslow are the safety needs. Maslow suggests that this need falls into two categories, (1) bodily safety and (2) psychological security. The first refers to the need to be secure from attack or aggression and to live one's life without being the object of physical threat. The second category is somewhat more subtle and refers to the psychological need for an orderly and predictable world. In children this need takes the form of a "preference for some kind of undisrupted routine or rhythm . . . (a preference) for a safe, orderly, predictable, organized world which he can count on and in which unexpected, unmanageable, or other dangerous things do not happen."[13]

This need is not absent in adults. Goffman for example has noted the elaborate staging and other devices utilized to control the interaction context.[14] He has called these normal attempts to control "stage managing" and found that they are a normal occurrence in social interaction. Carried to an extreme, however, the attempt to manipulate the environment for psychological security needs begins to resemble the compulsive personality described clinically by

[12] Angelica Balabanoff, *My Life as a Rebel* (New York: Harper, 1938), p. 204.

[13] A. Maslow, *Motivation and Personality* (New York: Harper, 1954), pp. 86–87.

[14] Erving Goffman, *The Presentation of Self in Everyday Life* (New York: Anchor, 1959).

Horney[15] and in the area of politics by George and George.[16]

When both physiological and safety needs are satisfied, what Maslow calls the higher needs emerge. Love needs refer to desire and need for human warmth, affection and inclusion by desired objects. The deleterious effects to human growth when these needs are not satisfied have been well-documented in animal studies by Harlow,[17] and for humans by Davis.[18] Organisms deprived of this need early in the life cycle grow up emotionally stunted, and never seem able to recover. The implications of the deprivation of this need for the political system may appear small at first glance, but a further look reveals its importance. A recently published psychoanalytic study of Adolf Hitler suggests that emotional deprivation had important consequences for his behavior as a political leader.[19] Closer to home, the resurgence of strong ethnic and racial self-group identification can be viewed as arising out of the same need.

The next set of needs to emerge arc the esteem needs. Maslow describes these needs in two ways. "First, the desire for strength, for achievement, for adequacy, for mastery, and competence, for confidence in the face of the world, and for independence and freedom. Second, the desire for reputation and/or prestige, status, dominance, recognition,

15 K. Horney, *Neurotic Personality of Our Times,* (New York: Norton, 1937), *passim.*

16 A. George and J. George, *Woodrow Wilson and Colonel House: A Personality Study* (New York: Dover, 1957).

17 H. Harlow *et al.*, "Manipulatory Motivation in the Infant Rhesus Monkey," *Journal of Comparative Physiological Psychology*, 49, 1956.

18 K. Davis, "Final Note on a Case of Extreme Isolation," *American Sociological Review*, 4, 1956.

19 Walter Langer, *The Mind of Adolph Hitler* (New York: Basic Books, 1972).

attention, importance, application."[20] The importance of this need in the study of politics has been suggested by a number of writers. In one study a group of political candidates were asked to describe why men sought effective office. What emerged was "a fairly clear picture of self-interest in which the most important elements were personal advancement and prestige.[21] The mastery of a particular area of endeavor is the basis for a positive evaluation of self by self. When significant others accord legitimacy to the area of mastery, self-esteem and positive evaluation by others coalesce.

Lastly, when all of these needs have been fulfilled, the need for self-actualization emerges. As Maslow has noted, "what man can be, he must be."[22] Once the other needs have been met then men can concentrate on realizing their potential. The relationship between self-actualization and political behavior has been analyzed by Knutson elsewhere.[23] Generally, the self-actualizing person is found to be more politically concerned, more tolerant and less likely to join extremist groups.

Maslow's need theory of personality development not only provides an important analytical tool for the analysis of political life, but it also provides political scientists with a personality model that is not linked exclusively with either psychopathology or unconscious motivations. Elsewhere, Greenstein has urged that "one of the great needs of contemporary political analysis is for convenient means of personal characterization that goes beyond political attitudes, but does not focus merely on deeper processes and struc-

[20] Maslow, *op. cit.*, p. 20.

[21] Robert Rosenzweig, "The Politician and the Career in Politics," *Midwest Journal of Political Science*, 2, 1957, p. 166.

[22] Maslow, *op. cit.*, p. 91.

[23] Jeanne Knutson, *The Human Basis of the Polity* (Chicago: Aldine, 1972).

tures."[24] I would like to suggest here that Maslow's theory provides such a model of personality.

Basic Beliefs

Our discussion of the nature of personal control stressed psychological needs and also basic beliefs. Basic beliefs, we suggested, originated in the attempt to satisfy basic psychological needs.

Basic beliefs are defined as a set of assumptions about the nature of reality and the world in which one lives, the validity of which is rarely if ever challenged.[25] Thus, basic beliefs represent a deeper level of psychic organization than do attitudes or opinions. Basic beliefs are suggested to be five in number.

First, beliefs about the nature of physical reality (for example, color, form, sound, space, and time). Second, beliefs about the potential for individual action in the world (personal control). Third, beliefs involving evaluations of the world in which one lives (that is, whether it is a friendly or hostile place). Fourth, beliefs about the other people who inhabit the life-space of the individual (that is, whether people are good and can be trusted). And fifth, beliefs about self-evaluations (that is, whether the self holds a positive or negative valence). These basic beliefs are interrelated in the acquisition process. By this I mean that I would hypothesize that several or all of these basic beliefs would vary together. For example, the belief that the world

24 Fred Greenstein, *Personality and Politics* (Chicago: Markham, 1969), p. 58.

25 Rokeach has developed a similar concept, which he calls "central beliefs," but neglects a discussion of where these beliefs originate. See Milton Rokeach, *The Open and Closed Mind* (New York: Basic Books, 1960), Chapter 2. Basic beliefs are also discussed by Lane, although in this case again, there is no mention made of psychogenesis. See Robert Lane, *Political Man* (New York: Free Press, 1973), Chapter 4.

is a place in which no personal control is possible (basic belief two) would be associated with the belief that the world is essentially a hostile place (basic belief three).

The suggestion that basic beliefs arise out of the attempt to satisfy human needs provides a new perspective on the whole debate in political socialization research about the impact of early learning. Most of the research on this issue has dealt with party preferences or political attitudes. Yet, as two well-known researchers in the area concluded after examining the results of a national sample of parents and children,

> it is clear that any model of socialization that rests on assumptions of pervasive currents of parent to child value transmissions of the type examined here *is in need of serious modification*. . . . Party identification . . . is a prime exception. The data suggest that with regard to a range of other attitude objects, the correspondences vary from, at most, *moderate support to virtually no support*.[26] (Emphasis added.)

Our model, however, suggests that what is learned in childhood that is politically important are not specific attitudes but basic beliefs about the world.[27] The hypothesis in political socialization research, that early learning affects later learning, depends on what it is that we specify is being learned. It may be entirely correct to argue at one and the same time that (1) a political attitude learned early in life will not shape subsequent attitude acquisition, and (2) that

[26] M. Kent Jennings and Richard Niemi, "The Transmission of Political Values from Parents to Children," *American Political Science Review*, 62, 1968, p. 183.

[27] For a more detailed statement on the relationship between psychological needs, basic beliefs, and political socialization see Stanley Renshon, "The Role of Personality Development in the Political Socialization Process," in D. Schwartz and S. Schwartz (eds.), *New Directions in the Study of Political Socialization* (New York: Free Press, 1974).

basic beliefs may shape subsequent political orientations and be highly resistant to change. We are suggesting that the emphasis on early learning in the political socialization process may prove to be essentially correct in its general form as long as one talks about basic beliefs and not specific attitudes for young children.

Several additional observations about basic beliefs should be mentioned. Although they do represent a deeper level of psychic organization than do attitudes, there are similarities insofar as they do have cognitive, affective, and behavioral components. What differentiates them from attitudes is their generality; they are beliefs about the nature of the world while attitudes are orientations toward specific objects.

The question that naturally arises at this point is why, if children do not have stable attitudes towards politics, should they be assumed to have stable beliefs about the world. The answer, we suggest, is that there is no reason to assume that children have no stable orientations because they have no political attitudes. For most politics is far removed from their daily existence. If as Converse[28] suggests the same is true for over half the adults in the nation, why should we assume it to be less the case for children? Since politics is so far removed from their lives ordinarily children acquire affective, but not cognitive orientations toward political objects.[29] Moreover, there is some evidence that even these affective orientations are a product of generalizations from affective orientations to more immediate objects, namely parents.[30] Yet, while politics may be distant, the world is not. As we suggested earlier in this chapter,

28 Philip E. Converse, "The Nature of Belief Systems in Mass Publics," in David Apter (ed.), *Ideology and Discontent* (London: Free Press, 1965), *passim.*

29 Fred Greenstein, *Children and Politics* (New Haven: Yale University Press, 1965), *passim.*

30 *Ibid.*

children do acquire information about the events and information in their life-space, so that basic beliefs can have a cognitive, as well as an affective, component.

Building on Maslow's model of human needs and our own discussion, we can now suggest the outlines of a personality system, with implications for the analysis of political socialization and political behavior. The components of such a personality system include (1) the basic human psychological needs, as defined by Maslow, (2) basic beliefs about the world, arising out of the attempt to satisfy these needs, (3) habitual patterns of relation to the world, built upon past methods for attempted need gratification,[31] (4) specific attitudes toward objects, generalized in part from basic beliefs, and (5) values—preferences based in part on need states and basic beliefs. This organizational schema is presented in Figure 1.

Figure 1 suggests to us that the need for personal control is one of the basic needs in Maslow's hierarchy. We previously noted that Maslow's second need was actually divided into two parts; one, the need to be safe from harm, and two, the need for an orderly, secure world. Taken to-

[31] Each individual builds up a repertoire of ways of obtaining satisfaction of his needs in the social context. Those that are perceived to have been successful are retained, and those that have not produced success are not. By the time an individual approaches his early adult years, these modes of relating to the world are largely fixed. There is of course the problem that what was successful at one stage of development will not prove to be so at a latter stage or in different circumstances. A number of psychologists have discussed this aspect of the individual, without however having related it to the attempt at need satisfaction. Jung's introversion-extroversion distinction is one attempt to analyze such differences in orientations to the environment.

There is, however, a further problem which those psychologists and political scientists who have utilized Maslow's need theory have not confronted. Granted that the need hierarchy exists within each person, how does he learn the appropriate objects of need gratification? It is insufficient to note that a person has a love need, for example, without also addressing the question of why and how the satisfaction of that need came to be associated with a particular context and a particular object.

FIGURE 1. THE PERSONALITY SYSTEM AND POLITICAL ORIENTATIONS

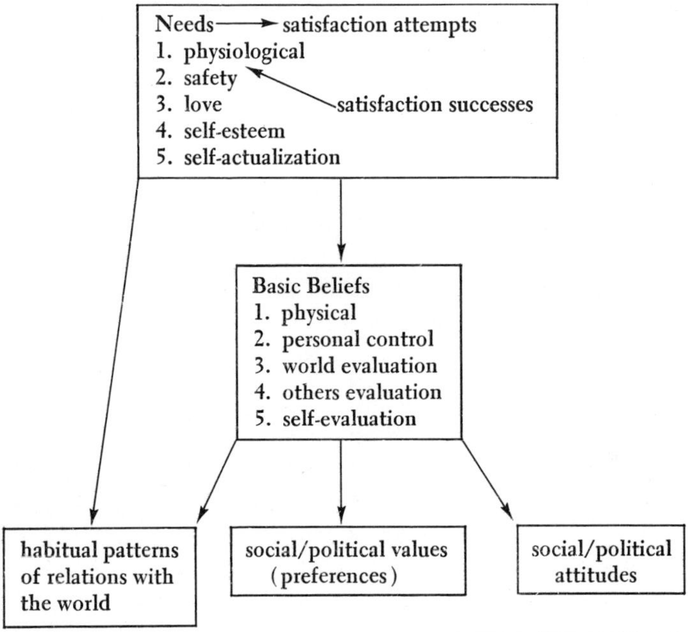

gether these aspects suggest a need to have control over relevant aspects of one's life-space. As one of the basic needs in the hierarchy, it serves as an organizing need for subsequent need satisfaction. That is, the potential to fulfill love, self-esteem, and self-actualization needs are dependent (for most people) on obtaining personal control. It is the basic belief that arises from the satisfaction or frustration of this need that we suggest has important implications for political life and the political system. This raises a number of questions, the most important of which is the specification of the link or links between personal control needs and beliefs and political attitudes and behaviors. Are psychological needs by definition political? If not, under what circumstances do they become politically relevant? What is the nature of the relation between these needs and beliefs when they become politically relevant and specific political attitudes and behaviors? It is to these questions that we turn in the following chapter.

Chapter Six

A NEED THEORY OF POLITICAL EFFICACY AND POLITICAL PARTICIPATION

The discussions in previous chapters suggested that there was within each of us a need to have some control over relevant dimensions of our social and psychological life-space. When perceptions of relevancy include the political system, then the link is forged between personal control and political efficacy.

More specifically, political efficacy is defined as *the belief that one has sufficient personal control over political processes to satisfy the need for control in relevant life areas.* Such a definition differs from previous definitional attempts in two ways: (1) it focuses attention on the concept of personal control with all of the attendant implications previously developed, and (2) it points to the psychological origins of the belief, namely the *need* for personal control.

Viewed from this perspective, political efficacy is an attitudinal manifestation of a basic personality orientation. Yet, in a sense, personal control is a necessary but insufficient ingredient of political efficacy, for it is only when the political system becomes salient that individuals are motivated to act. Thus, the concept of salience plays an important role in a need theory of political efficacy.

PERSONAL CONTROL AND POLITICAL SALIENCE

A great deal of research has simply assumed the salience of the political system and gone to present data on the relationships between attitudes and political behavior. Converse has suggested that such research in a sense creates attitudes where none had previously existed; and therefore has considerable problems of validity and reliability.[1] Another related problem, is the indirect measurement of political salience, which is very often measured by level of factual information,[2] attention to media,[3] or the importance of particular political events.[4]

Such measurement strategies may be perfectly adequate. Yet the concept of personal control suggests that salience can better be understood phenomenologically, that is, from the perspective of the perceived impact of the object in question on the daily life of the individual. In more specific terms, *the political system will be perceived to be salient to the extent that it is felt to have an impact on the individual's social or physical life-space—his day-to-day existence.* Such perceptions may arise out of three conditions: (1) The political system may be seen as the only source capable of supplying certain benefits in the form of either goods or services; (2) the decisional outputs of the political system may be viewed as interfering with the pursuit of an individual's values and goals; or (3) the political system may become salient because the individual believes he has an obligation as a citizen to pay attention to the processes of the political system. These three origins of political salience might be labeled political-reward salience, political-punishment salience, and political-obligation salience, respectively.

Political-reward salience arises out of the view that the political system has the capacity to accomplish goals which

[1] Philip E. Converse, "The Nature of Belief Systems in Mass Publics," in David Apter (ed.), *Ideology and Discontent* (New York: Free Press, 1964), Chapter 6.

[2] M. Seeman, "Powerlessness and Knowledge: A Comparative Study of Alienation and Learning," *Sociometry*, 30, 1967, pp. 105–123.

[3] A. Campbell *et al.*, *The American Voter* (New York: Wiley & Sons, 1960), Chapter 6.

[4] *Ibid.*

otherwise could not be obtained. In other words, the political system is viewed as the *only* system capable of accomplishing a particular task. This might be the case either because the political system is seen as having the legitimacy and authority to carry out a task or because the political system is viewed as the only system with the resources to carry out the task.

On the one hand, then, the enforcement of particular laws *could* be carried out by individuals, but there is substantial agreement that the political system and not the individual has the legitimate authority to make and enforce laws. Thus, "taking the law into your own hands" is viewed in this society as a serious breach of citizen behavior and is typically portrayed as occurring only after the almost total breakdown of enforcement procedures. The expected behavior in this type of salience would be an attempt to have the system either undertake new laws or more diligently enforce old ones. Thus, citizens who regard drinking as a great evil do not typically attempt to burn down bars but rather attempt to get the legislatures to legally restrict alcoholic distribution and consumption.

On the other hand, either the complexity or the magnitude of a particular problem may require the intervention by the political system with resources that are simply not available elsewhere. This is increasing the case in complex, highly morphogenic societies but also may occur in less technically and socially complex societies. For example, the attempt to find cures for physical disease requires a tremendous amount of capital expenditures for personnel and laboratory equipment. Such financial outlays may be outside the range of possibility for other societal institutions.

Another possibility is that the sources of a particular problem are so diverse and touch so many aspects of a society that only the political system can deal with them. This is especially true in complex societies which are highly differentiated, but increasingly interdependent. Thus, the problem of air pollution springs from a variety of sources in American life, and to deal effectively with the problem requires attention to many if not all of the problem sources. Typically, only the political system touches all or enough of the sectors of the social system to make a solution possible.

In the above examples, the basic consideration is that the political system is seen to have the *capacity* to act in a way that is perceived to be beneficial to the citizen. The citizen's role in this case is to induce *intent to act*, which when coupled with capacity will produce the desired results. Thus, political-reward salience is based on essentially positive orientations to and evaluations of the capacity of government to provide satisfactions to the citizen.

Such is not the case for political-punishment salience. In this condition the concern is not so much for what *might* be done, as for what *is* being done. Both reward- and punishment-oriented citizens might agree that the political system has a great impact on their daily lives; the difference between them lies in their evaluations of this social fact. For the punishment-oriented citizen the government's impact is seen to be deleterious, and the outputs of the political system are viewed as unwarranted infringements on the citizen's life.

For these citizens the problem is not so much to get the political system to do something more, but rather to get it to do less. Viewed from this perspective the government is not so much a means to a problem solution as it is the problem itself. These citizens might clearly agree with Jefferson that that "government which governs least governs best." The difference is that this is not so much a philosophy as an attitude reflecting the impact of government on their daily lives. The ability of the political system to raise an army by conscription, to tax individuals for social services to others, or to require that certain uniform standards of access to public education be met may all have negative impacts on large groups of people.

All these possibilities have in common the phenomena of direct impact from which there is usually little possibility of escape. In less politically centralized societies, interaction between government and citizen is more infrequent and might consist of occasional attempts to collect taxes or the usually unwelcome arrival of government soldiers.[5] In more centralized, bureaucratic societies, interaction is much more frequent and the possibilities for mutual influenceability or control are considerably greater. More importantly, the possibilities of avoiding the impact of the political system are decreased.

In reality, there is probably a considerable mix of the reward and punishment salience for many citizens. The important point is that it is the direct impact of the political system on their lives which makes politics salient, and therefore a sphere that becomes necessary for the individual to exercise some control over.

There remains one other source of political salience to be discussed, namely political obligation salience. In its purest form, the obligated citizen would view the political sphere as salient only because he feels his good-citizen role requires it. Because the origin of his concern with the political system is external (that is, social norms), rather than internal (that is, growing out of the impact on him personally), the political system, while salient, would be less likely to be a control-relevant sphere. This assumes, of course, that there are other areas with control relevance in the person's life to which he is more likely to commit his energy, time, and other resources. While this is probably the case for many citizens, there are no doubt others for whom the pull of citizen obligation is so strong that politics does become a control-relevant sphere. Thus, families with great traditions of political activity, such as the Rockefellers, the Lodges,

[5] D. Hinkley, *Village in Vietnam* (New Haven: Yale University Press, 1966).

or the Kennedys, may be more likely to be motivated to participate by political-obligation salience, than the ordinary citizen.

Of course very often one would expect to find this orientation combined with either political-reward or political-punishment salience, especially in more centralized political systems where the government has taken on greater responsibilities. Once the political system has become salient as a control-relevant sphere, the link has been forged between personal control and political action.

PERSONAL CONTROL, POLITICAL PARTICIPATION AND POLITICAL EFFICACY

Of course, to say there is a link between personal control and political participation is only a first step. It is important not only to understand that there is a link, but to explore the behavioral consequences of that link. We suggested that political efficacy was the belief that one *had* sufficient personal control over political processes to satisfy the need for control in relevant life areas. Viewed from this perspective, high political efficacy as a belief is logically preceded by (1) a need for personal control, (2) the perception that politics is salient, and (3) a successful history of attempts to gain some control through participation.

The importance of (3)—the history of participation—should be stressed. What distinguishes attitudes of political efficacy as a *norm*[6] from attitudes of political efficacy derived from the satisfaction of the need for personal control is some participation in the political process that is perceived to have been successful. Thus, an important dif-

[6] See the discussion in David Easton and Jack Dennis, "The Child's Acquisition of Regime Norms: Political Efficacy," *The American Political Science Review*, 61, 1967.

ference between those who have high political efficacy and those who do not is that the former will feel that their previous action has been successful, while the latter will feel it has not.

One might also suspect that another difference between those with high and low political efficacy would be found in participation rates. With the traditional conceptualization of political efficacy one might expect that the higher the personal control, the greater the frequency of participation; *however, a need theory of political efficacy suggests that the opposite might be the case.* That is, since political efficacy is viewed as arising out of the *satisfaction* of the need for personal control, and since the unfulfilled need for control is anxiety producing, one might expect *more, not less,* participation from those with low personal control and high political salience. For the people with feelings of low personal control and high political salience, the need for control would be unsatisfied, and one might expect renewed efforts to gain such control.

Clearly such continuous participation in the political system without satisfaction of control needs and increases in feelings of efficacy would be highly frustrating and anxiety producing. We might expect such frustration to lead to feelings of estrangement (that is, alienation) from the political system. Moreover, one might expect that individuals in these circumstances would be much more ready to participate in extreme forms of political activity, such as political violence, and more likely to believe in the efficacy of such extreme behavior.

For those who had achieved high political efficacy, one might expect less frequent, although certainly no cessation of political activity. Rather, since the need for personal control is being met, there would be less importance attached to participation in any particular event. Moreover, since past participation has been at least somewhat successful, one would expect less frustration and therefore less likelihood of participation in or belief in the efficacy of extreme political action.

This theory suggests then, that expansion of government activities into the daily lives of its citizens brings with it an increased need on the part of individual citizens to gain some control over political processes. Moreover, if the system is seen as unresponsive and participation as unsatisfying, the consequences for the stability of the system will be severe. Thus, the psychological need for control has important behavioral and attitudinal consequences for system stability, as well as system legitimacy. Of equal importance are its implications for democratic theory.

PERSONAL CONTROL AND PARTICIPATORY-DEMOCRATIC THEORY

In the introduction we suggested that political theory and political participation were closely related to democratic theory. We noted that the meaning of the low rates of citizen participation were under debate by political scientists, with some suggesting that low rates may be desirable or indicate substantial satisfaction, while others suggest that low participation rates are to be eschewed and may indicate potential system instability. In Chapters Seven, Eight, and Nine we will begin an empirical investigation of these issues and present the outlines of a possible answer to the debate. At this point, however, we wish to stop and assess the implications of our theory of personal control for participatory-democratic theory.

Traditionally, the justification of participatory-democratic theory has rested on a theoretical discussion of its functions and consequences. These functions may for convenience be grouped into three categories: (1) educational function, (2) legitimacy function, and (3) interest-articulation function.

The idea that participation in political life results in the education of the citizen is an old one in participatory-democratic theory.[7] Rousseau, for example, believed that a central function of participation was to educate the citizen to wider concerns. That is, in the process of attempting to gain the cooperation of others, he would be forced to acquire a wider conception of the public good,[8] since any position marked by narrow self-interest would fail to draw followers. Another classical theorist who saw the function of participation as an educative one was J. S. Mill. Mill argued that one of the most important dimensions of government was the degree to which it promoted the general mental advancement of the community. It was only within a context of popular, participatory institutions that Mill saw an "active," public-spirited character being fostered.[9] Finally, the educative function of participation has been summed up most recently and eloquently by Patemen:

> The major function of participation in the theory of participatory democracy is therefore an educative one, educative in the very widest sense, including both the psychological aspect and the gaining of practice. . . . Therefore, for a democratic polity to exist it is necessary for a participatory polity to exist, i.e., a society where all political systems have been democratized.[10]

The second broad function mentioned as a justification for participatory-democratic theory was its ability to foster the attribution of legitimacy to political systems. In part

[7] The discussion that follows owes much to Pateman's brilliant discussion of similar issues. See Carole Pateman, *Participation and Democratic Theory* (London: Cambridge University Press, 1970), Chapter 1.

[8] *Ibid.*, p. 25.

[9] *Ibid.*, pp. 28–29.

[10] *Ibid.*, p. 42.

the sense of legitimacy requires that the citizen perceive that both the regime and the regime outputs accord with his sense of the rules of the game. As Rousseau pointed out, it is the nature of the participatory process that no man can easily become the master of another and that all are equally subject to the law.[11] In this way the participatory process helps to assure that everyone plays according to the same rules of the game and thus helps to foster feelings of legitimacy.

There is also another perhaps more direct way that participation leads to feelings of legitimacy. Participation in the political process and the subsequent influencing of system outputs foster legitimacy by giving the citizen a sense of proprietary interest in the outcomes of the political process. Thompson suggests that

> the subjective element of legitimacy which a sense of proprietorship expresses does represent a vital function of participation. It contributes indirectly to the democratic objective by supporting a stable system in which processes required by other aspects of citizenship can operate. More importantly, citizenship theorists consider it a good to be sought for its own sake.[12]

Finally, the third function of participation revolves around citizen interest articulation. Actually this function has two sides. The first is to insure that the interests of the rulers do not prevail over the interests of the citizens. It is not only that rulers would purposely impose their interests at the expense of the citizen, although this was and is by no means an uncommon occurrence. Rather, participation is also seen as guarding against the assumption of the ruler that he knows what is best for the citizen. This is in turn

[11] *Ibid.*, p. 25.

[12] Dennis Thompson, *The Democratic Citizen* (London: Cambridge University Press, 1970), p. 63.

related to the other side of the articulation function, the consideration of citizen self-interest.

Even if rulers would never be disposed to impose their will on citizens, it would still be necessary to have substantial citizen participation, because each man is the best judge of his own interests. This is the famous "pinching shoes" argument used by Lindsay and other democratic theorists. According to Lindsay, "Only . . . the ordinary man can tell whether the shoes pinch and where; and without that knowledge the wisest statesman cannot make good laws."[13] Participation, therefore, is valuable because it allows the citizen to make his wishes known to the rulers. It is important to these theorists that participation becomes institutionalized, since "experts do not like being told that the shoes they so beautifully make do not fit."[14]

Thus, we see that participation has been justified as necessary because it fulfills at the least one of the three broad functions that we have outlined. Empirical or systematic theoretical support for these functions has not been easy to obtain. In part this is because most theoretical points are presuppositions rather than hypotheses about social reality. For example, in discussing the presupposition of autonomy—that citizens be treated as the best judge of their own interests—Thompson noted that

> autonomy and improvability are very much like absolute presuppositions. [They] serve . . . as regulatory principles in the theory. . . . Our acceptance of the presuppositions of a theory of democracy does not depend mainly on evidence from social science. A complete defense of the presuppositions of citizenship would require a portrayal, in literary and philo-

[13] A. D. Lindsay, *The Modern Democratic State* (New York: Vantage, 1922), p. 271.

[14] *Ibid.*, p. 276.

> sophical terms, of a vision of a society of autonomous and improvable men.[15]

While the presupposition of autonomy may not depend on social science, our confidence in it might be increased if we could bring some independent evidence to bear on the subject. It is at this point that a need theory of political efficacy makes its contribution to participatory-democratic theory. In Chapter Four we presented evidence to support the proposition that individuals have a need to control relevant aspects of their psychological and social life-space. We have herein suggested the conditions under which this need becomes transposed to the political system. If our theory is correct, then we have added another justification to participatory-democratic theory, but a justification that flows from empirical (in the Humean sense) assessment. That is, participation is important not only because it increases the system's legitimacy, not only because it educates the citizen, and not only because it serves as a vehicle for self-interest articulation, but also *because it may fulfill an individual's basic personality need to exert some control over relevant aspects of his life-space.*

Two points need to be stressed here. First, we do not propose that participation always leads to feelings of personal control in the political system. In order for personal-control needs to become transformed into feelings of political efficacy, the individual must have engaged in some action that is perceived *as successful.* Second, our theory suggests that, to the extent that the political system does not impact upon the individual's life, we would expect this need to have less relevance for political participation. It is my belief that this is not an important drawback to my justification for modern democratic theory. Certainly all of the industrialized and industrializing nations are characterized by large and increasing centralization of political authority. Even the

[15] Thompson, *op. cit.*, pp. 10–11.

relatively small and relatively unindustrialized lands of the South Pacific are undergoing increased centralization of political power.[16] The prospect is, then, that government will not decrease its role in the life of most world citizens, but on the contrary, will increase it. Therefore, as a justification for political participation, a need theory of political efficacy assumes greater importance.

Moreover, a need theory of political efficacy is related to another aspect of democratic theory. In the introduction we suggested that the question of what kind and how much citizen participation is desirable had been a concern of political theorists since the time of Plato. We went on to suggest that it was the last part and not the first part of the question that had been the concern of contemporary democratic theorists. Yet, a need theory of political efficacy also has implications for the attempt to determine the best form of political system.

Every theory of government rests on assumptions about human nature, and certainly democratic theory is no exception. The prescriptive statement that people *should* have some control over those who rule can be justified from two positions. On the one hand, it might be argued that such a statement by itself is a morally superior position based on superior values. Such an argument is easily criticized on the grounds of value relativism; that is, arguments about the relative merits of different positions are often a matter of personal preference and thus difficult to assess and compare.

On the other hand, one might argue that a certain position is more valid because it is based on a more accurate assessment of the human condition and human nature. More specifically, if it is true that people do have a need to control their life-space and if it can be empirically documented that a system which both allows for such control and is responsive to it will have the least alienated and most satisfied

[16] Ronald Force (ed.), *Induced Political Change in the Pacific* (Honolulu: Bishop Museum Press, 1965).

citizens, then the desirability of that form of government over other forms from the standpoint of the individual citizen will have received some substantiation.

The attempt to ascertain the degree to which citizens feel the system allows personal control and their subsequent evaluations of that system return us to the question we raised earlier: namely, the meaning of low participation rates and the relation between participatory motivation and participatory satisfaction. Before we begin our empirical exploration of these questions, it is necessary to first spend some time examining the acquisition of personal control.

A look at the socialization process underlying the acquisition of personal control and its transfer to the political system is important for several reasons. Firstly, the acquisition of personal control does not take place in a psychological vacuum. It is important to understand the cultural and social influences that shape it in a particular way in our present political culture. Secondly, the acquisition of personal control does not take place alone. Rather it is part of a complex of basic orientation acquisitions that must be understood in order to fully understand the social psychogenesis of political participation. Thirdly, a full theory of personal control and political efficacy requires an understanding not only of the psychodynamics involved but also of the psychogenesis of the need. With this in mind the next several chapters begin to explore the acquisition of personal control and the effect of the culture, social system, and family context. We will then be in a better position to turn to an exploration of the relation between personal control, political participation, and political satisfaction.

Chapter Seven

TOWARD A RECONCEPTUALIZATION OF POLITICAL EFFICACY

The suggestion that there is a need to reconceptualize the political efficacy domain in a way which would take into account the need for personal control allows us to see previous definitions of political efficacy in a new light. Recast from the vantage point of personal control, it appears that one common irreducible element of political efficacy is the perception of the self as having obtained sufficient mastery in the political arena: the perception that the individual feels he has a certain amount of control over the inputs and/or outputs of the political system. Such a belief implies that the self and not the environment is, in Heider's terms, the "locus of causality."[1] Concern with the consequences of the perception of the "locus of causality" has long played a major role in psychological research, and it is to this research that we now turn as a basis for the reconceptualization and revitalization of political efficacy.

The phenomenon of the perception of self as the locus of social causality has itself been studied in several ways. De Charms, for example, has used the terms "origin" and "pawn" to categorize differences in the perception of social causality. He defines an "origin" as a person who perceives his behavior to be the result of his own choice, while a "pawn" is a person who believes his behavior is being determined by external forces beyond his control.[2] In a series of papers, De Charms and his associates have demonstrated

[1] Franz Heider, *The Psychology of Interpersonal Relations* (New York: Wiley & Sons, 1958), Chapter 2.

[2] Richard De Charms, *Personal Causation* (New York: Academic Press, 1968), p. 273.

the behavior consequences of these feelings in several experimental situations.[3] Such work clearly has implications for the study of the psychological origins of political efficacy. Unfortunately, the usefulness of much of this work for the reconceptualization of political efficacy is somewhat limited by the selection and subsequent operationalization of the "pawn" concept, which suggests that one is the object of intentional manipulation. In our conception, it is clear that one can feel inefficacious and not be an "origin," without at the same time feeling manipulated.

More immediately relevant for our reconceptualization is the work of Julian Rotter. Utilizing the instrumental paradigm of learning theory, expectancy concepts, and an empirical definition of reinforcement, Rotter has developed what has come to be known as social learning theory.[4] Within this framework, Rotter and his associates have done extensive research in the area of generalized expectancies for internal versus external control of reinforcement, which is defined as

> the degree to which the individual perceives that the reward follows from, or is contingent upon his own behavior attributes, versus the degree to which he feels the reward is controlled by forces outside of himself, and may occur independently of his actions. . . . When a reinforcement is perceived . . . as . . . not being entirely contingent upon his action, then in our culture it is typically perceived as the result of *luck, chance, fate, as under the control*

[3] See, for example: R. De Charms, V. Capender, and A. Kuperman, "The 'Origin-Pawn' Perception," *Sociometry*, 3, 1965, pp. 241–258; R. De Charms and P. N. Dave, "Hope of Success, Fear of Failure, Subjective Probability and Risk-Taking Behavior," *Journal of Personality and Social Psychology*, 3, 1965, pp. 558–568.

[4] J. B. Rotter, *Social Learning and Clinical Psychology* (Englewood Cliffs, N.J.: Prentice-Hall, 1954).

> *of powerful others,* or as unpredictable because of the *great complexity* of the forces surrounding him.[5] (Emphasis added.)

The belief that rewards were contingent upon forces external to the individual Rotter has labeled *external control,* while the belief that reinforcements were contingent upon the individual's own behavior or relatively permanent characteristics has been labeled *internal control.* Rotter contends that an individual's history of reinforcements will significantly affect the degree to which personal action and reinforcement outcomes will generate internal-control beliefs. A reinforcer, according to Rotter, is anything "that changes behavior in some way by either increasing or decreasing the potentiality of its occurrence."[6] These include both internal reinforcements, which is defined as the subject's perception that an event has had some value for him and external reinforcements, which is an act or event known to have predictable reinforcement value for the group or culture to which the subject belongs.[7]

Based on these conceptions, Rotter and his associates developed a scale to measure the generalized expectancies for internal versus external control, commonly called and hereafter referred to as the I-E Scale. As Rotter notes,

> a careful reading of the items will make it clear that the items deal exclusively with the subject's belief about the nature of the world. That is, they are concerned with the subject's expectations about how reinforcement is controlled. Consequently, the test is

[5] J. B. Rotter, "Generalized Expectancies for Internal versus External Control of Reinforcement," *Psychological Monographs: General and Applied,* 80, 1966, p. 1.

[6] Rotter, *Social Learning . . . ,* p. 112.

[7] *Ibid.,* p. 112.

> considered to be a measure of a generalized expectancy.[8]

Rotter's original scale of 23 forced-choice items has been modified in terms of both number of items and item formats, yet the internal consistency and predictive validity of the scale have remained high.

If one indication of a theory's utility is the amount of research it stimulates, then Rotter's work certainly deserves high praise. A recent literature search listed over 200 articles dealing with internal-external control in such diverse areas as academic achievement,[9] interpersonal trust,[10] accident and suicide proneness,[11] and decision making under conditions of risk.[12]

Yet, in spite of the prolific amount of work Rotter's writing has inspired in various branches of psychology, his impact on political science has been rather small. To be sure, many political scientists are aware of the work of Melvin Seeman, one of Rotter's early associates at Ohio State, in the area of powerlessness and learning. Yet, only two of Seeman's articles deal directly with politics, and each of these is concerned with political information.[13]

[8] Rotter, "Generalized Expectancies . . . ," p. 10.

[9] V. C. Crandall *et al.*, "Children's Beliefs in Their Own Control of Reinforcements in Intellectual-Academic Achievement Situations," *Child Development*, 36, 1965, pp. 91–109.

[10] J. H. Itamsher *et al.*, "Interpersonal Trust, Internal-External Control and the Warren Commission Report," *Journal of Personality and Social Psychology*, 9, 1968, pp. 210–215.

[11] C. B. Williams and J. B. Nickels, "Internal-External Control Dimensions as Related to Accident and Suicide Proneness," *Journal of Consulting and Clinical Psychology*, 33, 1969, pp. 485–494.

[12] S. Liverant and A. Scodel, "Internal-External Control Dimensions as Determinants of Decision Making Under Conditions of Risk," *Psychology Reports*, 7, 1960, pp. 59–67.

[13] Melvin Seeman, "Powerlessness and Knowledge: A Comparative Study of Alienation and Learning," *Sociometry*, 2, 1967, pp. 105–123;

Thus, there has been as yet no systematic examination of internal-external control and either political behavior or politically relevant attitudes. One of the purposes of reconceptualizing political efficacy along the lines suggested in Rotter's work is to provide the beginnings of such systematic studies in the political arena.

It will be recalled that Rotter suggested that external-oriented attributions of causality were, in our culture, generally attributable to: (1) luck, (2) fate, (3) powerful others, and (4) great complexity. We now turn to a brief explication of these concepts, suggesting, where appropriate, their utility and implications for a psychologically grounded theory of political efficacy.

LUCK, CHANCE, AND SOCIAL CAUSALITY

Chance and luck both refer to the same class of serendipitous events; that is, those events that occur with little or no connection with the efforts of the individual. Viewed from the perspective of the individual, outcomes or reinforcements are seen as randomly occurring, with each particular occurrence having a probability of .5.

Rotter and others[14] have designed a series of experiments to explore subject performance under skill and chance conditions. In a typical experiment, subjects are divided into two groups and are presented with tasks that are secretly controlled by the experimenter and which are defined as "skill" or "chance" tasks, largely on the basis of previous

---

Melvin Seeman, "Alienation, Membership and Political Knowledge," *Public Opinion Quarterly*, 30, 1966, pp. 353–367.

[14] See, for example: J. B. Rotter *et al.*, "The Growth and Extinction of Expectancies in Chance Controlled and Skilled Tests," *Journal of Psychology*, 52, 1961, pp. 161–177; E. G. Phares, "Perceptual Threshold Decrements as a Function of Skill and Chance Expectancies," *Journal of Psychology*, 53, 1961, pp. 399–407.

cultural experience. For instance, one group will be given a dice-throwing task, usually considered to be regulated by chance or luck, while another group will be given an arithmetic problem or the task of throwing darts, both of which are generally considered to be personal-skill tasks. For each group, reinforcement schedules are manipulated by the experimenter so that they ranged from 50 percent (pure chance) to 100 percent reinforcement.

These experiments have demonstrated that when rewards are perceived as under the control of either the experimenter, chance, or random conditions, subjects will generally disregard past experience (that is, past reinforcement) and consequently learn less, decreasing their ability. Moreover, for those tests that were judged to be skill tasks, chance reinforcement had the effect of decreasing the number of trials to extinction. That is, when the subject was engaged in what he thought was a skill situation, but his rewards were unrelated to his efforts, his attempts to achieve a given task decreased.

Carried over to the political arena, the implications of these studies are clear. In our society, politics is usually thought of as a skill-controlled area; one in which individual and material differences in effort expended and personal skills will correspond in some degree to the magnitude and frequency of rewards obtained. Yet, in many ways, the relation between efforts and rewards in the political system is neither automatic nor temporally coterminous. Thus, if outcomes are perceived as chance-determined—with a .5 probability of occurrence—and if the behaviors themselves are not rewarding, then we would expect substantially less political participation.

FATE AND SOCIAL CAUSATION

Unlike the idea of chance in which the outcomes are random, the concept of fate implies that outcomes are (1) predetermined, (2) inevitable, and (3) known. The idea of predetermination suggests that a particular outcome or set of outcomes will occur and that their nature, magnitude, and implications for the individual have already been determined. Inevitability refers to the perception that these outcomes will occur regardless of attempts to divert them, and therefore, that it is futile to attempt to influence them. Finally, both inevitability and predestination rest on the assumption that both outcomes and their nature are known and knowable by the individual. Theoretically, there is no necessity that outcome need be deleterious, yet, in our society at least, the idea of fate has become associated with negative consequences for the individual involved.

Whatever the consequences, the central point is that action is viewed as pointless since the outcomes are predetermined and inevitable.[15] Carried over to the political system, this attitude set would substantially reduce political involvement and participation.

Historically, the belief in inevitability and predetermined outcomes has been associated with cultures in which strong beliefs in the supernatural, and the determination of human affairs by gods or other extraterrestrial beings are present. Where gods are viewed as actively engaged in human affairs, human initiative is lessened. Examples of this point of view in non-Western, nonindustrialized societies are numerous.[16] However, as we will suggest, this same point of view is currently present in the so-called advanced countries, but under a different guise.

In contemporary Western society, belief in the direct and

[15] There is, of course, the existential view that man must struggle against his fate and against the inevitable. See Arnold Kauffman, *Existentialism* (New York: Anchor, 1965).

[16] See, for example: Shwae Yuo, *The Burmese Way* (London: Nortlidge, 1937); Bronislaw Malinowski, *Argonauts of the Western Pacific* (London: Routledge, 1922); Raymond Firth, *Primitive Polynesian Economy* (London: Routledge, 1939).

active manipulation by gods and supernatural beings in daily living is probably minimal. However, this is not to suggest that the concept of fate has no applicability. The belief that powerful forces are at work determining the outcomes of our lives and efforts is not absent in modern societies. Rather the attribution of causation has changed from gods to society itself. The growth and complexity of modern societal systems has led to the reification of society by some, and the belief that larger forces are at work in the society over which they have no control, and therefore are inevitable. The phrases "a victim of society's neglect" and "slums breed crime" point to the assumption that the net effect of the size and complexity of social institutions and the processes they generate is to predetermine and stack the outcomes for certain groups of individuals.

POWERFUL OTHERS AND SOCIAL CAUSALITY

Of course, the individual need not attribute the determination of outcomes to impersonal societal forces, since there may be ample evidence available to him that differences in personal skills and resources, reinforced by differential access to influential social roles, leave most citizens with a decided disadvantage in the relative attempt to control outcomes. It is important to note that the belief in powerful others may realistically be made by most citizens, within a great range of personal skills and social positions, so that the problem is not so much the operation of this perception but the conditions under which it leads to fatalistic resignation.

One possibility is that the greater the perceived disparity between the personal resources position of the self vis-à-vis the powerful others, the greater the likelihood of withdrawal from contention. Carried to an extreme, this gap might result in the bitter, hostile perception that "they" have all the control and influence. In a sense, then, any attempt to influence, to have an impact, requires a leap of faith, both in oneself and one's abilities *and* in the responsiveness of other people.

Even a lack of personal skills and/or resources vis-à-vis others can be overcome, given the desire to make this leap of faith. Thus, recent protest tactics that attempt to overcome inadequate personal resources through a collective strategy[17] still presuppose a certain trust in the responsiveness of the political system. It is when this trust is absent that political participation becomes unlikely.

COMPLEXITY AND SOCIAL CAUSALITY

Complexity refers to three different but related notions: one is the number of parts in the system; the second is the nature of thc organization of these parts within the system; and the third is the rate of change of the system. Either of these separately or in conjunction will effect attempts to control the system. Past a certain point, the perception of complexity in a social system will decrease the perceived possibility of controlling or even influencing the system.

The political system provides an excellent illustration of the difficulties that complexity places on citizen participation and influence. The overwhelming majority of citizens in a political system are *at least* one step removed from the actual decision-making process. That is, they are not themselves involved in decision making, but must attempt to influence those who are so involved. Therefore, in order to effect some change, it first becomes necessary to locate those individuals within the system who can and do make decisions in the particular area of interest.

This may not be as easy as it appears at first glance. Those

[17] Michael Lipsky, "Protest as a Social Resource," *American Political Science Review*, 4, 1967, p. 1144.

dealing with large bureaucracies may experience the frustration of finding that authority and power are so diffuse that accountability is difficult if not impossible to assign. The practical consequence of the inability to focus responsibility is that citizens are powerless to effect change within a system. Even with the knowledge of where to focus one's energies, the attempt to effect change is difficult. Without such knowledge, energies can easily be dissipated in ineffectual and nonrewarding efforts. There are, of course, individual variations in the amount of psychic and physical energy available to citizens for political and other kinds of activity, but these differences appear to be more important for the persistence of the attempt than for the initial decision to become involved.

So far, we have talked of the number of components and their organization; but there is a third aspect that increasingly plays an important part in the perception of complexity, and that is the rate of system change. It is not the content of particular changes that we stress, although this is, of course, not unimportant; rather it is the amount and rate of change that we wish to focus upon here.

Everyone is aware that these are times of rapid technological and social change, yet the immensity of these changes is only dimly perceived by many people. Both social habits and social organization are undergoing rapid restructuring in response to the accelerating pace of technical innovation. In fields such as population growth, production of goods, consumption of energy, and information availability, not to mention breakthroughs in transportation, biology and cybernetics, the curve on a graph would appear the same; a gradual increase from the Middle Ages to the 1900's and a continual and rapid exponential acceleration from 1900 through the present.[18] The psychological effects of this

18 See, for example: Daniel Bell (ed.), *Toward the Year 2000* (Boston: Houghton Mifflin, 1968); Kenneth Boulding, *The Meaning of the 20th Century* (New York: Harper & Row, 1964).

phenomenon on people and the consequences for political institutions and political behavior have scarcely been examined,[19] yet several possibilities come immediately to mind.

When an individual is placed in an irregularly and rapidly changing situation, his ability to relate action to outcome decreases. The reasons for this are located in the complex interface between capacity and stimulation level. We know that there is a curvilinear relation between input level and performance, such that past a certain point increased input leads to overload and decreased performance.[20] As the number and complexities of choices increase, the individual may attempt to deal with the situation for a while by acquiring new information. But all information systems, including the human brain, have limits. The individual can cope with only so much. Of course, many individuals feel that it is futile to even attempt to cope, and for them the solution becomes psychological denial and behavioral withdrawal. Thus, in 1960, 59 percent of a nationwide sample agreed with the statement that "politics and government seem so complicated that a person like me can't really understand what's going on." By 1964, that percentage had increased to 67.[21] Those who agreed with this statement were significantly less likely to vote in the national election.

SUMMARY

In this chapter, it has been suggested that a reconceptualization and revitalization of political efficacy based on the concept of personal control might proceed along the lines suggested in the work of Rotter on internal/external control.

[19] But see the extremely suggestive work of Alvin Toffler, *Future Shock* (New York: Bantam, 1970), Chapters 1–3, 7, 13–16.

[20] M. Posner, "Components of Skilled Performance," *Science*, 21, 1966, pp. 1712–1718.

[21] John Robinson *et al.*, *Measures of Political Attitudes* (Ann Arbor: Institute for Social Research, 1968), p. 635.

We then briefly explicated and reviewed the implications for social and political life, of the attribution of causality to luck, fate, powerful others, and complexity. To this point we have suggested the concept of a need for personal control and provided some support for that concept. We have also suggested the ways in which this need originates and develops and we have referred to its links to political life. If our theories have any merit, then we would expect specific consequences to flow from either the satisfaction or frustration of this need. In subsequent chapters we will begin the empirical exploration of the personal control domain, but first it is necessary to say a few words about the design of this research.

Chapter Eight

RESEARCH DESIGN

Because of the lack of systematic research utilizing the concept of personal control, a study was designed and initiated to generate data which would allow us to examine some aspects of our model. Since we are interested in the acquisition of personal control, recent research[1] suggested that the need to study parents, as well as their children, was clear. Thus, the research strategy centered around the collection of data from two groups: a sample of college undergraduates and their parents.

Shortly before the congressional elections in November of 1970, the Princeton Plan was adopted by many schools. In its most general form this plan called for the suspension of classes during the week before elections in order to allow students to work within the political system for the candidate of their choice. At Pennsylvania, this plan took the form of an "unstructured period" during which classes were not officially cancelled but for which all absences were excused and all classwork was allowed to be made up by the students.

For this survey, a random sample of university undergraduates ($N = 423$) was selected from class lists supplied by the registrar. Interviews were held during the period to obtain data on the dimensions and demographic correlates of participation in the "unstructured period." That data has been reported elsewhere.[2]

Several weeks after the "unstructured period," plans were announced for a mass demonstration in Washington against

[1] M. Kent Jennings and Richard Niemi, "The Transmission of Political Values from Parent to Child," *The American Political Science Review*, 62, 1968.

[2] Allan I. Teger and Stanley Renshon, "Alienation and Motivation: New Directions in Student Political Behavior," paper presented to the Eastern Psychological Association Meeting, Boston, 1972. A copy of the questionnaire appears in Appendix A.

the war in Vietnam. Plans were made by this researcher to reinterview the respondents from the "unstructured period" sample immediately following the mass rally in Washington on April 24, 1971. Once again, personal interviews were conducted. To reduce stimulus variation connected with the interview, each interviewer participated in a training session before interviewing commenced. In addition, nightly meetings were held to discuss any interviewing problems that arose. A limit of one week was placed on the collection of interviews to guard against the possible impact of a dramatic external event during the collection period.

Within this period, a total of 300 interviews were conducted. A follow-up of the members who do not appear in the second survey indicated that five had graduated at midyear, ten had withdrawn or taken a leave of absence, and that the rest had moved and had given the registrar no new address. Only two people refused to be interviewed, and both of them cited the pressure of school work as the reason for the refusal.

The second interview was concerned with gathering attitudinal and behavioral indicators in the political efficacy domain, including data on childhood and high-school socialization experiences. A copy of the second interview appears in Appendix B. Both sets of interviews, then, were anchored to concrete political behaviors; in one case "traditional" political activity (working for the candidate of a political party), and in the other case a form of the "politics of protest."[3]

The implementation of the second part of our research design called for the collection of data from the parents of our undergraduate sample. Following the strategy utilized by the Survey Research Center for their pathbreaking High School Socialization Study,[4] we randomly selected a third of

[3] Jerome Skolnick, *The Politics of Protest* (New York: Simon and Schuster, 1970).

[4] M. Kent Jennings and Richard G. Niemi, *op. cit., passim.*

our respondents to be matched with father-only samples, a third to be matched with mother-only samples, and a third to be matched with both mother and father samples. A total of 555 questionnaires were sent out. Each packet contained a personally typed letter[5] on dean's office stationery[6] with a self-addressed, stamped envelope.[7] In addition, follow-up requests were made when necessary.[8] A total of 291 questionnaires were returned, giving a total response rate of 52 percent.

Thus, the sample consists of a total of 300 undergraduates and their parents. Of course, strictly speaking, the adult respondents do not constitute a real sample, but they play an important part in the research strategy, none the less.

No claim is made for the representativeness of the adult respondents. Indeed, no such claims are made for the undergraduate sample either. *It is felt that the most important thrust of this research lies in the relationships uncovered as indicators of future research possibilities.* It is hoped that the relationships uncovered will suggest the utility and importance of the basic belief in personal control arising out of a psychological need in the study of participation in the political system and orientations to it.

MEASUREMENT

The major concern of this research is the concept of a need for personal control and the basic belief that arises from it.

[5] Facilitated by the use of an IBM 10/20. See Arnold Linsky, A Factorial Experiment in Inducing Responses to a Mail Questionnaire, *Sociology and Social Research*, 49, 1965.

[6] G. Alan Rocher, "Effective Techniques in Increasing Responses to Mailed Questionnaires," *Public Opinion Quarterly*, 27, 1963.

[7] John T. Gullahorn and Jeanne E. Gullahorn, "An Investigation of the Effects of Three Factors on Response to Mail Questionnaires," *Public Opinion Quarterly*, 27, 1963.

[8] Donald Longworth, "Use of a Mail Questionnaire," *American Sociological Review*, 18, 1953.

As we suggested in our discussion of the revitalization of the political-efficacy concept in Chapter Eight, there exists in the psychological literature a scale designed expressly for the purpose of ascertaining the degree of a person's beliefs in personal control; namely, the internal-external scale devised by Julian Rotter. As a recent bibliography noted, this scale, or versions of it, have been utilized in over 800 separate studies since its introduction in 1966.[9] Its use in political research, however, has been slight.[10]

It seems appropriate to repeat that Rotter suggested that "a careful reading of the items will make it clear that the items deal exclusively with the subject's beliefs in the nature of the world . . . with how reinforcement is controlled. Consequently the test is considered to be a measure of generalized expectancy."[11] That is, Rotter's scale is designed to measure one of the basic beliefs—the belief in the controllability of the world. As such it is our basic operational measure of the level of the basic belief in personal control.

Several points need to be made here. Firstly, the scale deals only with the respondent's perceptions and feelings about his level of personal control; it in no way is a measure of "objective" control. Secondly, the scale does not measure the level of a respondent's need for personal control. Nor does this research contain a measure of this need. Rather our evidence for this need will come from the attitudinal and behavioral consequences that one could predict on the basis of the theory we have put forward. Since Rotter's scale measures a respondent's basic belief in his degree of

[9] W. Throop and A. P. MacDonald, "Internal-External Locus of Control: A Bibliography," *Psychological Reports*, 28, 1971, pp. 175–190.

[10] For a recent exception see Roberta Sigel, "Bases of Political and Civic Involvement Among Rural High School Youths: Internal-External Control and Involvement," paper presented to the American Political Science Association Meeting, Chicago, 1971.

[11] J. Rotter, "Generalized Expectations for Internal versus External Control of Reinforcement," *Psychological Monographs*, 80, 1966, p. 10.

control over his life-space, it is at the same time a general indicator of the degree of satisfaction of his need for personal control. That is, respondents with high levels of belief in their personal control are assumed to have satisfied their personal control needs to a large degree, while respondents with low levels of belief in their personal control are assumed not to have satisfied this need. We are well aware that these are not givens but assumptions to be tested in later research.

The scale in its present form consists of 29 forced-choice items, if which six are fillers. However, shorter versions of this scale have been utilized by a variety of researchers.[12] For our study a total of ten I-E items were used. Each item was selected because it had been used in at least several other studies employing shortened versions of the I-E scale and because it had demonstrated high homogeneity. These scale items appear in the Appendix. In addition all I-E items used for both the parents and the students had inter-item correlations of greater than .01. Illustrative items are as follows:

1. Some people feel that getting ahead today depends more on knowing the right people than on doing a good job. How do you feel?
2. Some people have said that given human nature there will always be problems of poverty and discrimination. How do you feel?
3. With the current job market some people feel that getting a good job is mostly a matter of being in the right place at the right time. How do you feel?

Each respondent was given a score based on the number of external items he endorsed, that is, responses that indi-

[12] R. Jessor *et al.*, *Society, Personality and Deviant Behavior* (New York: Holt, Rinehart & Winston, 1968).

cated that he felt he had no or little control over his life outcomes. Subjects scoring high on this scale were said to have high personal-control beliefs, while those who obtained low scores were said to have low personal-control beliefs. In addition, there was a moderate category for those respondents that fell into the middle range.

Since this is exploratory research, *we shall be interested throughout in uncovering relationships, rather than generalizing our results to populations.* Along these lines another note of caution is in order here. Although our interest is mainly with the high and low personal-control-belief respondents, this should in no way be taken to imply that "there are two personality types and that everyone can be classified as one or the other . . . but that there is a continuum so that persons have varying degrees of internality and externality."[13]

FURTHER QUESTIONS AND SCALES

In addition to basic beliefs in personal control, this study is concerned with a number of other, related areas. In Chapters Ten and Eleven we take up the question of the impact of various dimensions of family life on the acquisition of personal control. Each respondent was asked a series of questions about family life, including the following:

1. Are both your parents still living?
2. When you were growing up, who seemed to make most of the family rules?
3. Did (he, she, they) seem to be consistent in the application of these rules, or did you sometimes get punished for breaking a rule and sometimes not, depending upon the circumstances?

[13] Julian Rotter, "Internal and External Control," *Psychology Today*, 5, 1971, p. 58.

4. If you had a problem, which parent would you take it to?
5. Would you say that this person understood how you felt about things . . . all of the time . . . most of the time . . . sometimes?
6. How much freedom were you given to direct your own life, while you were growing up?

In addition, information was collected about the number of siblings and the respondent's birth order among those siblings. We should note that this data is recall data and thus subject to caution in interpretation. However, a recent empirical study has concluded that recall data for early family experiences is a great deal more accurate than previously thought.[14]

While we were interested in the socialization dynamics of personal control, we were also interested in psychodynamic aspects. That is, given a high level of personal-control belief, are we able to say that any other characteristics or attitudes of a politically relevant nature are associated with the satisfaction of this basic need? Do people with high levels of personal control differ from those with low levels of personal control with regard to faith in people, self-esteem, or attitudes of political alienation? In order to examine these and other questions, each respondent was asked a number of questions. Generally, these questions were of three types: (1) unstructured questions, (2) structured questions utilized to form scales and indices,[15] and (3) semantic differential evaluations of both the self and the government in Washington. From these questions the following scales and indices were formed for analysis:

[14] M. Yarrow *et al.*, "Reflections of Childhood: A Study of the Retrospective Method," *Monograph of the Society for Research in Child Development*, 35, 1970, pp. 1–35.

[15] All scale items intercorrelated at .01 or better. Complete wording of all scales and the complete questionnaire will be found in the Appendix.

1. *Faith in people*—The degree to which the respondent believes that people are basically good and can be trusted. This corresponds to one of the other basic beliefs.

2. *Faith-in-government*—The degree to which the respondent feels that the government in Washington can be trusted.

3. *Political blame*—The extent to which the respondent feels that current undesirable social, economic, and political conditions are the fault of either the nature of the political system or of individuals.

4. *System effectiveness*—The degree to which the political system is perceived as effective in meeting the needs of the individual.

5. *Government output evaluation*—The degree to which the outputs of the government in Washington (laws, administrative decisions) are perceived to be either punishing or rewarding.

6. *Political alienation*—The extent to which the individual feels that he is estranged from the political system because there is a wide gap between his values and those of the political system.

7. *Political time orientations*—The extent to which the individual would like to see certain policy decisions and implementations made immediately.

8. *Government accessibility*—The extent to which the respondent feels the government is accessible.

Indices 2 (faith in government), 4 (system effectiveness), 5 (government output evaluation), and 8 (government accessibility) were derived from semantic differential scales. This technique, developed by Osgood and his associates,[16] requires the respondent to evaluate a concept (in this case the government in Washington) along a seven-point continuum

[16] R. Osgood *et al.*, *The Measurement of Meaning* (Urbana, Ill.: University of Illinois Press, 1954).

with two opposite adjective pairs on each end as the anchor points. The technique has been utilized in hundreds of studies and has proved to be a valuable tool to tap orientations to specific objects.

These techniques were utilized to examine our respondent's attitudes and orientations to self, others, and the government. However, as many social scientists, beginning with LaPiere,[17] have pointed out, there may be great differences between attitudes and action. Much of the work in the area of psychology and politics has concentrated on intrapsychic dynamics and has given us an important picture of the way in which at least some psychological dimensions are related. To this point we will have been following the same path.

But important as intrapsychic dynamics are, it would be a mistake to minimize the importance of the behavioral implications. For this reason data was collected on political participation. We did not, however, limit ourselves to the traditional behaviors, such as voting or contributing money to a candidate, which appear frequently in the literature. In addition we gathered information about our respondents' less traditional forms of participation, such as demonstrations, sit-ins, and political violence. Thus, our participation data runs the range from trying to influence someone for a particular candidate or issue to engaging in some form of political violence, such as rock throwing or fighting. Here we are interested in finding out whether there are any differences in participation rates for individuals with their personal control needs satisfied and those whose control needs remain unsatisfied. If our theory is accurate, we would expect less participation from those with a satisfied need for personal control. Beyond this question we are also interested in ascertaining whether we can say anything about the types of political participation that we can expect from persons with

[17] R. LaPiere, "Attitudes vs. Action," *Social Forces*, 13, 1934, pp. 230–237.

satisfied or unsatisfied needs for personal control. Do those with less personal control take part in more violent types of political participation?

Continuing in our examination of political participation, the next chapter focuses on the perceived efficacy of political behavior. Each respondent was asked to rate the efficacy of a range of political behaviors, from voting to assassination. In view of the widespread association of youth with extremism, our data provides some insight into the nature of support for certain types of political behaviors. Here we asked under what psychological and experiential circumstances does one begin to support the use of violence as an acceptable political tool.

The last chapter will pause to review where we have been, and detail the political relevance of personal control. Here we will again return to the relationship between personal control and democratic theory, focusing on the psychological implications that this study has for political theory. Let us now turn to an examination of the acquisition of personal control.

Chapter Nine

SOCIALIZATION AND PERSONAL CONTROL:

SOME GENERAL PARAMETERS

Much of the discussion of the social context of behavior and socialization begins with an acknowledgment of the importance of various primary institutions, such as the family and schools. However, we wish to depart somewhat from this format to briefly discuss the impact of culture on personal control.

Like many concepts in the social sciences, the authoritative, definitive and agreed-upon definition of culture has yet to be published.[1] For our purposes, though, one useful way to view culture is as the set of learned, shared behavior configurations which includes temporal, spatial, and sequential assumptions about social reality.

The first part of that definition calls our attention to the fact that behavior patterns are learned, not genetically fixed, and that what is learned are behavioral sets, or "gestalts." The second part of the definition, however, should be emphasized, for it calls our attention to a known but seldom-explicated phenomenon, namely that because transmitted cultural patterns are so general, *in many cases they become assumptions about reality, as well as about a way of organizing reality.* Very often these assumptions are so basic and so taken for granted that they are never questioned; indeed, this is exactly what we mean when we say that a person or concept is culture-bound.

The concept of personal control that we have put forward, and the web of relationships that surround it are in no way

[1] A. L. Kroeber and Clyde Kluckhohn, *Culture: A Critical Review of Concepts and Definitions* (Cambridge, Mass., Harvard University Press, 1952), p. 9.

immune to this problem. The first and most obvious point to be made here is that the definition of what it is that constitutes "competent behavior" is itself culturally determined. Very often, these will reflect environmental necessity. Thus, among the Manus that Margaret Mead studied in the South Pacific, young boys are good swimmers long before they can walk.[2] This alerts us to the fact that few of the multiple possibilities of skill development are encouraged by a culture.

The implication of this fact is that a person or people might be competent in an area, only to be given no social rewards for their mastery. This can take place, of course, within cultures, as well as across cultures. One of the best illustrations of the former was noted by Malcolm X in his autobiography. There he talked about the difference between status hierarchies in the black and white communities. He discussed how he himself was the social type known in the black community as a "hustler" or "operator," and how he viewed himself as very competent—as a person with high personal control. Yet, this same person—Malcolm X—felt none of this competence vis-à-vis his dealings with the white community *until he excelled at a skill defined as "an area of competence in the white community, namely, political organizing.*[3]

A second, less obvious way that cultural assumptions influence personal control is by controlling definitions of what is difficult and what is not. Clearly, one feels more personal control and is accorded more competence for successfully mastering something "difficult" rather than something easy. What is very often not so clear is that attributions of "difficult-not difficult" are themselves learned. In our society

[2] Margaret Mead, *New Lives for Old: Cultural Transformations—1928–1953* (New York: Morrow, 1957), Chapter 3.

[3] Malcolm X, *The Autobiography of Malcolm X* (New York: Grove Press, 1964).

difficulty is defined in part by the degree of complexity; so that science, technology, and mathematics are viewed as difficult areas to master, while something like abstract art is considered relatively simple and therefore not particularly difficult to master. The first point to be made is that the relation between degree of complexity and attributions of difficulty in mastery are by no means universal.[4] Secondly, the degree of mastery required to produce a Mondrian, for example, can be appreciated only through an attempt to reproduce it.

We noted above that cultural transmissions include temporal, spatial, and sequential assumptions about social reality, and these also have their impact on personal control. The idea of sequence in behavior sets alerts us to the fact that not only are certain behaviors grouped together, but that they also have an order. Thus, dating may be viewed as having a certain number of steps which progress from hand-holding to getting married. Along the same lines, if we are going to use sickness as an excuse for breaking a date, we do so after, not a week before the date. The idea of sequence also affects personal control. In our society, the rule seems to be, "If we can, we should." That is, at the age when we are first biologically capable of mastery in a field, there is pressure to do so. Thus, many parents create a great deal of anxiety both for themselves and their children if the child does not learn to walk, talk, or control his bowels at what is considered the "correct age." One might also note that attributions of difficulty are also related to temporal sequences. Thus, if Johnny learns to read before others of his age, he is given special rewards; while if he learns to ride a bicycle at 23 he will get no special accolades.

This brief discussion of the relevance of culture for per-

[4] E. E. Bosworth, *Art and Illusion* (Princeton: Princeton University Press, 1966), Chapter 2.

sonal control has set the stage for a more detailed discussion of the impact of social-structure location on personal-control acquisition, and it is to this discussion that we now turn.

SOCIAL STRUCTURE AND PERSONAL CONTROL

The accident of birth into a particular family structures not only the acquisition of personal control but also life chances. Why this is so will become clearer in a moment. One of the most consistent findings in political-science literature is the positive relationship between socio-economic status and political efficacy,[5] both for adults and children from high SES homes. The same finding has been reported by Campbell for personal efficacy and SES.[6] Socioeconomic status is usually calculated by obtaining occupational, educational, and financial data, and there is usually a high intercorrelation among these three measures in our society, especially the first two. Thus, SES has usually been taken as a strong indicator of a person's (family) position in the social structure. Certainly, SES *is* a valid indicator of present position, *but it is sometimes overlooked that it is also a shorthand for a whole range of life and developmental experiences, attitudes and life-styles.* Ignoring these developmental aspects is like being interested only in the outcomes of a particular game; it is fine, but tells us nothing of how or why one produces a winning team. In other words, an emphasis on outcomes or end states obscures important developmental aspects of process.

In a sense, the difference between being born into a high SES family and a low SES family may be seen as the differ-

[5] See Lester Milbrath, *Political Participation* (Chicago: Rand McNally, 1965), Chapter 5, for a general review.

[6] A. Campbell *et al., The American Voter* (New York: Wiley & Sons, 1960), p. 512.

ence between being in an "expanding" choice system and a "limiting" choice system. By expanding choice we mean that one is more likely to acquire the attitudes, skills, and resources to develop and expand one's personal development and life horizons. By limiting choice system we mean that the development of certain attitudes, skills and resources will not reach that critical level needed to increase both one's life choices and chances. Viewed from another perspective, it is the difference between a homeostatic system and a morphogenic system.[7] Of course, certain values, skills, and resources have been differentially acquired in our society and their possessors have been rewarded, but we are only now beginning to understand the dynamics of this kind of psychological deprivation.

There is a folk maxim prevalent among the middle and upper classes that money cannot buy happiness. While this may be true, money certainly can provide growth potential. For example, the poor are likelier to live in smaller apartments than those who are not poor, and typically they must fit larger numbers of people into smaller amounts of space.[8] What this means in practical terms is that the child's exploratory behavior is limited because he will always be "getting under foot" in the limited space available, so that his world is that much more limited and his motivating curiosity not rewarded.[9] The middle- or upper-class child typically has fewer siblings or greater amounts of space in which to roam. Exploration is encouraged and rewarded, and the child's horizons and personal control grow accordingly.

[7] Walter Buckley, *Sociology and Modern Systems Theory* (Englewood Cliffs, N.J.: Prentice Hall, 1967), Chapters 1–3.

[8] John Clausen, "Family Structure Socialization and Personality," in Hoffman and Hoffman (eds.), *Review of Child Development Research* (New York: Russell Sage Foundation, 1966), p. 10.

[9] J. W. B. Douglass and J. M. Bloomfield, *Children Under Five* (London: Allen and Unwin, 1968), Chapters 3–5.

The influence of money also works in more direct ways. Taking swimming, dancing, and skiing lessons provides one with opportunities where practice will produce at least a certain amount of mastery and perhaps the attendant idea of "I can do it if I want to" (personal control). It is not that the higher SES child naturally is a better skier or swimmer than a lower SES child, it is just that his initial possibilities are greater, and therefore he is more likely to find something to master. One look at the number of blacks in high-school swimming or tennis teams should make this clear. The facilities that it takes to master some skill areas are simply unavailable to those without the requisite wealth.

Finally, wealth provides a certain psychological security against the costs of failure. Banfield has argued that one characteristic of lower-class families is that they live a crisis-oriented existence, where even small loss could be a disaster.[10] Such small margins of error promote habit, not development.

Of course, wealth is not the only benefit that a child who is born into a higher SES family possesses. There is also the matter of differential goals, values, and family socialization routines. In general terms,[11] middle-class parents stress curiosity, happiness and self-control. The goal of this training is to enable the child to learn to govern himself and also be able to fulfil his needs on his own initiative, including the need for personal control. Working-class parents, on the other hand, are more likely to stress obedience, neatness, cleanliness, with the emphasis on not transgressing against externally imposed rules. One indication of this tendency was explored by Rosen, who found a significant inverse re-

[10] E. Banfield, *The Moral Basis of a Backward Society* (New York: Free Press, 1958).

[11] The following points are discussed in M. L. Kohn, "Social Class and Parental Values," *American Journal of Sociology*, 64, 1959, pp. 337–351; and M. L. Kohn, "Social Class and Parent-Child Relationships: An Interpretation," *American Journal of Sociology*, 68, 1963, pp. 471–480.

lationship between mean age at independence training and social class.[12]

The importance of family values and reward structure is difficult to overstress. Many psychologists looking at the need for personal control have arbitrarily limited themselves to such areas as achievement motivation. Yet, if we examine these studies as a specific area of socialization for personal control, certain family characteristics stand out. Winterbottom has found that boys who scored high on N Ach had received demands for independence of action at an earlier age than those scoring low. Mothers of these children imposed fewer restrictions but imposed them earlier.[13] Another study of mothers of high achievers found that they had rewarded and encouraged attempts at achievement and tried to ignore children's requests for help. Moreover, they were more likely to spontaneously praise their children's efforts, even when the children did not seek approval.[14]

The third dimension of socio-economic position, occupational status, seems to affect socialization for personal control in two related ways. It seems clear that the attainment of a high-status occupation reflects a certain degree of accomplishment, and should therefore be associated with higher feelings of personal control. Moreover, the higher the occupational status, the more likely the position will be located in upper sections of the authority structure, with correspondingly greater personal autonomy and decision-making power, which should increase feelings of personal control.

[12] B. Rosen, "The Achievement Syndrome," *American Sociological Review*, 24, 1956, pp. 203–211.

[13] Marion Winterbottom, "The Relation of Need for Achievement to Learning Experiences in Independence and Mastery," in J. W. Atkinson (ed.), *Motives in Fantasy, Action and Society* (Princeton: Van Nostrand, 1958) pp. 445–479.

[14] M. J. Crandall, "Achievement," in H. Stevenson (ed.), *Child Psychology* (Chicago: University of Chicago Press, 1963), p. 429.

Thus, greater occupational status suggests that the need for personal control has been satisfied to some degree.

The role of occupation status also influences the acquisition of personal control by children, through the mechanism of identification. Identification refers to the process that leads the child to think, feel, and behave as though the characteristics of another person—for a young child, it is usually a parent—were his. At this early stage, it is not usually a conscious imitative process. The development of identification idea assumes that the child has some motivation to identify, namely that the model possesses attributes which he would like to have. Certainly, parents differ from their children in a multitude of important ways, yet we propose that the most important of these is the area of *personal control.*

It is already established that, with little discrimination, children tend to attribute great power and control to adults. Apparently, this tendency generalizes to perceptions of political figures like the president.[15] We suspect the attribution will be rather stronger if the parent is in a position which assumes a high degree of mastery, and there is some empirical evidence to support this. For example, Gold found that fathers' influences on their children varied directly with the prestige rank of his occupation,[16] while a study by Smelser found that boys from upper-class families or upwardly mobile families were higher on competence and autonomy and were more likely to see their fathers that way.[17] The same process appears to hold true for women also. Douvan found that mothers who held jobs connected with personal growth rather than family income addition were more admired and

[15] Fred Greenstein, *Children and Politics* (New Haven: Yale University Press, 1965).

[16] M. Gold, *Status Forces in Delinquent Boys* (Ann Arbor: Institute for Social Research, 1963).

[17] W. Smelser, "Adolescent and Occupational Choice as a Function of Family Socio-Economic History," *Sociometry*, 26, 1963, pp. 393–409.

perceived as more competent by their daughters.[18] Thus, there appears to be some evidence that personal control is one of the mechanisms underlying identification with parents and that increased control (as indicated by higher occupational status decision-making authority) should result in greater child-parent identification.

PERSONAL CONTROL AND LIFE-CYCLE DYNAMICS

Our model to this point has placed great emphasis on the impact of the early development of basic beliefs, arising out of the attempt to satisfy basic psychological needs. Does this mean that socialization ends after the child has acquired these basic beliefs, and that subsequent events have no impact? One way to approach these important questions is to focus upon two important themes, (1) continuities and (2) life-cycle dynamics.

Although basic beliefs about the nature of the world are acquired at an early age and are resistant to change, they are not impervious to it. That is, to the extent that later life experiences are congruent with basic beliefs and reinforce them, we would expect those beliefs to remain stable. However, to the extent that later experiences (including experiences with social institutions such as schools, armed forces, jails, and so on) are dissonent with basic beliefs, we would hypothesize that the potential for change in these basic beliefs would increase.

One other consideration seems relevant here, and that is that early and prolonged gratification of basic psychological needs enables an individual to withstand subsequent deprivation for longer periods of time. The individual who has always been able to develop and extend his personal control

[18] E. Douvan, "Employment and the Adolescent," in F. Nye and L. Hoffman (eds.), *The Employed Mother in America* (Chicago: Rand McNally, 1963), pp. 142–164.

will feel less need for control in any particular situation. In political life the leader who is confident of his ability to exert personal control may be able to endure greater periods of ambiguity in diplomatic affairs. On the other hand, persons whose needs have only been infrequently satisfied would be hypothesized to require extended periods of need satisfaction before being able to withstand subsequent deprivation.

Of course the person who has not acquired personal control beliefs during childhood can do so later on by a variety of methods. He may learn a particular skill or acquire fame, which will help him to exercise a greater degree of personal control (perhaps in sports or in politics), or he may attempt to gain the illusion of control by either centering or indulging in compensatory compulsive behavior. Centering refers to the narrowing of the stimulus field so that only a very small and select amount of input is allowed to reach the organism. With such narrow ranges of input, the possibilities of having personal control beliefs (in this limited area) are increased. Compulsive behavior to obtain personal control is similar to centering, except that (here) the person repeats sequences of behavior which suggest control, even though the behaviors are counterproductive in a particular situation.

Equally important are the changes in basic beliefs (such as personal control) that can take place for persons whose needs had been gratified during their early years. Given early gratification, we would hypothesize these individuals to be less likely to change their basic beliefs, even in the face of life-experience discontinuity. Yet, we should point out that less likely does not mean that it is improbable. Beliefs in personal control can be drastically changed by a number of events, including the death of a loved one or the unexpected onset of major illness, which may function to greatly reduce one's belief in personal-control possibilities.

Not only may interpersonal dynamics play a role in the continuity of basic beliefs, but larger societal forces and events play a role, also. For example, the onset of major economic depressions, wars, and other such disasters affect people's basic beliefs. Individuals caught up in these larger social events may experience a drastic change in their basic beliefs, including personal control. These changes may have direct implications for the political system, if that system is perceived to be involved either by action, potential action, or inaction. For example, the economic depression in Germany and the rise of Hitler could be interpreted in terms of the need for personal control. That is, we would hypothesize that the depression created a change in the basic beliefs about personal control for many members of German society and increased the salience of the need for personal control. In such a situation it is quite possible for a political leader to promise to impose personal control from the top down, because many people desire just that. Of course, economic depression need not inevitably lead to dictatorship, as the case of the United States illustrates. Yet, even here we can see evidence of the need for personal control at work. One need only look at the major realignment of American political party constituencies after the depression of 1929 to see some of the effects. In our case the depression brought a Roosevelt and not a Hitler. Yet, Roosevelt's promise to get the country moving again can be understood as a personal-control appeal. In effect, Roosevelt (and one might suggest every president since) has attempted to foster the impression that personal control is possible and that he had it.

Ronald Inglehart has also provided some empirical support of these remarks with his excellent work on the relation between values (based on Maslow's need hierarchy) and support for European integration. He has found that "cross-national differences in value choices (based on need satisfaction) have a fit with economic history."[19]

Finally, this discussion would not be complete without

[19] R. Inglehart, "The Silent Revolution in Europe," *American Political Science Review*, 4, 1971, p. 1017.

some mention of life-cycle dynamics. The pathbreaking work of Erikson[20] and others[21] alerts us to the fact that a person's passage through life may be viewed from the perspective of a number of different stages, each of which brings with it its own particular problems and its own opportunities for rewards. In fact it is possible to suggest that one confronts the problems of need gratification at each of the stages of life, with the attendant potential for changes in basic beliefs. As Erikson has shown, outplay of these life-cycle dynamics and attempts to come to grips with the problems they present can have revolutionary implications for the political system.[22] On the other hand, the end of the life cycle can bring with it either decreased or increased personal-control beliefs depending on the attitudes of the society toward the different stages (e.g., old age), and personal experiences.[23] In fact, the relation between personality development, need satisfaction, and the life cycle remains largely unchartered, but potentially exciting territory in political theory.

Having explored some of the general parameters in which socialization for personal control takes place, we turn now from macro to micro considerations. Chapters 10 and 11 stress the import of several dimensions of family life and their impact on the acquisition of personal-control beliefs.

20 E. Erikson, *Childhood and Society* (New York: Norton, 1950).

21 T. Lidz, *The Person* (New York: Basic Books, 1968).

22 E. Erikson, *Young Man Luther* (New York: Norton, 1958).

23 Thomas Agnello, Jr., "Aging and the Sense of Political Powerlessness," *Public Opinion Quarterly*, 37, 1973, pp. 251–259.

Chapter Ten

SOCIALIZATION AND PERSONAL CONTROL:

FAMILY AUTHORITY DYNAMICS

If family-life socioeconomic status provides the broad context in which the acquisition of personal control takes place, it still remains to specify the effects of particular dimensions of family life. These dimensions range from the authority-making structure of the family to the effects of sequential arrival of children. It should not be assumed, however, that each dimension has equal impact or that what impact there is does not fall differentially upon different children in the same family. In many ways the effects of family life parallel the effects of the society at large in that everyone is not treated equally. In the following pages the effects of family life on the personality dimension of personal control will be explored. We will be aided in this exploration by the answers each student respondent gave to a number of questions about different areas of his family life, including his family's decision making patterns, the types of punishment meted out at home, the nature, and degree of his family's emotional closeness, and his sibling relationships.

As was previously noted, our desire is not to concentrate solely on family socialization practices by themselves, but rather to examine them as one component of the process that relates personal control to political behavior. This and the following chapter will present some data on the family and the acquisition of personal control. Then we will go on to explore the relations among personal control, political attitudes, and political behavior.

AUTHORITY STRUCTURE

One of the most relevant dimensions of family life for the acquisition of personal control is those family dynamics dealing with the authority structure. Actually, family authority structure is not a unitary dimension; it comprises at least three different components: (1) the degree of autonomy allowed, (2) the rule maker or makers, and (3) the consequences of rule violation.

The authority structure is related to personal control in a number of ways. The acquisition of personal control requires that the individual confront and master a variety of situations. Each successful mastery increases the belief that what one does has an effect—that control can be exerted over one's life-space. Yet, the child grows up in a world populated by adults, who, by virtue of their strength, competence, and role, have a great deal of power over the lives of their children. This power carries with it problems and opportunities for the parents, as well as for the child, who is in the process of developing personal control. The dynamics can involve one or both of two types of restrictiveness: authoritarian restrictiveness and concerned restrictiveness.

In the former case, the parents rigidly control the child and stifle any behavior which is not considered appropriate. This is the classical authoritarian family authority structure. It results in a decreased range of opportunities for the child to develop his competence and mastery. Since the acquisition of personal control requires a wide range of mastery opportunities, the consequence of this type of authority structure is a decrease in the belief in personal control and an increase in the belief in external control.

The latter case involves the combination of anxious concern and a great amount of warmth—the classic components of parental overprotection. Such overprotection typically results in the attempt by parents to screen the child from activities or situations that the parents fear or find anxiety producing. Such concern is quickly transmitted to the child, with the result that he does not have the opportunity for the development of personal control, which he would have had if it had been necessary for him to master difficult situations. Again, the consequence will be a decreased belief in personal control.

We are suggesting that children who are allowed the greatest degree of autonomy should have feelings of internal control, while those who are allowed less autonomy should have feelings of external control. We asked each student respondent how much freedom he was given to direct his own life while he was growing up. The data are presented in Table 2.

TABLE 2. LOCUS OF CONTROL BY AMOUNT OF AUTONOMY

Degree of Autonomy	*Personal Control*			
	Low	*Medium*	*High*	*Total N*
None	25.3	61.3	13.8	135
Some	9.0	74.6	16.4	122
Great	7.7	61.5	30.8	39

gamma = .36 $x^2 = 19.74$ $p = <.001$

The results are generally consistent with the hypothesized relation between personal control and autonomy training. Those respondents who reported they were given a great deal of autonomy to develop their own lives while they were growing up are significantly more likely to have developed high personal control. Moreover, a closer examination of the relationship between personal control and degree of allowed autonomy provides some interesting insights into the differential impact of certain family dynamics.

It was previously suggested that the impact of family dynamics was differentially distributed within the family. One reason for this phenomenon is that parents have different expectations for each child. Such expectations are not only a function of the perceived capacities of the children, but also of more ascriptive dimensions of expectations and evaluations, such as sex-role expectations. An examination of sex differences in the socialization experience, especially the degree of allowed autonomy, gives us some understanding of what one author has called "the most thoroughly substantial finding in social science,"[1] that men are more likely to participate in politics than women. Empirically, this seems to be the case not only in the United States,[2] but in a variety of other countries, as well.[3] Of related interest is the finding that males are more likely than females to develop feelings of political efficacy. Apparently, this is also true both in the United States[4] and cross-nationally.[5]

In order to obtain some insight into the differential effects of the socialization process, we first cross-tabulated the degree of personal control by gender. As expected, we found that males were three times more likely than females to have high feelings of personal control (gamma = .29, $x^2 = 11.11$, $p = < .01$). If, as we suggested earlier, feelings of personal control may be a necessary but insufficient condition for political participation, then our data suggests that lower po-

[1] Lester Milbrath, *Political Participation* (Chicago: Rand McNally, 1965), p. 135.

[2] Robert Agger *et al.*, *The Ruler and the Ruled: Political Power and Impotence in an American Community* (New York: Wiley & Son, 1964).

[3] Erik Allardt and Pertti Personen, "Citizen Participation in Political Life in Finland," *International Social Science Journal*, 12, 1960, pp. 27–39.

[4] A. Campbell *et al.*, *The American Voter* (New York: Wiley & Sons, 1960).

[5] Gabriel Almond and Sidney Verba, *The Civic Culture* (Princeton: Princeton University Press, 1963).

litical activism among women may be related to a lack of personal control. Yet, while this may be an interesting perspective from which to view the relationship between sex and political participation, it still leaves unanswered the question of why women feel they have less personal control than men. One clue came from an analysis of the degree of autonomy allowed for both sexes.

One clue came from a study of Kagen and Moss.[6] After analyzing the results obtained from children in several longitudinal studies, they suggested that passive or dependent behavior is rewarded for girls, while boys were pushed toward independence and were often punished for showing dependence. One possible explanation, then, is that women are systematically allowed less autonomy, while growing up than are young boys, and that in turn leads to lower feelings of personal control. In order to see if this was the case, we cross-tabulated the degree of allowed autonomy by sex. As expected, we found that males were significantly more likely to have been allowed a high degree of autonomy while growing up. Girls were almost twice as likely as boys to have had little autonomy (gamma = .29, $x^2 = 10.71$, p = .001).

If, as we have indicated, the degree of autonomy is important in the facilitation of the acquisition of personal control, then perhaps one reason why women fail to develop feelings of personal control is that they are the objects of parental restrictiveness. It seems clear that this restrictiveness is related to ideas about what constitutes desirable feminine characteristics and behavior. A number of recent books have analyzed the nature of the feminine role and found it heavily weighted towards passivity.

The relations that we found to exist between autonomy training and feelings of personal control were further underscored when we examined the relationship between autonomy training and levels of personal control for each sex. For

[6] J. Kagen and M. Moss, *Birth to Maturity* (New York: Wiley & Sons, 1962), Chapter 2.

both males and females a greater degree of autonomy while growing up was strongly associated with high levels of personal control. In fact, the relationship was stronger for women than it was for men. In the controlled relationship the gamma for men was .31, while for women the gamma was .41. These findings suggest that the origins of differential rates for political participation for men and women may have less to do with feminine disinterest in politics than with parental expectations and socialization experiences. In short, the findings suggest one way in which socialization experiences structure orientations to life in general and politics in particular.

ALLOCATION OF DECISION-MAKING AUTHORITY

The second aspect of the family authority structure might be summed up with the question, who governs. The question raised here is what effect does the allocation of decision-making authority have on the acquisition of personal control? Essentially three allocation possibilities present themselves: (1) the traditional model of the male as head of the household, (2) the less common model of the woman as head of the household, or (3) the more democratic arrangement in which both husband and wife share the decision-making.

A number of studies have documented the social fact that in most American nuclear families it is the male who runs the household.[7] To be sure, some sociologists have suggested that there is an increasing amount of role ambiguity in the husband-wife relationship,[8] but recent empirical

[7] Morris Zelditch, "Role Differentiation in the Nuclear Family," in Talcott Parsons *et al., Family, Socialization and Interaction Process* (Glencoe: Free Press, 1955), pp. 339–342.

[8] Philip Staler, "Parental Role Differential," *American Journal of Sociology*, 67, 1961, pp. 296–311.

studies suggest that this has yet to be carried over to politically relevant spheres.[9] Since the father-dominant role is the most typical, indeed, one is tempted to suggest that it is a normative expectation for some; we hypothesize that personal control would be more likely to be achieved in father-dominant households, where the traditional expectations are met. There is some data which tends to support this analysis. At least one study has found that in families where the father is seen as dominant there is a greater tendency for the boys to show a preference for the male role and identify with their father.[10]

On the other hand, maternal dominance appears to be a source of maladjustment for some youths. Hoffman found that boys from mother dominant families had increased difficulty relating to peers, and that both boys and girls in these types of families identified more strongly with the mother.[11] Another study found that satisfaction with both parents and reported parental compatibility correlated negatively with power and dominance of the mother.[12] We would hypothesize, therefore, that in mother-dominated families the process of identification with the male and masculine socialization procedures would be decreased, leading to a decreased emphasis on autonomy training and therefore personal control.

Finally, it might be suggested that a democratic allocation

[9] M. Kent Jennings and Richard Niemi, "The Division of Political Labor Between Mothers and Fathers," *American Political Science Review*, 65, 1971, pp. 68–92.

[10] E. M. Hetherington, "A Developmental Study of the Effects of Sex of the Dominant Parent on Sex-Role Preference, Identification and Imitation in Children," *Journal of Personality and Social Psychology*, 2, 1965, pp. 188–194.

[11] L. W. Hoffman, "The Father's Role in the Family and in the Child's Peer Group Adjustment," *Merritt-Palmer Quarterly*, 7, 1961, pp. 97–105.

[12] L. S. Distler, "Patterns of Parental Identification," unpublished doctoral dissertation, U. of California, 1965.

of authority, in which both husband and wife share in the making of rules, might be a more suitable mechanism in the development of personal control. This consideration would suggest that in a household where power is shared and the subject of at least some give and take, children's perceptions that control is possible would be increased.

In order to explore this question, each respondent was asked the open-ended question, "When you were growing up, who seemed to make most of the family rules?" We then cross-tabulated the degree of personal control by the locus of decision-making responsibility. However, no support was generated for our hypothesis. Children raised in strong father families were not more likely to have high personal control; indeed, they were most likely not to have it. Children raised in families where both parents participated in the decision making were somewhat more likely to have high personal control, closely followed by families in which the mother had the rule-making powers. The results, however, were not significant even when we controlled for sex. Thus, we are led to conclude that the allocation of family decision-making authority is not an important component in the acquisition of personal control.

THE NATURE OF RULE ENFORCEMENT

Each family operates by a set of rules, whose existence over time presupposes some mechanisms for administering sanctions for violation. It has long been suspected that the type of discipline had consequences for the development of childhood personality and behavior[13]—however, it is only recently that these relationships have been empirically ex-

[13] D. M. Levy, *Maternal Overprotection* (New York: Columbia University Press, 1954), Chapters 4–6.

plored.[14] Some research has attempted to develop a general taxonomy of parental discipline,[15] while other research has concentrated on particular types of discipline and their effects.[16] As was previously suggested, the amount of autonomy versus restrictiveness has crucial consequences for the acquisition of personal control. There is, however, another important dimension which deserves consideration: that of rule consistency.

Each family develops a set of interaction patterns, some of which are explicit, others of which are not. In the case of family authority structures, a set of norms develops for family members; these norms become for them the boundaries of the permissible. The rules may consist of generally accepted social norms, such as "stealing is bad," plus a number of family-specific rules, such as no noise on Sunday mornings. A great deal of attention has been paid to the content of these rules,[17] but their implementation is equally important.

One of the facilitating mechanisms in the acquisition of personal control is a form of operant conditioning. That is, behaviors designed to manipulate and change the environment in some way will be rewarding, and therefore the tendency to engage in those actions increased. Yet, there is an important assumption contained in the operant conditioning model: life-space continuity. *In order for the same action to bring the same or similar results, the environment*

[14] Wesley Becker, "Consequences of Different Kinds of Parental Discipline," in M. Hoffman and L. Hoffman (eds.), *Review of Child Development Research* (New York: Russell Sage Foundation, 1964), pp. 169–208.

[15] E. S. Schaefer, "A Circumplex Model for Maternal Behavior," *Journal of Abnormal and Social Psychology*, 59, 1959, pp. 226–235.

[16] R. Sears *et al.*, *Patterns of Child Rearing* (Evanston, Ill.: Row, Peterson, 1957).

[17] See, for example, M. L. Kohn, "Social Class and Parental Values," *American Journal of Sociology*, 1959, 64.

must have remained sufficiently stable to make that action efficacious. Carried over to family life, this suggests that implicit/explicit rules about boundaries can never be acted upon if they are consistently changing. The implication of this is that the development of personal control presupposes a certain degree of life-space continuity. If one is allowed to play one Sunday morning, but punished for doing so the following Sunday, the establishment of boundaries is improbable. One needs to know the structure before one can master it. We therefore hypothesize that consistency in rule implementation should be positively associated with high personal control.

There is, of course, a voluminous literature on cognitive consistency,[18] much of it suggesting that people differ with regard to their need for consistency.[19] Even though people may differ, there is some work which suggests the importance of rule consistency in the socialization process.

A series of studies dating back to 1929,[20] as well as more recent studies,[21] have documented that a high incidence of erratic or inconsistently applied discipline, both within and between parents, is more likely to result in antisocial, aggressive behavior in children. These results are not surprising when viewed from the perspective of the hypothesized relationship and personal control and life-space consistency. It has already been suggested that the lack of personal control can be anxiety-producing and frustrating, or that aggressive behavior might be one consequence.

[18] An excellent review is to be found in David Glass, "Theories of Consistency and the Study of Personality," in E. Borgatta and W. Lambert (eds.) *Handbook of Personality Theory and Research* (Chicago: Rand McNally, 1968) pp. 788–850.

[19] N. T. Feather, "Acceptance and Rejection of Arguments in Relation to Attitude Strength, Critical Ability, and Intolerance of Inconsistency," *Journal of Abnormal and Social Psychology*, 69, 1964, pp. 127–136.

[20] C. Bert, *The Young Delinquent* (New York: Appleton, 1929).

[21] R. G. Andry, *Delinquency and Parental Pathology* (London: Methuen, 1960).

In order to examine the relation between personal control and rule consistency, we asked each respondent, after he had indicated who made most of the family rules, whether, "he (she or they) seemed to be consistent in the application of these rules, or did you sometimes get punished for breaking a rule and sometimes not . . . depending on the circumstances." The data are presented in Table 3.

TABLE 3. LOCUS OF CONTROL BY RULE CONSISTENCY

Nature of Enforcement	*Personal Control*			
	Low	*Medium*	*High*	*Total N*
Inconsistent	21.3	68.0	10.7	75
Consistent	10.6	67.5	21.8	223
gamma = .29	$x^2 = 6.30$ p =<.05			

The data appear to support the hypothesized relationship between rule enforcement consistency and the development of personal control. People who grew up in homes where rules were consistently applied are much more likely to have high levels of personal control. Controls introduced for sex resulted in no change in the relationship, suggesting that consistency behavior does not arise out of differential sex-role expectations as is the case with the degree of allowed autonomy.

SUMMARY

This chapter has explored the impact of some aspects of the family structure on the acquisition of personal control. Three dimensions of this structure—degree of autonomy, allocation of decision making, and rule-enforcement consistency—were systematically examined. Two of these three dimensions were found to have important relationships to the acquisition of personal rather than external control. High degree of childhood autonomy and consistency in the enforcement of rules were found to significantly associate with the acquisition of high personal control.

In a sense, then, the findings provide some support, not only for the particular propositions advanced, but also for the strategy of inquiry initiated by Adorno[22] and more recently by Lane,[23] of linking family experiences to politically relevant personality orientations. In the following chapter, we will continue the explanation of the domain, focusing on other aspects of the role of family dynamics in the acquisition of personal control.

[22] T. Adorno *et al.*, *The Authoritarian Personality* (New York: Harper, 1950).

[23] Robert Lane, *Political Ideology* (New York: Free Press, 1962).

Chapter Eleven

SOCIALIZATION AND PERSONAL CONTROL:

FAMILY EMOTIONAL DYNAMICS

Just as each family has an authority structure, there exists for each family an emotional structure, made up of the affective dimension of family life. A number of theorists have suggested that love and emotional warmth are preconditions for human development,[1] and experimental studies by Harlow,[2] Davis,[3] and others have provided additional support for that contention. There is also some evidence to support the importance of family affective relationships in the development of certain political attitudes and behaviors. For example, Keniston in a study of alienated students found that their fathers were recalled as cold, rigid, and withdrawn men.[4] These studies suggest the importance of the emotional side of family life for the socialization experience.

Families in which there is a high degree of emotional closeness provide an atmosphere in which the attempt at and the development of personal control may take place without excessive fear of the consequences of failure. Strong positive attachments among family members make the family in effect like a safe haven; a secure place to which the child can return in time of need. Not only does emotional closeness among family members provide a secure base from

[1] John Bowlby, *Attachment* (New York: Basic Books, 1966).

[2] H. Harlow *et al.*, "Learning Motivated by Manipulation Drive," *Journal of Experimental Psychology*, 40, 1950.

[3] K. Davis, "Final Note on a Case of Extreme Isolation," *American Sociological Review*, 4, 1956.

[4] Kenneth Keniston, *The Uncommitted* (New York: Basic Books, 1965), Chapter 5.

which control attempts may be made, but it is also the framework within which intrapersonal and interpersonal trust may begin. This relationship between emotional closeness and the development of personal control on one hand and both intrapersonal and interpersonal trust on the other, is an important one. It is also of more than passing interest to political scientists, for it has important theoretical implications for the understanding of political participation.

It was previously suggested that personal control was acquired through the successful confrontation with and mastery of a variety of situations. The growth of personal control is also accompanied by growth in self-trust and self-confidence, both in one's accomplishments and in one's capacities. In a sense then, the development of personal control and trust in one's self are symbiotic, as well as synergistic. Moreover, the development of trust in self precedes trust and is an important component of trust in others.[5] Confidence in the capacity to manage one's self and one's social relationship allows that leap of faith about the good will of others, without which interpersonal relations become ritualized games.[6] It is at this point that the emotional closeness of the family, personal control and intra/interpersonal trust coalesce.

In effect, the family relationship is the child's first interpersonal relationship. It is here that the child begins to work out for himself a balance between personal control and trust and reliance upon others. Emphasis upon either to the exclusion of the other is a potentially serious problem. On the one hand, in the political arena, a lack of personal control and excessive reliance upon others provides perfect candidates for followers of strong political leaders of all

[5] William Fey, "Acceptance by Others and Its Relationship to Acceptance of Self, and Others," *Journal of Abnormal and Social Psychology*, 50, 1955, pp. 274–276.

[6] Erving Goffman, *The Presentation of Self in Everyday Life* (New York, Anchor, 1959).

varieties. On the other hand a high degree of personal control without that component of faith and trust in other people may lead to a single-minded desire to manipulate in order to control, a characteristic not uncommon in some political leaders.[7]

Yet, there is another way in which intrapersonal and interpersonal trust have implications for political life. Every act of citizen participation requires a leap of faith by the individual. If it is the unitary act of voting, then one has to have some faith in the responsiveness of the government to make the act more than a ritual. The same is true for any collective undertaking, from working to elect a candidate to attending a mass-demonstration. There is already empirical evidence to support the contention that there is a political analogue to interpersonal trust,[8] but this is only part of the relationship.

Not only must there be some trust in the responsiveness of the government, but one also must have some faith in the people with whom one takes part. For those with very low feelings of trust in other people, the possibilities of satisfactory collective activities would be minimized, since they would probably attribute others' activities to nothing more than personal aggrandizement. That is, people would be viewed as participating for selfish reasons, rather than because of any attempt to improve the collective good. Participation with such people would be essentially unsatisfying, especially when we consider that agreeable interaction with like-minded people is an important dimension of political participation.[9]

[7] Alexander George and Juliette George, *Woodrow Wilson and Colonel House: A Personality Study* (New York: Dover, 1964).

[8] Robert Agger *et al.*, "Political Cynicism: Measurement and Meaning," *Journal of Politics*, 23, 1961, pp. 477–506.

[9] Steve Brown and John Ellithorp, "Emotional Experiences in Political Groups: The Case of the McCarthy Phenomenon," *American Political Science Review*, 2, 1970, pp. 349–366.

Since the family emotional structure is suggested to provide an important context within which personal control and intrapersonal trust are acquired, as well as more generalized interpersonal trust, each respondent was asked the following two questions: (1) If you had a personal problem, which parent would you take it to? (2) How often would you say this person understood how you felt about things? The answer to the first question indicates the degree of trust and openness that our respondents placed in their parents, since the likelihood of sharing a personal problem with someone who is not trusted is small. Answers were then coded according to whether the respondent answered that he would take his problems to his mother, father, or both parents, or whether he would not feel free to share them with either parent. We then analyzed the relationship between this indication of trust and the degree of personal control. The results were in the suggested direction, but were not statistically significant. That is, children who reported that they would take their problems to their mother, father or both parents were more likely to develop feelings of personal control (gamma = .19), but again the results were not statistically significant, and therefore do not provide conformation of the hypothesis.

The second question asked was an attempt to tap the degree of perceived empathy of the respondent's parents. One basis for a mutually satisfactory relationship is the ability to empathize, that is, the ability to put oneself in another's place. It certainly feels likely that we would feel emotionally closer to someone who "understood" us than to someone we felt did not. Here again our hypothesis is that those parents with higher empathy (as perceived by our respondents) would have been more likely to have produced an emotional environment necessary for human growth in general and personal control in particular. The results are presented in Table 4.

The data in Table 4 provide stronger support for the

TABLE 4. LOCUS OF CONTROL BY PARENTAL EMPATHY

Degree of Parental Empathy	*Personal Control*			
	Low	*Medium*	*High*	*Total N*
Low	22.6	73.6	3.8	84
Medium	12.2	65.8	22.1	132
High	9.4	68.8	21.9	83
gamma = .35	$x^2 = 11.46$ p = < .02			

hypothesized relationship between parental empathy and the acquisition of personal control. Individuals growing up in homes in which parents were perceived to have high or medium empathy were more than six times as likely than those from homes where parents were rated low in empathy, to have developed high feelings of personal control. Thus it appears that parental empathy plays at least some role in the development of personal control by providing an atmosphere in which mastery attempts may be made without excessive fear of the consequences of failure. This mastery in turn leads to the acquisition of personal control.

Some additional light is shed by examining the effects of two other variables, autonomy training and rule consistency, upon this relationship. When we control for the degree of autonomy allowed during childhood, the gamma jumps from .35 to .46 in the high childhood autonomy condition, while decreasing to .14 in the low childhood autonomy condition. The same results are found when we controlled for consistency of rule enforcement. In the consistent enforcement condition, the gamma jumped from .35 to .56, while in the inconsistent enforcement condition, it decreased to .19. These findings suggest the importance of both autonomy training during childhood and the nature of rule enforcement, for the relationship between family empathy and the acquisition of personal control. What these controls do not tell us unfortunately, is the relative importance of each of these variables for the acquisition of personal control. Fortunately, a multivariate technique for ordinal data does exist which allows us to explore these relationships in greater depth, and we shall do so at the end of this chapter.

In our previous discussion we suggested that family emotional closeness would be significantly associated with a greater degree of faith in people. The reasoning was that since family members were the first and at least for the early years the most significant individuals, beliefs developed at this time would be important for future orientations.

Paralleling our findings of the relationship between family emotional closeness and personal control, we found no significant relationship between taking a problem to a parent and faith in people (gamma = .07). However also paralleling other findings we found a significant association between high parental empathy and greater faith in people (gamma = .22, $x^2 = 10.77$, p = <.05). Individuals in our sample who reported that their parents were high in empathy as likely as those reporting low parental empathy to have a high degree of faith in people. When we examined these results, controlling for degree of allowed autonomy and rule consistence no significant alteration of the results was in evidence.

These findings suggest that the family emotional structure plays an important role in the development of personal control. The extent of this role is a question to which we shall shortly return.

FAMILY COMPOSITION AND PERSONAL CONTROL

The most general aspect of family life is the dimension of family composition. Typically in the United States, this means a nuclear family composed of husband, wife, and children. The major departure from the norm occurs when one or both parents are absent because of either divorce or death.

The death of a parent at any age is a traumatic experience, but it is even more likely to be so when the child is young.[10] The advent of death, like the advent of disease, is something over which little control can be exerted. Moreover, from the existential perspective, one function of death is to serve as a reminder of the limits of human control,[11] and indeed, there is some indication among our respondents that this is the case. Although the Chi-Square was not significant, there was a moderate tendency for those respondents who reported that one of their parents had died to have external rather than personal control (gamma = .21) This suggests that the impact of serendipitous events does have consequences for the socialization process, and more specifically, the acquisition of personal control.

The other aspect of family composition is family size, which some research has suggested is closely related to child rearing practices, especially the family authority structure. Bossard, for example, has suggested that the large family places more emphasis on cooperation and conformity, and places a high value on hierarchical organization and leadership.[12] As we have seen in Table 4, autonomy rather than conformity is a facilitator of personal control. Yet, it is also possible to suggest that a large family implies a decrease in the amount of time that can be devoted to any particular member, in a sense freeing members from strict control.

In order to explore this dimension of family life, we asked

10 Rollo May *et al.* (ed.), *Existence: A New Dimension in Psychiatry and Psychology* (New York: Basic Books, 1958), Chapter 5.

11 H. Feifel, "Death Relevant Variable in Psychology," in R. May (ed.), *Existential Psychology* (New York: Random House, 1960), p. 62.

12 H. H. S. Bossard and E. S. Boll, *The Large Family System* (Philadelphia: University of Pennsylvania Press, 1956), Chapters 3–5.

each respondent to list all of his brothers and sisters along with their ages. We then analyzed the relation between family size and the various dimensions of family life. No significant associations were found between family size and any component of family relations, including authority structure and emotional ties.

While family size is one aspect of the family there is a sequential aspect of family membership that is equally important, namely birth order.[13] The impact of birth order to both personality development and socialization experiences has been the subject of voluminous research by psychologists and sociologists interested in the socialization experience.[14] In part, this research originates in the realization that life experiences within the same family will vary subtly, but significantly, for different children. In Chapter Eight, the effects of different socialization experiences, based on sex-role expectations, were suggested to have an important impact on the acquisition of personal control. Here, we hypothesize that sequential arrival into the family will have an impact on the socialization experience and the acquisition of personal control.

BIRTH ORDER AND PERSONALITY DEVELOPMENT

The first systematic work in the relationship of birth order and personality development was begun by Alfred Adler,

[13] For a more fully developed discussion of birth order as a research variable in political socialization, see Stanley Renshon, "Birth Order, Personality and Political Socialization," in D. Schwartz and S. Schwartz (eds.), *New Directions in Political Socialization Research* (New York: Free Press, 1974).

[14] See the review in E. E. Sampson, "The Study of Ordinal Position," in B. Mayer (ed.), *Advances in Experimental Personality Research* (New York: Academic Press, 1964).

one of Freud's disciples. Adler observed that the personalities of the oldest, middle, and youngest children in the same family were likely to be very different, a fact that he attributed to the distinct experiences that each child has as a family member.[15]

Adler believed that the first child was likely to receive all of the parents' attention until the time that a second child was born, thus engendering feelings of insecurity throughout the elder child's life. The middle child was seen by Adler as ambitious, and continually attempting to surpass older siblings; while the youngest child was seen as constantly spoiled and very likely to become a neurotic adult.

Subsequent research has not systematically confirmed Adler's theory of birth order and personality development, but it has documented that there are subtle but important differences in the socialization experience of children that are a function of sequential arrival into the family. In part, these differences are a reflection of parental expectations and learning, as well as the accumulation of experience.

Schachter and others have suggested that the first child receives more attention and love because of the parents' inexperience and insecurity.[16] This combination of anxious concern and high affectivity are the classic components of parental overprotection discussed earlier. Schachter's thesis, then, is that this type of behavior is a function of parental inexperience and should be less likely to occur with later children. Carried over to the area of personal control, the hypothesis would be that first born children will be likelier to have low personal control beliefs because of limited allowance for autonomy. However, it has also been suggested that first-born children are expected to be responsible parent sur-

[15] A. Adler, *What Life Should Mean to You* (Boston: Little, Brown, 1931), pp. 144–154.

[16] S. Schachter, *The Psychology of Affiliation* (Stanford: Stanford University Press, 1959).

rogates[17] and, in many cases to become responsible adults earlier,[18] i.e., that that should have increased autonomy.

The few empirical studies that have been attempted have generally come up with conflicting findings. Thus, Sampson and Handcock found a significant correlation between degree of autonomy and first-born position,[19] while a study by Sears found that mothers tended to rate their first born as more independent.[20]

Our sample was divided into three categories: only children, children in the first half of their families, and children in the last half of their families. The data are presented below in Table 5.

The data suggest that there are clear and significant differences among our respondents which are related to the rather

TABLE 5. LOCUS OF CONTROL BY BIRTH ORDER

	Personal Control			
	Low	*Medium*	*High*	*Total N*
Only child	36.0	48.0	16.0	25
First half of family	18.8	67.3	13.9	165
Last half of family	10.2	70.2	19.5	108

gamma = .26 $x^2 = 11.22$
$p = < .05$

[17] E. E. Sampson, "Birth Order, Need Achievement, and Conformity," *Journal of Abnormal and Social Psychology,* 64, 1962, pp. 155–159.

[18] B. C. Rosen, "Family Structure and Achievement Motivation," *American Sociological Review,* 26, 1961, pp. 574–585.

[19] E. E. Sampson, *op. cit.,* p. 197.

[20] P. Sears, "Doll Play Aggression in Normal Young Children: Influence of Sex, Age, Sibling Status, Father's Absence," *Psychological Monographs,* 65, 1951, pp. 1–41.

fortuitous event of sequential entry into the family. Only children are clearly the most likely to have low personal control. Apparently the pressures of parental expectations and concern suggested by Schachter have some validity for these respondents. Children who have siblings, but who are temporally located in the first part of the family are slightly more likely than their "only child" counterparts to have developed moderate personal control. But it is really within the last half of the family that one finds the strongest appearance of personal control. Children born into the last half of the family are more likely to have personal control than are only children or children in the first part of the family. This suggests that birth order, like sex, is linked to the process of differential socialization experiences, the results of which may be seen in differential personality development. Moreover, an interesting finding emerges when we analyze the relationship between birth order and personal control, controlling for sex. The strength of the relationship between birth order and personal control (gamma = .26) increases somewhat for males (gamma = .38) when we control for sex. Yet for females, the introduction of controls for sex has the effect of washing out the relationship (gamma = .09).

This suggests the relationship between personal control and later arrival into the family does not hold for women. Women are equally likely to lack personal control and are not advantaged by being the latter part of the entry order. This would appear to indicate that sex-role expectations outweigh the effects of increased parental experience in dealing with children, as suggested by Schachter. One explanation for this can again be traced back to the crucial aspect of the family authority structure: degree of allowed autonomy.

In order to gain further insight into this relationship, we cross-tabulated the respondent's birth order and the degree of allowed autonomy while growing up. As expected, we found a significant correlation (gamma = .21, $x^2 = 6.68$, p = .05) between later arrival into the family and greater autonomy allowed during childhood. This suggests that sequential arrival into the family will have important consequences on socialization experiences, such as the degree of allowed autonomy. This in turn has effects on the acquisition of personal control. Our findings do suggest, however, that the impact of birth order on the politically relevant socialization experience obtains for males but not for females. That is, it appears that sex-role training and expectations are strong enough to overcome family practice associated with greater experience.

THE DIRECT TRANSMISSION OF PERSONALITY ORIENTATIONS

To this point we have been dealing with what might be called the indirect transmission of personality orientations. That is, the analysis so far has implied a model in which the influence of the parents upon the children is mediated through family structural dynamics, such as decision making and emotional closeness. There is, however, another very interesting possibility, and that is the direct transmission of personality orientations from parents to children. Typically, the study of the transmission of political orientations has concentrated on either political opinions or political attitudes.[21] However, if we follow Rokeach's suggestion that opinions represent the topmost layer of psychic organization, attitudes the next deepest level, and beliefs and needs at the most basic and deepest level,[22] then it is not surprising that the results have not been overwhelming. The highest level of

[21] For an excellent example of this type of attempt, see M. Kent Jennings and Richard Niemi, "The Transmission of Political Values from Parent to Child," *American Political Science Review*, 62, 1968, pp. 169–184.

[22] Rokeach, *op. cit.*, Chapters 1–3.

relationship found by Jennings and Niemi was that of parent-child party identification[23] (tau-B = .47), while parent-child scores on the political attitude of political cynicism were weakly related (tau-B = .12).[24]

The nature of our sample allows us to explore the possibility that what is really transmitted from parents to children are basic personality orientations, some of which, such as personal control, have important political consequences. As we noted in Chapter Six, the parents of our respondents were each sent a questionnaire which contained a shorter version of the questionnaire which their children had answered. Included were the same items used to create the personal-control scale for the undergraduate respondents. We therefore created a personal-control scale for the parent sample identical to that used for their children. The data are presented in Table 6.

The data suggest that parental personal-control beliefs are an important determinant of the children's personal-control beliefs. The moderately high gamma suggests that

TABLE 6. CHILD PERSONAL CONTROL BY PARENT PERSONAL CONTROL

Parent	*Child Control*			
	Low	*Medium*	*High*	*Total*
Low	29.8	57.1	13.1	42
Medium	14.7	70.6	14.7	109
High	7.6	63.6	28.8	33
gamma = .34	$x^2 = 10.47$ $p = < .05$			

[23] Jennings and Niemi, *op. cit.*, p. 173.

[24] *Ibid.*, p. 178.

there is indeed a strong relation between parents' personality orientations and their child's, at least in the case of personal control. The results, of course, are only suggestive, but they do point to the importance of future research on the role of the transmission of personality orientations on political attitudes, opinions, and behaviors.

THE MULTIVARIATE ANALYSIS OF THE ACQUISITION OF PERSONAL CONTROL

Of course, what we would like to be able to do is to measure the relative impact of these variables on the acquisition of personal control. In order to measure the effects of the several dimensions of family structure on the acquisition of personal control, some form of multivariate analysis is clearly suggested. Yet, each statistical technique is explicitly based on a set of underlying assumptions about sampling procedures and level of measurement, which must be met before the techniques can be properly utilized. For example, partial and multiple correlations techniques require data that is interval level, a condition which we do not feel is met by most survey data, including this data set. Moreover, if one utilizes partition design as a method of statistical control, as the numbers of variables simultaneously controlled increases, the number of respondents within each group tends to become dangerously small, unless the sample size is extremely large. What would be hoped for, then, is some sort of multivariate technique which assumes only ordinal level data, and which would allow us to assess the relative explanatory weights of several independent variables on a dependent variable.

Fortunately, such a technique is available in the form of the Multiple Classification Analysis Program (M.C.A.) developed at the Institute for Social Research at the University of Michigan by Andrews, Morgan, and Sonquist.[25] The program uses a technique similar to multiple regression using dummy variables, which allow the researcher to assess the relative power of several predictor variables in a dependent variable. The program's algorithm allows the use of predictor variables of nominal level or stronger. The predictors may be correlated with each other, and they need not be linearly related to the dependent variable.

The program itself provides the researcher with several sets of statistics, including eta and beta measures of each independent variable. Eta is a general measure of the ability of an independent variable to predict the values of the dependent variable under consideration. When squared, it indicates the proportion of the total sum of squares as explained by the predictor variables. Thus, eta is analogous to a simple correlation coefficient.

Beta is the other summary statistic provided by the program. It provides a measure of the ability of an independent variable to explain variation in the dependent variable, after adjusting for the effects of all the other independent variables. Thus, in a sense, beta is analogous to a partial correlation coefficient. Beta gives a generally clear picture of the relative strengths of the independent variables in predicting variations in the dependent variable.

Finally, a third statistic, R^2 is computed by the program. This statistic is an unbiased measure of the total effects of the independent variables, taking into account the degrees of freedom, in the attempt to explain variance in the dependent variable. Thus, it is an oll-over indicator of how well one could predict the values of the dependent variable once the values of the independent variables are known. Table 7 below presents the results of the multivariate analysis of the impact of the family in the acquisition of personal control.

[25] Frank Andrews, *et al.*, *Multiple Classification Analysis: A Report on a Computer Program for Multiple Regression Using Categorical Predictors* (Ann Arbor: Institute for Social Research, 1967).

TABLE 7. RELATIVE WEIGHTS OF THE FAMILY VARIABLES ON THE ACQUISITION OF PERSONAL CONTROL

	ETA	*BETA*
Who Made Rules	.56	.11
Rule Consistency	.35	.31
Autonomy Allowed	.46	.37
Trust in Parents	.20	.12
Parent Empathy	.34	.10
Parental Personal Control	.41	.84

Multiple R(adjusted) = .597
Multiple R(Squared) = .356

When we examine the Eta statistics in Table 7, we see that many of the variables, with the exception of the trust in parents dimension, have relatively high degrees of association with the acquisition of personal control. At first glance this would appear to suggest that most of the variables we have examined are of some importance in understanding and predicting personal control. However, a close look at Table 7, especially the Beta statistic allows a more precise view.

With the effects of all of the other variables held constant, the strongest single predictor of our respondent's level of personal control was their parents level of personal control. This finding would appear to underscore the importance of parental personality configurations for the transmission of politically relevant personality orientations to their children. This in turn suggests that one potentially rich field of future exploration in political socialization would be the study of the impact of parental personality on children's politically relevant personality dimensions.

After parental personal control, the two most important

structural variables are degrees of allowed autonomy while growing up and rule enforcement consistency. Both of the emotional closeness dimensions were found to have rather low predictive value when the effects of the other variables were taken into account, while the allocation of family decision-making power appears to play little role in the acquisition of personal control.

It is well to remember that our analysis deals only with the acquisition of personal control. We would expect and indeed hypothesize that different dimensions of family life would have differential impact on different personality dimensions. For example, if one were to examine the acquisition of interpersonal trust, one might hypothesize that the emotional structure dimension that we examined would have high predictive power, while perhaps rule consistency might not. In any case these matters are empirical questions; our point here is only to suggest that there is no theoretical reason to assume that the dimensions of family-life impact similarly upon all politically relevant personality dimensions.

We hypothesized and found that high personal control was associated with degree of parental empathy, sequential arrival into the family, and parental personal-control beliefs. A multivariate analysis of the relative predictive value of all our socialization variables suggested that parental personal-control beliefs were the single best predictor of personal-control beliefs among our adolescent respondents.

In the following chapters we turn our attention from the acquisition of personal control to some politically important interpersonal correlates of personal control. These interpersonal correlates in turn will then be examined in relation to the political system.

Chapter Twelve

THE SELF, PERSONAL CONTROL, AND THE POLITICAL SYSTEM

To this point, the focus of this analysis has been on the conceptualization, psychological origins, and acquisition dynamics of personal control. This focus has been necessary to develop a viable social-psychological theory of political efficacy. Just as important, however, is the fact that the basic personality orientation of personal control has politically important attitudinal and behavioral consequences. These consequences flow not only from the nature of the need itself, but from its relation to a complex network of attitudes toward the self and others. We will draw together some themes and present some empirical findings in order to begin to document the relationship between the self, personal control, and the political system.

INTERPERSONAL TRUST, SATISFACTION, AND PERSONAL CONTROL

In the previous chapter, we suggested the importance of childhood autonomy in the acquisition of personal control. Insofar as parents attempt to screen or keep the child from participating in situations that they find anxiety producing, the message is transmitted to the child that there are a number of situations which he should both fear and avoid. Yet, while avoidance behavior may reduce anxiety in the short run, it is not always available as an option, especially in some political situations.

More importantly, the failure to experience reliance and trust in oneself may give rise to an anxious mistrust of one's environment, including other people. Since the environment is perceived as unmodifiable due to a lack of resources or skills, the individual may view himself as at the mercy of his environment. This is especially true where avoidance may not be possible. Such lack of control is extremely anxiety producing.[1]

We suggested, however, that the growth of personal control was facilitated by confrontation with and mastery of challenging situations. Trust in oneself and one's abilities can only develop through successful mastery of interpersonal and environmental challenges. Furthermore, we suggested that after trust in oneself has developed, there is more likely to be trust in others, and that this trust in others has important implications for political participation.

We said that for those in whom trust in others is low, the possibilities for satisfactory collective activity would be minimized. Since individuals with low trust in others would deny that there can be altruistic origins of behavior in others, collective activity would be seen as simply self-serving. Of course, it is possible that there are individuals for whom the ends of an action are more important than the motives that others bring to the collective activity. Yet, there is some evidence that agreeable interactions with like-minded others is an important component of political activity.[2]

There is also another way in which interpersonal trust is related to political activity. The extension of self-trust to others is sometimes paralleled by an extension of trust in others to trust in social institutions,[3] including political

[1] See, for example, Bruno Bettleheim, "Individual and Mass Behavior in Extreme Situations," *Journal of Abnormal and Social Psychology*, 38, 1943, pp. 447–451.

[2] Steven Brown and John Ellithorp, "Emotional Experiences in Political Groups: The Case of the McCarthy Phenomenon," *American Political Science Review*, 2, 1970, pp. 349–366.

[3] M. Rosenberg, "Misanthropology and Political Ideology," *American Sociological Review*, 21, 1956, pp. 690–695.

institutions.[4] In a sense, this may be seen as a logical extension of trust in self. The belief that leaders and institutions are responsive to citizen initiative and action is implicit in most acts of participation. Most attempts to influence imply trust in one's abilities and in the responsiveness of public men and institutions. If, as has been suggested, these attitudes are strongly related to personal control, then another important link between personal control and political behavior will have been established.

In order to analyze the relationships among these variables, each respondent answered several questions dealing with his level of faith in people, as measured by several items from the Rosenberg Faith-in-People scale.[5] We then cross-tabulated the relationship between personal control and faith in people. As we hypothesized, there was a significant positive association (gamma = .30, $X^2 = 9.45$, $p = <.05$) between feelings of personal control and the degree of faith in people. Respondents with high personal control were more than three times more likely to feel that people could generally be trusted than their counterparts with low feelings of personal control. These results were not unexpected in view of our discussion of the origins and nature of the acquisition of personal control. Is it the case, however, as we have indicated, that these feelings of interpersonal trust generalize to the political system?

Respondents were asked to evaluate the government on a number of adjuctive pairs, including (1) honest–dishonest, (2) open–closed, and (3) trustworthy–untrustworthy. These items, when placed together in an index, may be viewed as an indicator of a respondent's general level of trust in government. A respondent that evaluated the government as dishonest, closed, and untrustworthy would be indicating a

[4] Robert Agger *et al.*, "Political Cynicism: Measurement and Meaning," *Journal of Politics*, 23, 1961, pp. 690–695.

[5] Rosenberg, *op. cit.*, p. 691.

substantial lack of trust in government. The relationship between personal control and faith in government is presented in Table 8.

TABLE 8. FAITH IN GOVERNMENT BY PERSONAL CONTROL

Personal Control	*Faith in Government*			
	Low	*Medium*	*High*	*Total N*
Low	60.0	18.0	22.0	50
Medium	35.8	51.1	13.1	199
High	20.8	43.8	35.4	50
gamma = .34	$x^2 = 31.41$ $p = < .001$			

Once again, the data suggest that there is a strong relationship between personal control and faith in government. The results are especially striking on the negative evaluation or low faith-in-government category. The overwhelming majority of the respondents with low personal control have little faith in government. Also interesting is that the highest percentage of respondents appear in the medium, or middle, category. This requires some further explication. The semantic differential ranges from one to seven, with one being the highest score on a pole of an evaluation and a seven the other highest pole. Thus, it is conceivable that four is the midpoint category indicating a perceived balance between the two extreme poles. For example, on the honest-dishonest dimension, a one would represent most honest, while a seven would represent most dishonest. A score of four might indicate that the evaluation was basically balanced between the two alternatives.

Viewed from this perspective, the respondents with high or medium personal control were slightly more likely to hold a balanced or mixed evaluation of the government, seeing it neither on one extreme or the other. Of course, respondents with high personal control were much more likely than those with low personal control to hold favorable evaluations of the government.

We hypothesized that those people who had high personal control would have more interpersonal trust and that this trust could be generalized to evaluations of the political system. This suggests that those individuals with low trust in people would be more likely to have been unsatisfied with political activity. The point to be made here is that satisfaction with past participation originates in part from the social aspects of political participation. The rewards obtained by working toward collective goals with like-minded people are an important ingredient in political behavior.[6] To examine the relationship between this satisfaction and the interpersonal trust associated with personal control, we asked each respondent the following question: "Thinking back to when you have become involved in politics . . . how often have things turned out the way you wanted them to?" Percentages from zero to 100 were placed below the question, and the respondent was asked to place a check after the appropriate percentage. The answers were then grouped into three categories, (1) less than 50 percent of the time (2) 50 percent of the time, and (3) more than 50 percent of the time. No suggestion is being made here that what is being tapped is the "actual" percentage of past rewards. Rather this is an attempt to obtain a general indication of the subject's perceived reinforcement schedule in political participation. The relation between faith in people and prior political reinforcement schedule was both positive (gamma = .21) and statistically significant ($X^2 = 14.88$, $p = <.01$). The data suggest that individuals who reported that they were satisfied with the results of their

[6] Brown and Ellithorp, *op. cit., passim.*

participation were six times as likely to have a high degree of faith in people as were those who reported being unsatisfied with their past political activity less than 50 percent of the time. So it appears that interpersonal trust is related to satisfaction with political activity as we suggested in our previous analysis.

Another important point related to satisfaction remains to be made here, and that is the relation between personal control and life satisfaction. We indicated that the concept of the need for personal control had important implications for democratic theory. More specifically, it was suggested that if people did have a need to control their life-space, and if it could be empirically documented that when such control was available, citizens were less alienated and more satisfied, then the normative desirability of forms of government which increased personal-control possibilities would have received some substantiation, at least from the perspective of the citizens.

This is not an argument for the general desirability of democratic values over others, for such an argument depends on a complex series of means-ends relationships and is beyond the scope of this research. Rather, the point here is that if one begins with the assumption that maximizing citizen satisfaction is a value end of democratic political systems, and the means to this end is some form of government-citizen relationship in which the latter has control over the former, then demonstrations of the relation between personal control and personal and political satisfaction become relevant.

In effect, this demonstration will take place on several levels; firstly, with the individual vis-à-vis himself, and secondly, in his relations to the political system. It has previously been hypothesized that a lack of personal control over one's life-space is anxiety producing; but does it follow that the attainment of personal control is positively valued by individuals? If, indeed, individuals who have personal control are not happier or more satisfied than individuals with external-control beliefs, then the suggestion that the acquisition of personal control is inherently rewarding will have to be modified. In order to analyze the relationship between personal control and satisfaction, a semantic differential section was included in the survey instrument which asked the respondent to evaluate himself on a number of dimensions. Important for our purposes is the adjunctive pair, happy-unhappy. Our theory suggests that individuals with high personal control would rate themselves as happier than individuals with low personal control, since the theory suggests that it is intrinsically rewarding to have such personal control.

When we cross-tabulated the degree of personal control by the reported degree of happiness, the associations were both substantial (gamma = .31) and statistically significant ($X^2 = 15.48$, $p = <.001$). The data does suggest that respondents with high degrees of personal control do rate themselves as happier, while those with low degrees of personal control are more likely to rate themselves as unhappy. The statistically significant relationship provides some support for our theoretical statement that feelings of personal control are intrinsically rewarding.

Furthermore, this suggests that citizens with feelings of high personal control will be happier and more satisfied than citizens who lack such feelings. Whether this satisfaction is generalized to the political system is a question we will explore in both the following section and in the next chapter.

PERSONAL CONTROL AND DIMENSIONS OF ORIENTATIONS TO THE POLITICAL SYSTEM

We have already seen that individual citizens' feelings of personal control will have some consequences for the evaluation of the political system, specifically the amount of faith in government. Clearly, evaluations of the political system may proceed along a variety of different lines, some of which are the focus of this particular section.

In the last section we suggested that individuals with a high degree of personal control were personally more happy than those with low feelings of personal control. But does this personal satisfaction extend to evaluations of the political system? There is already some indication that it does, for in fact the three adjuctive pairs used to form the faith-in-government index may be viewed as evaluations of the government. Closer to the point, however, is the relation between the citizen with high personal control and his evaluation of the political system in which he operates.

Since the American political system is in theory a representative system in which mechanisms exist through which the citizens can have some control over political processes, it remains to be determined whether citizens who have high personal control will in any way differ from those citizens with feelings of external control in their positive or negative evaluations of the political system. If it is the case that citizens with high personal control evaluate the government much more favorably than those without such control, a link will have been made between citizen satisfaction with the political system, the nature of the political system (allowing for personal control) and personal control.

On the one hand, presence or occurrence of personal control presents prima-facie evidence that such control is possible within the context of this political system. On the other hand, feelings of external control may originate in either the inability of the individual to gain control because of personal shortcomings or the inability to gain control because the system does not allow it.

In order to make any suggestions about the differences in evaluation of the politcial system between those with personal or external feelings of control, which originate in the *nature* of the system itself, it is first necessary to find the locus of perceived responsibility for external control. For if individuals with external feelings of control place the responsibility on themselves, then their evaluation of the government, while interesting in itself, will tell us nothing about the comparative evaluations of political systems that allow or discourage personal control. However, if individuals with feelings of external control place the blame on the social system rather than upon themselves and their individual failings, then some suggestions can be made about the evaluations of political systems that are *perceived* to allow personal control as opposed to those which are perceived not to allow such control.

Fortunately for our purposes, there is a way to distinguish between the locus of responsibility for external control. Gurin and her associates at the University of Michigan have developed an index which they call individual versus system blame.[7] In essence, this scale measures the degree to which respondents attribute undesirable social conditions to the nature of the system itself or to individual failure.[8] Although this scale is similar to the personal-control scale we have used throughout, it is not the same. The control scale we have used throughout specifically measures the amount of control an individual *feels he has,* while the Gurin index attempts to find *the locus of responsibility for the state of the system.* A factor analysis by Gurin provides empirical evidence of the separability of the control and blame scales.[9]

We present no hypothesis about the relation of personal control to political blame attribution, for, as Gurin suggests, "rather than predicting a relationship between personal control and individual-system, it might be more fruitful to ex-

7 Patricia Gurin *et al.*, "Internal-External Control in the Motivation Dynamics of Negro Youth," *Journal of Social Issues*, 55, 1969, p. 45.

8 The exact wording for each item used in all scales and indices utilized in this study appear in the Appendix.

9 Gurin *et al.*, *op. cit.*, p. 36.

pect the relationship to vary under different conditions."[10] The results are presented in Table 9.

TABLE 9. POLITICAL BLAME ATTRIBUTION BY PERSONAL CONTROL

Personal Control	*Political Blame*		
	Individual	*System*	*Total N*
Low	43.8	56.3	48
Medium	68.5	31.5	194
High	75.0	25.0	48
gamma = .36	$x^2 = 12.71$ $p = < .001$		

The results suggested that, in this sample, individuals with low personal control are significantly more likely to attribute the state of the system to the nature of the system itself, rather than to individual feelings of the skills and capacities of individuals. Moreover, the level of the gamma provides greater confidence of the separability of the two scales.

The data suggest that individuals with low personal control do attribute responsibility for the way things are to the system and not to individuals, presumably including themselves. Therefore we might suggest that the individuals with low personal control would attribute their own lack of control not to individual failings on their part, but to the nature of the system itself.

Given the finding that individuals with low personal control appear to blame the system rather than themselves, it remains to explore the evaluations of government outputs by our respondents. We previously hypothesized and found that

[10] *Ibid.*, p. 51.

individuals with high personal control were more personally happy, which we suggested provided some support for the thesis that having personal control was rewarding. Our hypothesis here is that a government that is perceived to allow and make possible personal control will be positively valued and be evaluated as more effective and beneficial, than one which is perceived to be structured so as to decrease the opportunities for personal control. More specifically, we hypothesize that individuals with high personal control will evaluate the government as highly effective and highly beneficial. Each respondent was asked as part of the semantic differential evaluation of the government to give his reaction to the following two adjective pairs: effective-ineffective and rewarding-punishing. Tables 10 and 11 present the data for the evaluation of the political system on the ineffective-effective and rewarding-punishing dimensions.

These tables indicate that the political system is evaluated differently by citizens with high and low personal control. The government is evaluated as much more effective by respondents with high personal control, while citizens with external feelings of control are not only more likely to give a negative evaluation, but are also less likely than respondents

TABLE 10. PERCEIVED SYSTEM EFFECTIVENESS BY LOCUS OF CONTROL

Personal Control	*System Effectiveness*			
	Low	*Mixed*	*High*	*Total N*
Low	47.9	29.2	22.9	48
Medium	18.3	52.2	29.9	197
High	6.4	40.4	53.2	47
gamma = .43	$x^2 = 34.69$ $p = < .001$			

TABLE 11. EVALUATIONS OF GOVERNMENT OUTPUTS BY LOCUS OF CONTROL

Personal Control	*Outputs*			
	Punishing	*Mixed*	*Rewarding*	*Total N*
Low	18.8	43.8	37.5	48
Medium	7.1	70.5	22.4	197
High	8.5	85.1	6.4	47
gamma = .22	$x^2 = 22.27$ $p = < .001$			

with high personal control to view the government as having limited (mild) effectiveness. The moderately high gamma correlation suggests a strong relationship between locus of control and positive evaluations of government.

When we move to an analysis of the evaluation of the outputs of the political system, an interesting set of findings emerges. Once again, those respondents with low feelings of control are much more likely to perceive the outputs of the political system as punishing rather than rewarding. Interestingly, this difference does not extend to evaluations of the system as rewarding. Indeed, respondents with external feelings of control are slightly more likely than respondents with personal control to evaluate the outputs as rewarding. The major difference seems to occur in the center category. Respondents with high personal control are much more likely to have a balanced evaluation of political system outputs, as sometimes being rewarding and sometimes not, rather than placing all of the output evaluations in one category. So it appears that respondents with high personal control are not only individually happy but are also more likely to hold positive evaluations of the political system providing some empirical support for one of the underlying assumptions of democratic theory:

people are happier and more satisfied with the government when they have some control over what it does.

A note of caution should be sounded at this point: Future research aimed at explicating the causal sequence involved here will of necessity involve extended panel studies. The cross-sectional nature of our data limits our ability to make strong causal statements with solid empirical grounding. In this sense our data and analysis of the interrelationships among personal control and other variables should be taken as suggestive rather than definitive.

In the next chapter, with the examination of a number of political attitudes, we will continue the exploration of the relationships between personal control and political orientations.

Chapter Thirteen

SOME POLITICAL ATTITUDE CORRELATES OF PERSONAL CONTROL

In the last chapter, focusing on the evaluation of political objects, we began to explore the relationships between personal control and political orientations. This chapter will continue that focus by examining the relationships between personal control and political attitudes. By attitudes we mean "the enduring, persistent organization of predispositions towards an object."[1] The literature on political attitudes is immense[2] and growing, but there has been less work on the relation of political attitudes to human needs.[3]

Generally, needs may be thought of as a more basic and underlying psychic disposition than attitudes,[4] and there is already some evidence that unfulfillment of particular needs, such as the need for personal control, will cause perceptual if not behavioral distortions.[5] It is important, then, to understand what relationships, if any, exist between the need for personal control and the organizations of predispositions toward the political system. We have already examined several of these political attitude sets, including faith in government and individual versus system attribution of blame, and in both cases found strong associations between

[1] Gordon Allport, "Attitudes," in Martin Fishbein (ed.), *Readings in Attitude Theory and Measurement* (New York: Wiley & Sons, 1967), p. 8.

[2] A useful starting place is the bibliography in Fred Greenstein, *Personality and Politics* (Chicago: Markham, 1969), pp. 154–184.

[3] But see the work of Jeanne Knutson, *The Human Basis of the Polity* (Chicago: Aldine, 1972), Chapter 4.

[4] A. Maslow, *Motivation and Personality* (New York: Harper, 1954).

[5] James Davies, *Human Nature and Politics* (New York: Wiley & Sons, 1963).

these attitudes and personal control. In this chapter we will focus specifically on the relationships between personal control and selected sets of political attitudes. Some of the political attitudes are:

1. Personal control—the extent to which the individual feels he has control over relevant life-space areas (higher score = personal control).
2. Political alienation—the perception that one is estranged from the political system because there is a gap between one's personal values and the values of the political system (higher score = higher alienation).
3. Political time orientations—the extent to which the political outcomes that the individual would like to see occur are immediately desired (higher scores = results wanted sooner).
4. Faith in government—the extent to which the government is viewed as honest and trustworthy (higher score = less faith in government).
5. Governmental accessibility—the extent to which the political structure is viewed as open to change (higher score = greater accessibility).
6. Government effectiveness—the extent to which the government is seen as a powerful and effective structure (higher score = greater government power).
7. System vs. individual blame—the degree to which the state of the system is attributed to the nature of the social and political system itself or to individual failings (higher scores = higher individual blame).

PERSONAL CONTROL AND POLITICAL ALIENATION

The last chapter suggested that individuals with personal control were much more likely to favorably evaluate the government than individuals with external feelings of control. Another perspective on the same set of self-polity relationships may be seen by examining the relationship between personal control and political alienation.

Both political and social alienation have been conceptualized in a number of ways. Seeman, in an early examination of the concept, suggested five alternate meanings of alienation: powerlessness, meaninglessness, normlessness, isolation, and self-estrangement.[6] Later empirical research by Neal and Rettig provides some support for a separation of the different meanings advanced by Seeman.[7] In practice, however, empirical investigations have concentrated on different dimensions, each of which is called alienation.

Thus, for those who follow Seeman, alienation means powerlessness,[8] for those who follow Srole, it refers to a syndrome of isolation, despair, and powerlessness,[9] while for others, alienation is defined as the belief that politicians do not care and cannot be trusted.[10] Yet, as Schwartz has pointed out, there is a core meaning to the term alienation, which he suggests is "estrangement—a perception that one does not identify oneself with the political system."[11] Moreover, other researchers have reached similar conclusions. Olson has suggested that, "alienation might be defined formally as an attitude of separation or estrangement be-

[6] M. Seeman, "On the Meaning of Alienation," *American Sociological Review*, 24, 1959, pp. 783–789.

[7] A. Neal and S. Rettig, "On the Multidimensionality of Alienation," *American Sociological Review*, 31, 1967, pp. 54–64.

[8] M. Seeman, "Alienation, Membership, and Political Knowledge," *Public Opinion Quarterly*, 30, 1966, p. 353.

[9] Leo Srole, "Social Integration and Certain Corollaries," *American Sociological Review*, 62, 1969, p. 86.

[10] W. Gamson, "Stable Unrepresentation in American Society," *American Behavioral Scientist*, 12, 1968.

[11] David Schwartz, *Political Alienation and Political Behavior* (Chicago: Aldine-Atherton, 1973), p. 9.

tween oneself and some salient aspect of the social environment,"[12] while Srole has suggested that alienation is, "a generalized, pervasive sense of self to others, belongingness at one extreme—compared with . . . self to other, alienation at the other pole of the spectrum."[13]

Our measure of political alienation reflects this core meaning. Each respondent was given a political alienation score based on his answers to the following three item index: (1) Do you believe that the government represents people with your political and social beliefs? (2) Does the government seem unable or unwilling to do the things that you think need to be done? And (3) when you think of your ideas and the ideas and actions of the federal government in general, do you feel there is . . . no gap . . . a small gap . . . a fairly wide gap . . . a very wide gap?

It was suggested above that the relationship between political alienation and personal control provided an important perspective on individual–polity relationships. Certainly the relationship has important implications since it is clear that identification with the values and outputs of the political system is part of what Easton regards as "diffuse support" which is important for the stability and persistence of the political system.[14] It would be suspected that since individuals with external control are more likely to blame the system than themselves (see Table 9), we would hypothesize that they would be more likely to be politically alienated. Table 12 suggests that this appears to be the case.

The results provide some support for our hypothesis that individuals with low feelings of control are much more likely to be highly alienated, while individuals with high personal control are much more likely to have low alienation.

[12] Marvin Olsen, "Alienation and Political Opinions," *Public Opinion Quarterly*, 29, 1965, p. 203.

[13] Leo Srole, *op. cit.*, p. 710.

[14] David Easton, A *Systems Analysis of Political Life* (New York: Wiley & Sons, 1965), p. 220.

TABLE 12. POLITICAL ALIENATION BY LOCUS CONTROL

Personal Control	Political Alienation			
	High	*Medium*	*Low*	*Total N*
Low	55.3	42.6	2.1	47
Medium	28.0	62.5	9.5	200
High	29.8	51.1	19.1	47
gamma = .33	$x^2 = 18.86$ $p = < .001$			

This is not to suggest, however, that individuals with personal control are completely satisfied with the government, for the majority of the high personal-control respondents expressed at least some alienation from the political system. When we analyzed this relationship, controlling for blame attribution, the relationship remained stable. Given the lack of association between political alienation and attributions of blame, it would appear that there is some support for the importance of feelings of personal control in the generation of political-alienation attitudes.

We also analyzed the personal-control and political-alienation relationship holding faith in government constant, and we found that the relationship between alienation and personal control is relatively unaffected by levels of faith in government. In conditions of high and low faith in government individuals with low personal control are still more likely to be highly politically alienated.

Not surprisingly, individuals with high political alienation had decided lack of faith in the government. The association was extremely strong (gamma = .46) and statistically significant ($X^2 = 31.74$, $p = .001$). Also not very surprising was the relationship obtained between political alienation and an index of government effectiveness. This index was made up of two semantic differential pairs; ineffective–effective and impotent–powerful.

This index is a measure of the respondent's evaluation of the government's power plus his estimation of its effectiveness. Clearly, in order to be effective, a certain degree of power is needed, although power itself does not guarantee effectiveness. The relationship between political alienation and government effectiveness was moderate (gamma = .27) and statistically significant ($X^2 = 12.25$, $p = <.02$). Again, this result is not very surprising, since it is entirely plausible that an individual who felt estranged from the values or outputs of the political system could hardly evaluate the government as effective.

Given that the highly politically alienated have a low sense of trust in the government and are more likely to negatively evaluate its effectiveness, the relationship between political alienation and government influenceability does come as somewhat of a surprise. In the semantic differential section, each respondent was asked to evaluate the government along the following three dimensions: (1) active–passive, (2) initiating–reacting, and (3) decisive–indecisive.

These items were combined to form a government responsiveness index. Thus, if a respondent viewed the government as active, initiating, and decisive, there would be less opportunity to influence. If the government were viewed as more passive, reacting, and indecisive, the possibilities for influence might increase. This is not the same as trust in the government, for one cannot trust the government to take certain actions on its own and still feel that the government is open to be influenced in its course of action. Of course, it is also possible to distrust the government and feel that it is not open to influence attempts.

The results in Table 13 suggest that although the politically alienated do not trust the government, they still believe that it is open to attempts at influence. As one looks down the column from low to high alienation, one finds a

TABLE 13. GOVERNMENT INFLUENCEABILITY BY POLITICAL ALIENATION

Political Alienation	*Possibility of Influencing Government*			
	Low	*Medium*	*High*	*Total N*
Low	24.6	63.1	12.3	33
Medium	7.0	69.0	23.8	185
High	7.3	58.7	33.9	109
gamma = .28	$x^2 = 16.57$ $p = < .01$			

continual increase in the perception that the government is open to influence.

This interesting result provides one possible means of resolving a set of contradictory findings which have linked political alienation to nonvoting[15] and low political interest,[16] as well as to protest voting[17] and sit-ins.[18] Apparently, the belief in the openness and responsiveness of the government to political influence by an individual may be a factor in an individual's decision to withdraw from or to participate in the political system. That is to say, political alienation, defined as self-polity value estrangement, may not lead to withdrawal from participation *if the government is viewed as potentially accessible to people with alienated political views,* even though these views would most likely not be accepted.

15 Edward McDill and Jeanne Ridley, "Status, Anomia, Political Alienation and Political Participation," *American Journal of Sociology,* 67, 1962, p. 205.

16 Melvin Seeman, "Alienation, Membership, and Political Knowledge," *Public Opinion Quarterly,* 30, 1966, p. 353.

17 McDill and Ridley, *op. cit.*

18 Schwartz, *op. cit.,* Chapter 6.

Turning to an examination of the impact of personal control on these orientations to the political regime, the results parallel those discussed previously for political alienation. We have already suggested and presented some data to support the proposition that individuals with a high sense of personal control are significantly more likely to have a higher degree of trust in government.

A glance at Table 14 suggests that they are also more likely to rate the government as more effective.

TABLE 14. GOVERNMENTAL EFFECTIVENESS BY LOCUS OF CONTROL

Personal Control	*Governmental Effectiveness*			
	Low	*Medium*	*High*	*Total N*
Low	34.0	40.0	26.0	50
Medium	14.2	46.3	39.5	198
High	4.2	39.6	56.3	48
gamma = .38	$x^2 = 21.09$ $p = < .001$			

This finding is not unexpected in view of our previous discussion of the relationship between locus of control and the nature of the political system evaluation. These data would seem to support the hypothesis that individuals with feelings of high personal control are more likely than those without it to hold positive evaluations of the political system, and that these positive evaluations grow out of the perceived nature of the system itself.

A somewhat different finding emerged when the relationship between locus of control and governmental accessibility was examined. It was found that the most highly politically alienated individuals were the most likely to believe that the government was accessible to influence. We suggested that it was not implausible that a politically alienated individual could perceive a gap between his values and those of the government and still believe that the government was accessible to influence attempts. But what of the relationship between personal control and the perception of government accessibility?

We have already presented data to suggest a significant inverse relationship between level of personal control and political alienation and a significant positive association between degree of political alienation and degree of perceived government accessibility. If feelings of political alienation and beliefs in personal control are closely related dimensions, we might then expect that the greater the feelings of personal control, the lesser the perceived accessibility of government. On the other hand, if political alienation and personal control are distinct dimensions, we might expect that the lower the personal control, the less the perceived influenceability of government. Table 15 presents the relationship.

The data suggest that there is a significant positive association between the degree of personal control and the percep-

TABLE 15. GOVERNMENT ACCESSIBILITY BY LOCUS OF CONTROL

Personal Control	*Accessibility of Government*			
	Low	*Moderate*	*High*	*Total N*
Low	30.0	44.0	26.0	50
Medium	8.1	65.2	26.7	199
High	2.1	75.0	22.9	48
gamma = .18	$x^2 = 26.15$ $p = < .001$			

tion of government accessibility. A look at the table suggests only small differences in the high category. In the low category, however, individuals with low feelings of personal control are overwhelmingly more likely to perceive that the government is not open or accessible. Interestingly, individuals with high feelings of personal control are much more likely to have a balanced assessment of government openness, with the largest percentage of these respondents falling in the middle categories. The findings are related to our previous discussion (page 173) about the relationship among personal control, political alienation, perceived government accessibility, and political behavior.

Apparently, knowledge about political alienation alone does not yield enough information to allow the making of any general statements about participation or withdrawal from the political system. Our data suggests that, insofar as one is politically alienated, withdrawal may depend on the degree of personal control and the perceived influenceability of the system. Since respondents with high personal control do not dramatically differ from respondents with low personal control in perceiving the government as high in accessibility, we might suggest that high political alienation and high personal control coupled with beliefs in government accessibility would be no bar to participation, but that political alienation and low personal control, coupled with perceptions that the government is not accessible, might result in withdrawal from the political arena.

Another vantage point from which to view the same results is to suggest that high political alienation coupled with feelings of personal control will tend to generate or be consonant with beliefs of government accessibility, while high political alienation coupled with low feelings of personal control will generate or be consonant with beliefs in the inaccessibility of the government to influence.

PERSONAL CONTROL AND POLITICAL TIME ORIENTATIONS

Time and space have been called the basic organizational principles of reality by at least one scholar.[19] Yet, surprisingly, the subject has received little attention in political science.[20] To be fair, one can point to studies of social change[21] and some excellent work in the study of political generations,[22] all of which have an inherent time component. However, in these cases the emphasis has been on an objective rather than subjective time component.[23] That is, though events contained within an analytically selected set of time intervals, equally important but less examined is the element of subjective time as it is experienced by the individual. Many people are aware of how time appears to speed up or slow down, depending on our enjoyment of what we are doing. Viewed from an outside perspective however, an hour is no more or less than sixty minutes. Yet, as many students both undergraduate and graduate and even professors can testify, an hour lecture can be either 60 minutes long, or much longer.

The study of subjective time in political life is an important dimension of political analysis. For example, there is some evidence that subjective time speed up is one com-

[19] See A. Toffler, *Future Shock* (New York: Bantam, 1971).

[20] For an exception to this see Pat McGeever, "The Sources of Impatient Demands," unpublished Ph.D. dissertation, University of Pennsylvania, 1971.

[21] William Ogburn, *On Culture and Social Change* (Chicago, University of Chicago Press, 1964), *passim.*

[22] Neal E. Cutler, "Generation Maturation and Party Affiliation: A Cohort Analysis," *Public Opinion Quarterly*, 33, 1970, pp. 583–588.

[23] A good discussion of the problems involved in selecting political generations is to be found in W. Klecka, "Identifying Political Generations," unpublished ms., Northwestern University, Department of Political Science, pp. 2–11.

ponent of political crisis.[24] Another example has to do with the political implications of the perception of the rapidity of social change. Certainly individuals experience social change differently, and we might suggest that this would have important implications for political theory and political behavior. Might it not be the case, for example, that individuals who are experiencing (at least perceptually) very rapid social change would be most likely to support status quo social programs? During the last election, it was suggested that the Democratic candidate, Senator George McGovern, was defeated in large part because people were tired and afraid of more social change; a position that he had become identified with by too many of the electorate.

While these examples may give some idea of the importance of time orientations in political analysis, there is a more specific way in which they are related to personal control and political participation.

One of the results of early and substantial need gratification is the ability to withstand subsequent need deprivation.[25] In more concrete terms, individuals who have their control needs satisfied early in their life, are more able to tolerate and work within situations where they lack a high degree of personal control. If the individual builds up a reservoir from which to draw, it means that he is less susceptible to short-term fluctuations in his need satisfaction. The implication of need satisfaction in this area for politics is both interesting and important.

Given the nature of our political system, including the vertical layering of officials and the horizontal layering of interested parties for any issue, it is a rare political act that gains the individual the intended satisfaction in short order. This is especially true for people who participate to bring

[24] See the discussion of the Cuban missile crisis in T. Sorenson, *Kennedy* (New York: Harper and Row, 1965).

[25] Maslow, *op. cit.*, Chapter 4.

about changes in particular policies, but holds for other participations, as well. Given the inertia and bureaucratic layering, adherence to the idea of "Peace *Now*!" or "Freedom *Now!*" while perhaps philosophically justifiable, is bound to result in disappointment. Even if there is unanimity among all relevant publics and public officials (a rare case, indeed), change is often slow in coming. This means that the citizen must expect, and also be able to tolerate, delays in the gratification he desires from the political system.

Not all motivation to participate in politics requires this toleration for gratification delay. For example, the individual who participates to discharge his civic responsibility, obtains gratification of that motivational impulse as soon as he presses the lever. The discharge of civic responsibility, however, is not typically related to the psychological need structure of the individual, and therefore may be easier to satisfy. The individual attempting to gain a greater measure of control over his life must be able to tolerate delays, especially as we have suggested, if the political area has become the control relevant sphere.

In order to gain some insight into the dynamics and political implications of time orientations, we constructed a time index based on the following two questions:

1. It has been suggested that it is no longer necessary to keep our troops stationed in Western Europe. How willing would you be to support an *immediate* substantial reduction of our troops there?

2. Different groups are working to end our involvement in Vietnam, but there is disagreement about how quickly we should leave. How willing would you be to support a total withdrawal of U. S. troops by the end of 1971?

Each respondent answered the above question by noting if he were very willing, somewhat willing, or very unwilling to see the above policies put into effect immediately. Thus, he could agree with the policies, while at the same time not subscribe to the immediate time element specifically cited in each question. For example, one might agree that the U.S. should leave Vietnam but be unwilling to support total immediate withdrawal.[26]

Respondents were placed into one of three categories: (1) very politically patient, (2) somewhat impatient, and (3) very impatient. The results, presented in Table 16,

TABLE 16. POLITICAL TIME ORIENTATIONS BY LOCUS OF CONTROL

Personal Control	*Political Patience*			
	Low	*Medium*	*High*	*Total N*
Low	73.1	25.0	1.9	52
Medium	43.8	52.2	5.9	203
High	27.1	62.5	10.4	48
gamma = .48	$x^2 = 24.19$ $p = < .001$			

detail the relationship between locus of control and political time orientations.

An examination of Table 16 suggests that individuals with a high sense of personal control are significantly more likely to be more politically patient, while those individuals with low feelings of personal control are overwhelmingly more likely to desire immediate political gratification. Here

26 This index should be interpreted with the greatest caution. It is meant only to be an exploratory indicator and not a sophisticated scale. I am aware of the limitations of the index but included it because it suggests some important, previously neglected dynamics.

again it is interesting to note that the majority of the high personal control respondents are located in the moderate category. As was the case with evaluations of the political system as well as self-polity evaluations (political alienation), the high personal control respondents appear to be more likely to be moderate in both their orientations and evaluations. The picture that appears to emerge of the high personal-control respondents is not one of uncritical acceptance of political system personnel and outputs, but is rather the attempt to transcend dichotomous attributions and evaluations. We shall have more to say about this in the final chapter.

Another vantage point from which to view the importance of subjective time is to examine the relationship between political alienation and political time orientations. We have already suggested that there is a significant inverse association between level of personal control and degree of political alienation (see page 173) and a significant positive association between level of personal control and political patience. From these associations we would expect a negative association between political alienation and political patience. That is, since individuals with high personal control are able to delay political gratification and since those with high personal control are less politically alienated, it might be suggested that the ability to withstand the inevitable frustration with the pace of change that is inherent in mass political systems would be one factor helping to reduce the perception of self-polity differences. The data is presented in Table 17.

A glance at this table suggests that respondents with high political alienation are significantly more likely to have low political patience. In fact, this finding offers the possibility of a new way in which to explain the origins of political alienation. It may be that the conflict between the necessity for immediate political rewards (in the form of changed policies) and the inability of any complex multilayered political sys-

TABLE 17. POLITICAL TIME ORIENTATIONS BY POLITICAL ALIENATION

Political Alienation	*Political Patience*			
	High	*Medium*	*Low*	*Total N*
Low	15.2	54.5	30.3	33
Medium	17.4	52.6	40.0	190
High	.09	35.8	63.3	109
gamma = .43	$x^2 = 23.58$ $p = < .001$			

tem to produce such instant changes, may result in the generation of political alienation attitudes, or at least exacerbate them.

Our discussion to this point has assumed that being politically impatient is bound to result in a degree of frustration. Another way to gain some perspective on this relationship is to examine the association between political patience and degree of satisfaction with past participation. Each respondent was asked the following question: "Thinking back to when you became involved in politics . . . how often have things turned out the way you wanted them to?" Percentages from 0 to 100 were placed below the question and the respondent was asked to place a check after the appropriate percentage. The answers were grouped into three categories: (1) less than 50 percent of the time, (2) 50 percent of the time, and (3) more than 50 percent of the time. If it is true that being politically impatient is frustrating, we would expect these respondents to have reported a significantly lower degree of satisfaction with their past participatory experience. The results are presented in Table 18.

The data appears to support the contention that political impatience gives rise to frustrated feelings about politics

TABLE 18. PAST PARTICIPATION REWARDS BY POLITICAL TIME ORIENTATIONS

Political Patience	*Past Rewards*			
	Less Than 50%	*50%*	*More Than 50%*	N
Low	70.0	18.5	11.5	130
Medium	46.6	24.4	26.0	131
High	50.9	11.1	38.9	29
gamma = .35	x = 16.98 p= <.01			

and political participation. Respondents who scored high on political patience were significantly more likely to report that they were satisfied with the results of their participation more than 50 percent of the time, while those with low political patience were overwhelming more likely to report that they were satisfied with the results of their participation less than 50 percent of the time. One would suspect that this syndrome of low personal control, high political alienation, and high political impatience would have important implications for participatory orientations in the political system. In the following two chapters we shall turn our attention to the linkage between the feeling of personal control and its attitudinal correlates and participatory orientations.

Chapter Fourteen

PERSONAL CONTROL AND POLITICAL PARTICIPATION

The last several chapters have focused on the relationship of personal control to political attitudes, but as some social scientists are fond of pointing out, personality and attitudes are not the same as behavior. In some cases they might not even be related. For example, in a now classic study by LaPiere, it was found that there was little correspondence between the answers to questions concerning the lodging and other services that would be offered to Chinese guests and the actual treatment the Chinese received.[1] More recently, this finding has been replicated by Becker,[2] who has called into question the relation among attitudes, opinions, and behaviors. But there are studies which indicate that the intention to vote is strongly associated with the report of actually voting,[3] and others that show a strong correspondence between political ideology and actual voting preference.[4] The mixture of results would seem to indicate that the relation between psychological variables and actual behavior is a rather complex one.[5] It is the purpose of this chapter to explore some of the linkages between personal control and political participation.

[1] R. T. LaPiere, "Attitudes Vs. Action," *Social Forces*, 13, 1934, pp. 230–237.

[2] W. C. Becker, "The Matching of Behavioral Ratings and Questionnaire Personality Factors," *Psychological Bulletin*, 57, 1960, pp. 201–212.

[3] A. Campbell *et al., The American Voter* (New York: Wiley & Sons, 1960).

[4] H. Leventhal, "Authoritarianism, Ideology and Political Candidate Choice," *Journal of Abnormal and Social Psychology*, 69, 1964, pp. 539–549.

[5] See the discussion in Greenstein, *Personality and Politics* (Chicago: Markham, 1969), Chapter 2.

PERSONAL CONTROL AND POLITICAL SALIENCE

We have suggested that political salience is an important link between personal control and political behavior. That is, since political efficacy was defined as the belief that one had sufficient personal control over political processes to satisfy the need for personal control in *relevant life areas,* the questions remained how and to what extent politics becomes a control-relevant area. One answer is that the political sphere becomes control relevant *to the extent that the political system is felt to have an impact on the individual's social or physical life space—his daily existence.*

This is essentially a phenomenological definition of political salience, which begins with the assumption that political impact, like beauty, is in the eyes of the beholder. It also leads away from the indirect assessment of salience by such measures as attention to media or level of factual information. Although we would hypothesize that phenomenological salience and attention to media are related, there is no reason to believe that one needs to have high levels of factual information or sustained attention to the reporting of political events in order to feel affected by the political system.

As part of the attempt to assess the perceived impact of the federal government, each respondent was asked the following question: "Thinking about the federal government, how much affect do you think its activities, the laws passed and so on, have on your life?" In addition, each respondent was then asked the following question about the local government: "How much affect do you think its activities, the laws passed and so on, have on your life?" Answers to these two questions were used to form an impact-of-politics index, which was the measure we utilized to assess political salience.

When we examined the relationship between political

salience and attention to political events, we found there was a strong (gamma = .32) and statistically significant ($X^2 = 37.76$, $p = < .001$) association to political events. However, there was only a very small association (gamma = .02) between perceived impact of government and a measure of political information about the positions of candidates in a hotly contested local and regional election.

Our discussion in Chapter Five suggested that politics would become a control-relevant sphere to the extent that it would be perceived to have an impact on the individual's life. Given this contention, how can we characterize the distribution of political salience for our respondents? Approximately 38 percent of our respondents thought that the impact of the federal government on their daily lives was "great," while another 46 percent perceived the impact to be moderate. Only 12 percent of our respondents perceived the federal government to have a small impact on their daily lives. Switching to the impact of the local government, approximately 10 percent of our respondents saw the local government as having a "great" impact on their lives, while 79 percent saw the local government as having a moderate impact. Only 10 percent of our respondents saw the local government as having little or no impact on their lives. In terms of the distribution of political salience, our data suggest that for approximately 90 percent of our respondents the political system is seen as a control-relevant sphere.

These figures about the distribution of political salience for our respondents are of more than passing interest. One major criticism leveled at the survey research conducted over the last two decades is that, by focusing on political issues, it tends to produce a temporary and in some senses an artificial sense of political salience. This argument has been most eloquently advanced by Converse in a series of papers.[6]

[6] See Philip Converse, "Attitudes and Non-Attitudes: Continuations of a Dialogue," in E. Tufte (ed.), *The Quantative Analysis of Social Prob-*

While it is possible that taking a survey does temporarily increase the salience of political attitudes and orientations, our data about the perceived impact of the political system does provide some independent assessment of the importance of the political system to our respondents.

Another way of evaluating the impact of the political system is to examine the relationship between levels of personal control and the perceived impact of the political system. Does impact vary as a function of personal control? That is, do those with more personal control perceive the political system to have more of an impact on their lives, and those with low personal control perceive the political system to have less of an impact? Our discussion of the motivational implications of the political efficacy concept in Chapter 6 is relevant here. We suggested that the definition of political efficacy, as a feeling of effectiveness and capacity in the political sphere, assumes that people participate in areas in which they have effectiveness. Put another way, it assumes that politics becomes salient to people as a result of *their feelings of effectiveness* rather than as a result of *the impact of the political system upon their lives.* In order to ascertain the nature of this relationship we cross-tabulated the impact of the federal government by the degree of personal control. The degree of association is small (gamma = .11) and statistically nonsignificant ($X^2 = 5.67$, p = N.S.). In fact, the overwhelming majority of our respondents at all levels of personal control perceive the political system to have at least a moderate impact on them. Only 11 percent of the respondents saw the government as having little or no impact. This suggests that for all three control groups (low, medium, and high) politics is a control-relevant sphere, since it is perceived to have an impact on their daily lives.

---

lems (Reading, Mass.: Addison, 1970); "The Nature of Belief Systems in Mass Publics," in D. Apter (ed.), *Ideology and Discontent* (New York: Free Press, 1964).

Of course, individuals exist in relation not only to the federal government system, but also to the more spatially proximate local political system. Thus, a complete picture of the individual's political salience should also take into account his relation to the local government. As we had done for the perception of the federal political system, we cross-tabulated the impact of the local political system by the degree of personal control. Somewhat to our surprise we found a moderate (gamma = .20) and statistically significant relationship ($X^2 = 16.24$, $p = <.001$) between personal control and the perceived impact of the local government. Individuals with low personal control were significantly more likely to report that the local government had a "great" impact on their daily lives than were those respondents with high levels of personal control. Thus, we might assume political systems (both local and national) to be salient, control-relevant arenas. Yet respondents with low personal control are somewhat more likely to see both levels as salient.

While this information allows us to suggest that the government and politics is perceived to have an impact, it does not by itself allow us to suggest the nature of that impact.

The discussion in Chapter Five suggested to us that there were essentially three types of political salience orientations: (1) political-reward salience, (2) political-punishment salience, and (3) political-obligation salience. Political-reward salience originates in the perception that the political system is the only source capable of supplying certain benefits in the form of either goods or services. Political-punishment salience originates in the perception that the outputs of the political system may be viewed as interfering with the individual's values and goals. And political-obligation salience originates in the feeling that one *ought* to pay attention to politics in order to be a good citizen.

After the question about the perceived impact, each respondent was asked: "Are you satisfied with that or do you wish that the federal government had . . . more . . . less . . .

or the same impact on you?" Only 10 percent of our respondents suggested that they wished the impact of the federal government were greater, while approximately 22 percent indicated they were relatively satisfied. By far the largest group of the respondents (68 percent), however, desired less of an impact. For most of our respondents it appears that the type of salience involved is political-punishment salience; they saw the government's impact on their daily lives as essentially negative. When we cross-tabulated the nature of impact by the degree of personal control, the association was small (gamma = .15) and statistically nonsignificant ($X^2 = .63$, p = N.S.). At all levels of personal control, over 80 percent of the respondents desired less impact on their daily lives by the federal government.

With regard to local government, approximately 19 percent of our respondents indicated they would welcome additional impact, while almost 35 percent indicated that they were satisfied with the nature of the impact of the local government. Forty-eight percent of the respondents indicated that they would want less local-government impact on their daily lives. When we cross-tabulated the level of personal control by the nature of local government impact, we found a strong (gamma = .42), statistically significant ($X^2 = 11.70$, $p = <.01$) relationship. Individuals with high levels of personal control were much more likely to be satisfied with the existing level of impact, while respondents with low personal control were significantly more likely to desire less impact.

Thus, a major difference emerges in the political-salience orientations of individuals with different levels of personal control. Individuals with low personal control feel that both the national and local government have an important impact on their lives and in both cases wish to decrease that impact. That is, at both levels political-punishment salience appears to be operating. Individuals with high personal control feel that the federal government has an important impact on their lives and wish it had less of an impact. At the local level, however, these respondents are more likely to perceive the government as having a moderate impact and are apparently willing to allow an increase in the extent of that impact.

Important from our point of view is that the overwhelming majority of our respondents find politics salient; they feel that the outputs of the political system have an impact on the way they live their daily lives. To the extent that politics impacts upon the individual's life, it becomes a control-relevant sphere.

The results further suggest that while the political salience is generally high for both groups, it appears that politics is even more salient for the low personal-control group, since both levels of government has an important but negative impact on the daily lives of these respondents.

The whole question of salience is important not only for the reasons advanced so well by Converse, but also because the syndrome of high political salience coupled with low personal control has important consequences for political behavior. It is to this important area that we now turn our attention.

PERSONAL CONTROL AND POLITICAL PARTICIPATION

It is by now a commonly held assumption that the more politically efficacious are more likely to participate in politics, at least in campaign activities. Indeed, there are a variety of studies which have empirically documented the relationship between a high sense of political efficacy (as measured by the Survey Research Center Scale discussed in Chapter Two) and political participation in campaign activities.[7]

The data we will present is, *if not a direct contradiction of*

[7] See Campbell *et al., op. cit.*

the above statement and assumption, at least a substantial challenge to the traditional view of the relationship between political efficacy and political participation. Unlike the traditional view of this relationship, a need theory of political efficacy suggests that low personal control, coupled with high political salience would be associated with *greater not lesser rates of participation.* That is, since political efficacy is viewed as arising out of the *satisfaction* of the need for personal control and since the lack of personal control is anxiety producing in a control-relevant area, our theory hypothesizes that *more not less participation* will be associated with those who have low personal control (given high political salience). For those who have achieved high political efficacy (high personal control given high political salience) our theory would predict less frequent although certainly no cessation of political activity.

The same basic assumptions about efficacy and political participation have been made in those few studies that have examined the relationship between Internal-External locus of control (our operationalized measure of personal control beliefs) and the attempt to influence the environment, including in some cases the political system. For example, Gore and Rotter[8] suggested that an individual who has external feelings of control (what we have called low personal control) will not attempt to influence his environment. In another study, Rotter and his associates suggest that "within the normal range of adjustment it may be hypothesized that individuals with a high belief in the external control of reinforcement might be relatively passive in any attempt to change the world."[9] In one of the few studies of the relation of Internal-External control and political participation, Thomas found that "Perceived

[8] P. Gore and J. Rotter, "A Personality Correlate of Social Action," *Journal of Personality*, 31, 1963, pp. 58–69.

[9] J. Rotter et al., "Internal versus External Control of Reinforcement: A Major Variable in Behavior Theory," in N. E. Washburne (ed.), *Decisions, Values, and Groups* (New York: Pergamon, 1962), p. 475.

internal causality [what we have called high personal control], as measured by the I-E Scale, was found to be non-significantly associated with any of the measures of political participation of the parent sample, *with five of the six correlations being in the opposite direction from that predicted by social learning theory.*"[10] *In other words, Thomas found exactly what a need theory of personal control predicts, namely, that those with low personal control may participate more under certain conditions than those with high levels of personal control.*

As had previously been demonstrated, both high and low control respondents have high political salience, indeed for the latter the salience of politics is somewhat greater. Thus, for both groups politics is a control-relevant sphere. This being the case, it is now possible to explore the relationships between the level of personal control and political participation. Each respondent was asked if he had ever: (1) worked for a political party, (2) worked for a particular candidate, (3) worked for a community organization dealing with a social issue, (4) been an officer in any political organization, (5) tried to influence someone about an issue or candidate, (7) written to a public official to voice his opinion, (8) signed a petition for or against some issue, (9) attended a protest rally of any kind, (10) broken a law to dramatize feelings about an issue, (11) taken part in a sit-in, or (12) been involved in any physical confrontation (pushing, shoving, and so on) during any of the above. These behaviors appear to be fairly representative of the possible range of political behaviors, ranging from the traditional to the newer forms of participation. Respondents were asked how frequently they had engaged in each behavior. The one glaring omission was, of course, voting. (This item was included in the survey, but since most of the respondents were under the legal voting age when this survey was taken, the voting item was deleted from the analysis.)

[10] E. L. Thomas, "The I-E Scale, Ideological Bias, and Political Participation," *Journal of Personality*, 38, 1970, p. 285.

Table 19 provides some support for our hypothesis about locus of control and rates of participation. *In ten of the twelve classes* of political behavior, individuals with low personal control are more likely to have participated than individuals with high personal control. Thus, over 90 percent of our cases are in the predicted direction. Moreover, in six of these ten cases the differences in participation rates were statistically significant. This effect is particularly in evidence when we examine the last four participation modes, but is *not limited to these.* That is, individuals with low personal control are more likely to have reported that they took part in mass demonstrations, physical confrontations, and sit-ins, but they were also significantly more likely to have worked for a political candidate, contribute money to a campaign, or to write to a public official—all traditional political behaviors.

An objection to these results could be made on the basis of the nature of the participation data. After all, it might be suggested, these are not real behaviors, and they may be biased by faulty recall or social desirability. If this is a real problem, it is certainly not unique to our data, but fortunately there is an independent check that can be made on the results.

The data collections were centered around two particular political events: one a traditional political campaign and the other a mass demonstration.

The first of these events began shortly before the congressional elections of 1970. Stirred by student unrest, many schools adapted the so-called Princeton Plan. In its most general form this plan called for the suspension of classes during the week before the election, in order to allow students the opportunity to work within the political system for a candidate of their choice. At Pennsylvania this plan took the form of an "unstructured period" during which classes were not officially canceled, but for which all absences were excused. Interviews were conducted with the respondents

TABLE 19. POLITICAL PARTICIPATION BY LOCUS OF CONTROL

Acts	*Do respondents with low personal control participate more?*	*Chi-square*	*Gamma*
1. Worked for Party	Yes	N.S.	.16
2. Worked for Candidate	Yes	$p = <.05$	.41
3. Worked for a Community Organization	Yes	N.S.	.08
4. Had been an Officer	No	N.S.	−.15
5. Contributed Money	Yes	$p = <.05$	.24
6. Tried to Influence	No	N.S.	−.07
7. Wrote to a Public Official	Yes	$p = <.05$	.45
8. Signed a Petition	Yes	$p = .07$	.06
9. Attended Mass Demonstration	Yes	$p = <.02$	.65
10. Broke Law	Yes	$p = <.05$	.71
11. Took Part in Sit-in	Yes	$p = <.05$	.50
12. Involved in Physical Confrontation	Yes	$p = <.05$	.70

in the week immediately following the elections. Each respondent was asked if and in what ways he had participated in the "unstructured period."

The second set of interviews were conducted immediately after an April 24, 1971, mass demonstration against the war in Vietnam. This mass demonstration was carried out in Washington, D.C., and was extremely well attended. As an example of this kind of political participation, the April 24 demonstration was in no way atypical. As part of the interview each respondent was asked if he had gone to Washington to participate in the demonstration.

The two concrete types of political participation—the traditional and the somewhat less traditional generated a set of events within which we may examine the relationship between locus of control and participation. The results are presented in Table 20.

TABLE 20. PARTICIPATION IN THE "UNSTRUCTURED PERIOD" AND THE MARCH ON WASHINGTON

Personal Control	*Unstructured Period Participation*			*Washington March Participation*		
	Yes	*No*	*(N)*	*Yes*	*No*	*(N)*
Low	26.1	73.9	(46)	74.8	25.2	(46)
Medium	14.9	85.4	(198)	61.5	38.5	(200)
High	17.0	83.0	(47)	44.7	55.3	(47)
gamma = .16		$x^2 = 3.49$ p = N.S.		gamma = .33		$x^2 = 8.47$ p = < .02

In both cases the data are in the predicted direction, although only one set of results are statistically significant. For participation in the "unstructured period," those respondents with low personal control were somewhat more likely to have participated than those respondents with either medium or high degrees of personal control. For participation in the march on Washington, those respondents with low personal control were significantly more likely to have taken part than those respondents with high personal control. These data provide additional support for the results obtained in Table 19 and its interpretation.

Several additional points about political participation and personal control need to be made. We have suggested that individuals with low personal-control beliefs would have less trust in themselves and therefore less trust in others. We further suggested that this lack of intrapersonal and interpersonal trust has important political implications, namely, that because other individuals could not be trusted, participation in collective social and political activity would be more likely to be an unsatisfying experience. If this is the case, we would expect that individuals with low personal control would be significantly more likely to report that they had not been satisfied with the results of their past political participation. Moreover, we would expect that their expectations of future rewards from political participation would also be significantly lower than those respondents with high personal control. In order to check this assertion we cross-tabulated the degree of personal control by the degree of satisfaction obtained from past participation in the political system and also the degree of anticipated future satisfaction. The results appear in Table 21.

An examination of the left side of this table, provides some support for the relationship we suggested would be found among personal control, interpersonal trust, and participatory satisfaction. Even though individuals with low personal control (and high political salience) are more likely to have participated more, they appear to have enjoyed it less. Our data suggest that individuals with high personal control were overwhelmingly more likely to report that, when they have become involved in politics, things have

TABLE 21

Personal Control	*Past Rewards*				*Future Rewards*		
	Less than 50%	50%	*More than* 50%	(N)	*Less than* 50%	50%	*More than* 50%
Low	81.1	13.5	5.4	(47)	75	12.5	12.5
Medium	58.5	22.2	19.3	(190)	46.9	29.1	45.1
High	42.9	16.7	40.5	(57)	29.5	25.0	45.5
gamma = .43	$x^2 = 18.55$ $p = < .01$				gamma = .44		$x^2 = 22.18$ $p = < .001$

worked out the way they wanted over 50 percent of the time. For respondents with low personal control, the opposite has been true. These respondents are significantly more likely to report that when they have taken part in politics, things have turned out the way they wanted less than half the time. The major point that emerges about participatory satisfaction then, is that individuals with low personal control, although they participated more frequently, are much less likely to have been satisfied with the outcomes.

Moreover, not only is their level of past satisfaction low, but their future expectations for participatory rewards is also low. Immediately after the question dealing with past satisfaction, we asked each respondent, "Now looking ahead five or six years, how often do you think things will turn out the way you want them to when you get involved in politics?" The results obtained in answer to this question appear on the right side of Table 22.

The data suggests that individuals with low personal control feel that not only have they been unsatisfied with their past political participation, but that the level of satisfaction in the future is unlikely to improve. Individuals with high personal control, although they have participated less frequently are not only more satisfied with their past participation rewards, but also expect the level of rewards to remain satisfactory. Thus, differences emerge between respondents with high and low personal control for both the reconstruction of their past and their anticipation of the future. One might suspect that this combination of frequent and unsatisfying participation would be extremely frustrating. In the following chapter we will present some evidence to suggest that this combination does have important implications for the selection of political action.

We can obtain another perspective on political participation by examining its association with civic obligation, which, in the absence of other incentives, provides a minimal motivation. We suggested that the reason for this is that civic obligation is a social norm and therefore is external to the human need structure. As a contrast and as a further check on the relationship we found between personal control and political participation, we cross-tabulated our index of civic obligation by the range of political behaviors described previously.

The civic-obligation index was made up of the following three questions: (1) Do you feel that each citizen has the obligation to work for better government? (2) Do you feel that each citizen should always take the time to vote? (3) Do you feel that it is not important to vote when your party does not have a chance to win? The index of civic duty was uncorrelated with our personal-control scale (gamma = .01), so that Table 22 allows us to examine and compare the motivating effects of civic obligation.

As we can see from the table, in only 3 of the 12 cases are respondents with high degrees of civic obligation more likely to participate in the political system. (This compares with the 10 out of 12 total we obtained for the motivating power of low personal control.) It is interesting that each of these cases involve traditional modes of political participation; namely, working for a political party, trying to influence an individual on an issue or for a candidate, and contributing money. Of equal interest is the finding that a high sense of civic obligation is significantly and negatively correlated with breaking laws to dramatize opposition to a law or policy, taking part in sit-ins, and taking part in violent confrontations.

It should be remembered that low personal control was significantly associated with a variety of behaviors, both of the more and the less traditional types. This leads us to conclude that personal control is a more powerful motivator of political activity than civic obligation. We expect this to be the case, since the need for personal control is part of the basic life-need orientations of individuals, and unlike the

TABLE 22. POLITICAL PARTICIPATION BY CIVIC OBLIGATION

Act	*Do individuals with high civic obligation participate more often than those with low civic obligation?*	*Chi-square*	*Gamma*
1. Worked for Party	Yes	$p = < .01$	.24
2. Worked for Candidate	No	$p = < .01$	.15
3. Worked for Community Organization	No	N.S.	−.09
4. Had been an Officer	No	N.S.	.08
5. Contributed Money	Yes	$p = .05$	.29
6. Tried to Influence	Yes	$p = .02$	.34
7. Wrote to Public Official	No	N.S.	.15
8. Signed petition	No	N.S.	.13
9. Attended Mass Demonstration	No	N.S.	−.06
10. Broke a Law	No	N.S.	−.31
11. Took Part in Sit-in	No	$p = < .01$	−.22
12. Involved in Physical Confrontations	No	$p = < .02$	−.38

civic-obligation norm is not external to the individual's needs.

THE MULTIVARIATE EXPLANATION OF POLITICAL PARTICIPATION

To this point we have examined the effects of personal control and several other variables on each other and on political participation. Given our two concrete cases of political participation, namely working in the "unstructured period" and taking part in the march on Washington, it would be interesting to compare the effects of a number of variables that we have been discussing on these two types of participation.

In order to assess the relative impact of a number of the variables we have discussed, we again utilized the Multiple Classification Program (MCA) described in detail in Chapter Eleven. The analysis was run twice, using the same set of independent variables, the first time using participation in the "unstructured period" as the dependent variable, and the second time using the march on Washington as the dependent variable. The results are presented in Table 23.

An examination of this table provides some interesting findings. First, let us examine beta coefficients for the political salience group, remembering that this statistic indicates the predictive power of this independent variable with the effects of all of the other variables taken into account. Political interest, operationalized as attention to political events, has only a moderate explanatory power. The perceived impact of the government on the daily lives of the respondents emerges as a slightly more powerful predictor than political interest for both participatory modes.

The salience variable most clearly associated with participation in the "unstructured period" is satisfaction with the impact of the local government, which is in the .5 range.

The satisfaction with the impact of the federal government is minimal, both before and after controls are introduced. This finding is not unexpected, since the "unstructured period" did take place during an off-year election, in which few national offices were at stake and the concentration was on the governor's campaign. This finding is clearly reversed when we examine the march on Washington. Here, as expected, it is the satisfaction with the impact of the national government which has the most explanatory power

TABLE 23. RELATIVE EXPLANATORY POWER OF VARIABLES LINKED TO PARTICIPATION

	Participation in Unstructured Period		*March on Washington*	
	Eta	*Beta*	*Eta*	*Beta*
Political Interest	.861	.228	.636	.293
Impact of Government	.159	.312	.631	.330
Satisfaction with Impact (Federal)	.159	.332	.333	.334
Satisfaction with Impact (Local)	.785	.559	.281	.273
% Past Rewards	.188	.149	.388	.773
Political Alienation	.594	.521	.974	.113
Faith in People	.939	.716	.665	.448
Civic Obligation	.118	.118	.644	.106
Political Patience	.159	.139	.662	.125
Personal Control	*.170*	*.705*	*.494*	*.906*
Faith in Government	.107	.103	.652	.286
Government Effectiveness	.229	.287	.668	.728
Government Influenceability	.221	.273	.653	.590

Multiple R (adjusted) = .61
Total explained variance = .36

Multiple R (adjusted) = .66
Total explained variance = .43

also in the .5 range. This march was clearly directed at influencing the national government. Thus the increased importance of federal government impact and its evaluation is not surprising.

When we turn to an examination of the other independent variables, several surprises emerge. The frequency of past rewards was not a strong predictor of participation in the unstructured period but did prove to be a very strong predictor of the march on Washington. These relationships, however, are not as uniform as the data suggest at first glance.

Along with Eta and Beta, the M. C. A. program provides for each category of each predictor, the mean value of *y* for that category, and the deviation of the category mean from the grand mean, adjusting for the effects of the other predictors. By examining the unadjusted category deviations, one can tell whether the predictor has any relation to the dependent variable, and, if so, whether this relationship is positive, negative, curvilinear, or of another form. The adjusted deviations show these relationships after the effects of the other predictors have been held constant.

When we analyzed the deviations for past rewards and participation to determine the nature of the relationship, an interesting finding emerged. For participation in the unstructured period, those who had been rewarded either less than half the time or half the time were more likely to participate. It appears, then, that those who have been satisfied in the past felt less need to participate in this off-year election. When we examine the march on Washington, however, a different pattern emerges. Both those with minimal past satisfaction (less than 50 percent of the time) and those with maximal past satisfaction (more than 50 percent of the time) were more likely to take part, while those who perceived themselves as being rewarded half the time were less likely to participate.

One explanation of this finding is that any political event

draws together people who have arrived there by virtue of different routes and different political and psychological orientations. If we think of each person as occupying a "political track," which is made up of his personality orientations, family socialization experiences, and life socialization experiences, then any study that focuses on a particular event will have a snapshot effect. That is, people who are brought together by virtue of their participation may be similar only insofar as their participation. Their reasons for participating, and thus, the effects of participation upon them, may very well be very different. Consequently, it might not be surprising that the same event could attract those with both low and high past reward structures; the latter group might be there because of past successes, while the former group might be there in anticipation of future ones. Perhaps future research will be able to determine whether and under what circumstances certain political events draw people with a similar "political track."

Turning to some of the other independent variables, several important findings emerge. For both participatory modes, faith in people emerges as a relatively strong predictor. In the uncontrolled relationship the coefficients are quite high and remain moderately so in the controlled relationship. As we suggested, faith in people was a necessary component for satisfactory collective social and political activity. Civic obligation on the other hand, had very low predictive power for both participatory modes. This finding parallels our results in Table 23 on the motivating power of civic obligation.

The political analogue of the faith-in-people variable is the trust-in-government index. Our data suggest that it is a relatively weak predictor in one case of participation, the "unstructured period" mode. For the march on Washington it has moderate explanatory power, approaching the .3 level. Perhaps working for a candidate requires one to have faith essentially in that candidate, while taking part in a mass demonstration aimed at the government requires a more generalized faith.

Another independent variable with mixed impact is the political alienation variable. In both cases, the uncontrolled correlation is moderate to high. However, when controls are introduced, the explanatory power of political alienation for the march on Washington drops dramatically. For participation in the "unstructured period," political alienation remains a strong predictor variable. Both governmental effectiveness and influenceability were moderately related to participation in the "unstructured period." However, for the march on Washington both of these independent variables had moderate to high explanatory power. The finding about government influenceability is not surprising for the mass demonstration and is perhaps similar to our finding about faith in government for this participatory mode. In order to take part in this type of action, it is probably important that the government is viewed as open to influence and at least potentially responsive and effective. This type of orientation is perhaps less needed when one is not attempting to change policy directly by oneself, but is attempting to do it indirectly, by electing a sympathetic candidate.

Finally, our data suggest that *for both participatory modes the degree of personal control is the single most powerful predictor variable in the controlled relationship.* For both types of participation the correlations are extremely high. In both cases when we examined the adjusted deviations to determine the nature of the relationship, we found that individuals in the low personal-control category were more likely to participate. This finding provides additional support for the importance of feelings of personal control for political participation and political life in general.

To this point, we have almost come full circle. We began with the exposition of a need for personal control, delineated its dimensions, and then discussed its ontology. From there we turned to an examination of the psychopolitical correlates of this need and then attempted to link these personal-control beliefs and related sociopolitical attitudes to political participation. There remains, however, one further link to be established, and that is the relationship between personal control and its syndromatically related correlates and the selection of political action. Our findings suggest that individuals with low personal control participated more frequently but were less satisfied, the classic configuration of frustration. Does this frustration have any implications for the selection of political action? It is to this important point that we turn our attention to in the following chapter.

Chapter Fifteen

PERSONAL CONTROL AND THE EFFICACY OF POLITICAL ACTION

Thus far we have focused upon the nature, acquisition, correlates, and participatory implications of personal control. Yet, there remains one further link to explore, and that is the effect of past participation on subsequent political actions as modified by personal control. This is not an area that has received a great deal of attention in political-science research. The link between the decision to participate, the mode of participation selected and the subsequent satisfaction obtained has for the most part been simply assumed. Thus, we know from a variety of studies that the efficacious tend to vote more, but there is little knowledge of the level of satisfaction that this and other political behavior bring to the citizen.

These are important areas of concern, for discussion about the meaning of political behaviors (that is, high voting turnout means satisfaction with the political system) rests on assumptions *both* about the efficacy of behaviors and their ability to satisfy the original motivation to participate in the political system. Yet, because this area has not been systematically explored, it is not known for whom and under what circumstances voting will give more satisfaction than physical confrontation.

As suggested in the previous chapter, increased participation need not indicate political satisfaction, indeed, it may indicate just the opposite. What is needed, then, is an examination of the perceived efficacy of particular behaviors —a systematic examination of the differences in perceived efficacy of behaviors arising out of differences in levels of personal control, as well as past experiences.

In a sense this is an examination of the political behavior sources of what Easton has called diffuse support.[1] Others have examined the diffuse support for particular institutions, such as the American party system,[2] the institution of elections,[3] and legislative institutions,[4] but no one as yet has focused on the diffuse support afforded various political behaviors, nor on the psychological conditions under which this support might change.

According to Dennis, diffuse support "is an orientation of good will towards an object which does not depend on specific benefits derived from the object."[5] Or as Easton puts it, "it is a type of support that continues independently of specific rewards which the member feels he may obtain by belonging to the system."[6] Yet, as Dennis notes, "repeated failure of the institution to provide acceptable outcomes is one of the conditions that undermines diffuse support and in the long run weakens the institution itself."[7] If this is true of the institutions, we would certainly suggest it to be the case for political behavior.

For most people political behaviors are instrumental, that is, they are a means to an end. The end, of course, is the satisfaction of the original motivation to participate. If the original motivation is citizen duty, then the act of participa-

[1] See David Easton, *A Systems Analysis of Political Life* (New York: Wiley & Sons, 1965), *passim*.

[2] Jack Dennis, "Support for the Party System by the Mass Public," *American Political Science Review*, 60, 1966, pp. 600–615.

[3] Jack Dennis, "Support for the Institution of Elections by the Mass Public," *American Political Science Review*, 64, 1970, pp. 819–835.

[4] G. R. Boynton *et al.*, "The Structure of Public Support for Legislative Institutions," *Midwest Journal of Political Science*, 12, 1968, pp. 168–180.

[5] Dennis, *op. cit.*, p. 823.

[6] David Easton, *A Framework for Political Analysis* (Englewood Cliffs, N.J.: Prentice-Hall, 1965), p. 125.

[7] Dennis, *op. cit.*, p. 823.

tion itself will satisfy the motivation to take part in the political process. However, if participation originates in the desire to gain rewards from the political system or to obtain some personal control over the political sphere when it becomes control relevant, then the behaviors must be capable of producing the desired result.

It seems probable that attachment to particular institutions and to particular behaviors is one outcome of early political socialization.[8] In a sense then, both political institutions and political behaviors begin with what Hollander would call "idiosyncratic credit,"[9] or the accumulation of good will against which one might draw in time of difficulties. While loyalty to institutions and forms of participation begins as a norm, the institutions and forms must, as Dennis suggests, eventually stand the test of perceived results. This would appear to be especially true with participation originating in the desire to gain some measure of personal control in the political arena. This means that eventually institutions, as well as particular political behaviors, must satisfy the desire for results or lose "credit" or "support," and eventually be thought of as inefficacious.

The consequences of viewing particular behaviors as inefficacious are dependent on the original motivation to participate. If one has been motivated to participate in the political process in order to obtain material rewards (pensions, increased benefits, and so on), then behavior which fails to produce the desired outcomes may result in a decision to withdraw from the political field or to select some other behavior to produce the desired results. The important point is that withdrawal from the political system is a pos-

[8] Robert Hess and Judith Torney, *The Development of Political Attitudes in Children* (Chicago: Aldine, 1967), *passim.*

[9] Steve Hollander, "Idiosyncratic Credit," in J. David Singer (ed.), *Human Behavior and International Politics* (Chicago: Rand McNally, 1966).

sibility, especially if the material rewards may be obtained in other arenas.[10]

On the other hand, if the individual is seeking control in an area that has become control relevant, withdrawal is not a viable alternative. This is especially true in the political arena in which the outputs of the government are not easily avoided for extended periods of time. This is essentially the case in a modern, highly complex and centralized country such as the United States. This suggests that an individual seeking personal control in the political sphere is to some extent "locked in" to the political system. Given this process, participation and the selection of a mode of action will in part be a function of past experiences. These observations are presented diagrammatically in Figure 2.

We might speculate that an individual begins his political participation career with a certain need level for personal control and a moderate but expandable sense that the government has an impact on his daily life. Given the need to gain some personal control in the political arena, the individual might select a particular behavior that he feels will be efficacious in satisfying his motivation to participate. It is likely that these first participatory behaviors will be of the more traditional mode, since without prior personal experience the weight of prior learning will prevail.

Other than by direct experience, an individual has two possibilities for receiving data about the efficacy of particular behaviors. On the one hand, he can gain information via social norms. In this case a child would hear from his parents or school that voting, for example, is an efficacious behavior and accept that as a social fact. On the other hand, he could use his own direct experience of events or others to evaluate behaviors. Thus, one young person might see that in his neighborhood picketing brought about changes while in another neighborhood a person might see that

[10] Peter Blau, *Exchange and Power in Social Life* (New York: Wiley & Sons, 1967), Chapter 7.

money was extremely efficacious. These two sources of information could obviously be either consonant or dissonant with each other.

It seems likely that for a majority of the population of any country the beginning political behaviors will be of a more traditional variety. In fact, one characteristic of a revolutionary situation occurs when a sufficient number of people in the society, either through their direct experience or their evaluations of the experiences of others, come to believe that traditional nonviolent behaviors are ineffective. This means that in the United States, adherence to social norms about the efficacy of traditional behaviors such as voting, campaigning, and so forth, will be the dominant theme for most citizens.

FIGURE 2. A FLOW CHART OF THE EFFECT OF POLITICAL PARTICIPATION ON THE SUBSEQUENT SELECTION OF POLITICAL ACTION

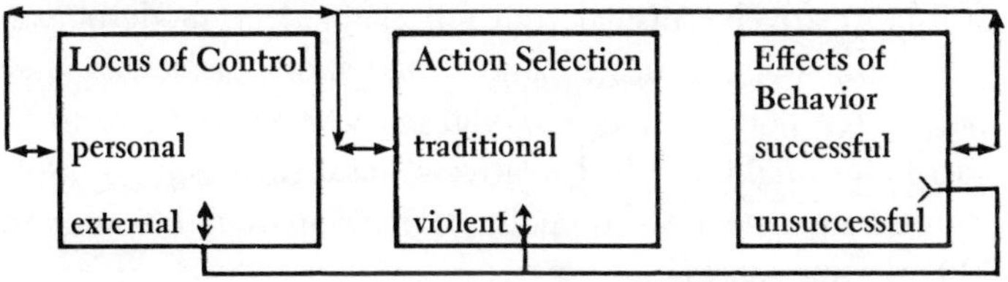

The flow diagram depicts these relationships and their component parts. It is wise to caution here that it is only analytically that one can separate "independent" and "dependent" variables. Viewed from this perspective, "independent" and "dependent" partake of some of the qualities of Weber's ideal types. What this analysis suggests is the importance of multidirectional causality in the analysis of political behavior.

A further word should be said about the nature of the perception of the effects of political action. Here it is clear we are talking about two components: one a ratio of success to failures and the other the political time dimension we discussed earlier.

The time dimension refers to the length of time that will be tolerated between the behavior and some outcome. Some groups, for example, working to change the direction of foreign policy, see their efforts of necessity extending over 20 years or longer. Others wish to see immediate changes in foreign policy. Clearly these differences in orientation will lead to different evaluations of how successful a particular behavior has been.

The other component to be examined is the relationship between the number of successes and failures and the propensity to select new modes of political action. Thus, if we examine two people who engage in the same number of political acts, as well as the same type, we would expect to find different tolerances for different ratios of success/failures. Thus, if one individual had engaged in ten political acts, only four of which were viewed as successful, he might still be relatively satisfied, and not change the mode of participation. On the other hand, some individuals who take part in ten political acts and who perceive six of them to be successful might still feel relatively unsatisfied and go on to a more extreme form of political participation in order to obtain some success.

Clearly what is called for in order to study this problem more closely is an extended panel study with repeated assessment of the relevant variables. This is unfortunately beyond the scope of this particular study. However, data were collected which should allow us to make some tentative explorations of the model presented.

Each respondent was asked the following question as part of the interview schedule:

> There are many different ways to try to influence the government; but people today are often in disagree-

> ment about which ones are effective. How effective would you say that each of the following is in making the government pay attention to what people think?

Answers ranged from one (most effective) to five (least effective). The behaviors, the mean scores and the ranks are given in the following table.

Table 24 presents quite a few surprises and challenges a

TABLE 24. MEAN SCORES AND RANKS OF EFFICACY OF BEHAVIORS FOR ENTIRE SAMPLE

Behaviors	*Mean*	*Rank*
1. Voting	2.29	1
2. Contributing Money	2.71	2
3. Mass Demonstrations	2.78	3
4. Being an Informed Citizen	2.89	4
5. Picketing	3.07	5
6. Political Parties	3.08	6
7. Writing to Officials	3.18	7
8. Personally Influencing	3.18	7
9. Sit-ins	3.20	8
10. Breaking a Law	3.43	9
11. Attending Political Meetings	3.43	9
12. Violence During Protests	3.96	10
13. Assassination	4.00	11

great many stereotypical images. To begin with, in spite of all the demonstrations, sit-ins, and marches of the last five years, voting is still felt to be the most efficacious behavior. This is at the same time both encouraging and somewhat troubling. It is encouraging because in spite of all of the talk and attention focused on sit-ins, demonstrations, and occasional violence among adolescents, there is still apparently a great deal of commitment to what has traditionally been the most basic form of political participation in the United States.

Yet there is also something troubling about the fact that most of these respondents have never actually voted. This presents the possibility that what is being tapped is not based on the test of actual utilization, but may revolve around normative expectations about the efficacy of the vote.

After voting, the next two efficacious behaviors come as somewhat of a surprise. Making campaign contributions to the political system emerges as the second most powerful behavior, according to our respondents. Here again, one suspects that we are dealing less with the personal experience of the respondents, than with their general opinions about the role of money in political life. Approximately 20 percent of the respondents reported that they had contributed money, but at this stage of their financial development it seems unlikely that these sums are sufficiently large to gain them much influence.

Also of some surprise is the listing of mass demonstrations as the third most efficacious form of behavior. Considering that the mass demonstrations of the types seen in Washington over the last five years has never been a typical political activity, the high ranking of this mode suggests that what was atypical ten years ago is now a fully established and institutionalized behavioral possibility. Of equal interest here is the finding that while mass demonstrations are considered efficacious, the boundaries of the permissible for this mode do not apparently include political violence.

In the last six years there has been a great deal of talk in this country about violence and youth. One of the task force reports to the National Commission on the Causes and Prevention of Violence dealt specifically with student violence,[11] and in a great many minds students, mass demonstrations, and violence are indiscriminately lumped together. Our data casts considerable doubt upon this union. Our range of behaviors include two that specifically mention or have to do with political violence; taking part in some violence during a protest and political assassination. These behaviors are ranked 12th and 13th respectively. Thus, engaging in violence during a protest is ranked next to last, even though mass demonstrations, is ranked third as a form of protest. Even the nonviolent behavior of breaking a law to demonstrate opposition to a policy is ranked 10th out of 13. Thus, our data suggest that the stereotype of the violence-prone young person is in need of substantial modification.

Another way of examining the data which holds considerable interest is to ask what beliefs and political attitudes are associated with the perception of certain modes of political activity as efficacious. Table 25, on following page, presents the Pearsons correlations between some of the variables we have been examining and the perception of certain behaviors as efficacious. In addition, it includes the rank orderings of the behaviors, given certain political orientations. It is to this data that we now turn.

The discussion of civic obligation at the start of this chapter suggested that this orientation might be an exception to the rule of the instrumentality of efficacy testing. That is, we suggested that if civic obligation was the original motivation to participate, then the motivation would be satisfied by the act itself, rather than any outcome. This was placed in contrast to other motivations in which participation was a means to an end. This suggests that for the civically motivated, a great variety of (traditional) behaviors will be considered efficacious, since what matters is not what the

[11] Jerome Skulnick, *The Politics of Protest* (New York: Simon & Schuster, 1970).

TABLE 25. PEARSON CORRELATIONS AND RANK EFFICACY RATINGS FOR POLITICAL ORIENTATIONS AND POLITICAL BEHAVIORS

Behaviors	(1) *Civic Obligation*	(2) *Personal Control*	(3) *Political Impatience*	(4) *Political Alienation*	(5) *Past Reward Satisfaction*	(6)*	(7)*	(8)*	(9)*	(10)*	(11)*
Voting	.19**	.52**	–.21**	–.13*	.23**	1	1	1	4	1	1
Personal Influence	.19**	.10	.01	.01	.01	8	7	8	6	7	7
Writing to Officials	.14**	.29*	–.18**	–.12*	.19**	7	8	5	12	10	10
Giving Money	.07	.20*	–.05	.05	.10*	2	3	3	2	2	3
Political Meetings	.16**	.21*	–.14**	–.01	.17*	11	10	10	10	11	11
Political Parties	.15*	.23**	–.10*	–.06	.10*	6	5	6	9	6	9
Informed Citizen	.26*	.24*	–.13*	–.14*	.12*	4	2	2	5	8	5
Picketing	.07	.08	.01	–.01	.03	5	6	9	3	4	4
Sit-ins	–.01	.13*	.06	–.01	–.02	9	9	7	7	9	6
Mass Demonstration	–.05	.09	.05	–.07	–.07	3	4	4	1	3	2
Breaking Law	–.05	–.07	.15*	.18**	–.05	10	11	11	8	5	8
Violence	–.01	.08	.07	.17**	–.06	12	12	12	11	12	12
Assassination	–.10*	–.09	.05	.13**	–.01	13	13	13	13	13	13

* = Significant at .01
** = Significant at .001 or better

6 = Ranks for total sample
7 = Ranks for high civic duty
8 = Ranks for high personal control
9 = Ranks for low personal control
10 = Ranks for high political alienation
11 = Ranks for high political impatience

behavior produces in terms of material rewards or personal control but the fact that one participates at all.

Column one of Table 25 provides some support for this view. Of the seven traditional behaviors listed (voting, trying to influence someone, writing to public officials, giving money, attending political meetings, working for a political party, and being an informed citizen), all seven are in positive relationship with the degree of civic obligation, and six of the seven are statistically significant. Turning to their relative rankings in column seven we find that the traditional civic virtues of voting, being an informed citizen, and giving money are the three most efficacious behaviors. Mass demonstrations are ranked as the fourth most efficacious behavior, slightly below the rating given for this behavior by the total sample.

One can gain some perspective by comparing these findings to the different patterns that emerge for the other orientations, for example personal control. Paralleling the findings for the relationship between civic obligation and the efficacy of behavior, respondents with high personal control are likely to rate a range of behaviors as efficacious. In fact, there is a positive correlation for 11 out of the 13 behaviors. In addition seven of these associations are statistically significant, and the magnitude of relations is generally stronger for personal control than for civic obligation. One other difference should be mentioned, although the results are not statistically significant, and that is the negative relationship between civic obligation and the efficacy of violence, mass demonstrations, and sit-ins, and the corresponding positive associations between personal control and these same behaviors. Although these results are not statistically significant, they point to the observation that individuals with personal control apparently view a wider range of behaviors as efficacious than do civically motivated respondents.

When we take a look at the structure of ranks for respondents with high civic obligation (column seven) and high personal control (column eight), few differences emerge. Both rank voting as the most efficacious behavior and both rank being an informed citizen and giving money the second and third most efficacious behavior, respectively. At the other end of the spectrum, both agree that breaking the law, taking part in violence and political assassination are the three least effective political behaviors. What differences that do occur are relatively minor and appear to be of little consequence.

We can begin to note changes however, when we examine the behavior rankings for those respondents with low personal control (column nine). Unlike both high civic-obligation and high personal-control respondents, those with low personal control do not see voting as the most efficacious behavior. For these respondents it drops from first to fourth. These respondents believe that mass-demonstrations are the most efficacious behavior, an opinion shared by no other analytical group that we examined. Another difference emerges in the second and third ranks for these groups. The high civic-duty and personal-control groups agreed that being an informed citizen and giving money were the next two most efficacious behaviors. The low personal-control group rates money as the second most efficacious political behavior. An even greater difference emerges for the next ranked behavior. While the other two rate money as the third best, the low personal-control group rates picketing as the third most efficacious behavior. Picketing is rated sixth and nineth respectively for the two other groups.

Emerging from these figures is the sense that respondents with low personal control are more likely to rate the less traditional and more direct forms of participation (money is an obvious exception) as more efficacious. By direct we mean those behaviors characterized by face-to-face interaction, as opposed to the analytical grouping of those who take part in the same action but are unconnected with each other (like voting). This can be seen by examining another set of behaviors at the bottom of the continuum. Respondents with low personal control rate sit-ins higher in effectiveness than do high civic-duty respondents. Moreover, breaking a law to demonstrate a point is ranked three degrees higher for these respondents than for the other two groups. Even taking part in violence is rated slightly higher by the low personal-control group. From these results we can begin to see the way in which the deprivation of human needs operates to shape the structure of support for particular modes of political behavior.

A very different perspective can be obtained by turning to an examination of column three which presents the relationship between the efficacy of political behaviors and the degree of political impatience. When we examine the first seven behaviors, those that are more traditional, we find that for six of these, there is a negative correlation between the perceived efficacy of the behavior and the degree of political impatience. In five of the six traditional behaviors, the associations are statistically significant! The data suggest that the politically impatient respondent is not satisfied with the efficacy of any of the traditional modes of participation. This finding is in accord with our previous discussion. We suggested that for the politically impatient politics would be extremely frustrating, since immediate rewards are rarely forthcoming in the political system. Our data also suggest that the politically impatient are also significantly more likely to think that breaking a law to dramatize opposition to a particular policy is efficacious.

It might be thought that the politically impatient would be more likely to believe that violence would bring about the desired results, since their impatience would heighten their frustration. However, the data suggest this is not the case. Although there are small positive correlations between political impatience and taking part in violence and political assassination, they are not statistically significant. Moreover, when we examine the rankings for these two behaviors (column eleven), they rank last and next to last in perceived efficacy.

In contrast to the feeling of high political impatience which was significantly associated with lower amounts of past rewards, the respondents who are characterized by substantial past rewards for political participation (column five) generally follow the pattern of the high civic-duty and high personal-control types. That is, there is a positive association with the more traditional behaviors, which in six of the seven cases is statistically significant. Of equal interest is the finding that there is a negative (but statistically nonsignificant) association between past reward satisfaction and the perceived efficacy of the less traditional forms of participation. This finding gives some support for the model of behavior selection outlined on page 213. It appears to be the case that past satisfaction with traditional behaviors does not predispose one to the more direct, less traditional forms of behavior.

So far in our discussion, we have yet to come across any trait associated with the perception of violence as efficacious. We have in fact saved that question for last. When we discussed political alienation, we suggested that it was the feeling of distance and separation between what the individual wished to be happening in politics and what he thought the government was doing. We also presented data which suggested that a high degree of political alienation was significantly associated with low personal control and a high degree of political impatience. Given this confluence of factors, we might expect that political alienation would be associated with the acceptance of violence as an efficacious behavior. An examination of column four suggests that this is indeed the case. Column four presents a pattern of associations unlike the previous patterns we have discussed. Examining the traditional behaviors first, we find that in five of the seven there is a statistically significant negative correlation between political alienation and the perception of behavior efficacy. When we examine the total number of negative associations, we find that in 8 of the 13 cases, there is a negative association.

The data suggests that individuals with high alienation are less likely than any other group to see both the traditional and nontraditional behaviors as inefficacious. Not only are the traditional behaviors so viewed, as they are, for example, with politically impatient respondents, but this negativism also extends to some nontraditional behaviors, as well, such as sit-ins and mass-demonstrations. In fact, the only behaviors that are viewed as efficacious by those respondents with high alienation are breaking laws, engaging in political violence and political assassination. It thus appears that this syndrome of alienation, with attendant orientations and life experiences (for example, low past satisfaction with political rewards) plays a role in allowing the individual to psychologically accept the possibility of the use of violence. We should like to stress, of course, that psychological acceptance should not be equated with behavior, and we have no wish to suggest a one-to-one relationship between the two. What we do mean to suggest, however, is that the psychological acceptance of the use of violence may be a prerequisite for its later use. We should also note that while there is a statistically significant correlation between political alienation and the perception of violence as efficacious, violence is still rated very low in the overall efficacy ranks (column ten) for the highly politically alienated.

THE MULTIVARIATE EXPLANATION OF THE PERCEPTION OF VIOLENCE AS EFFICACIOUS

While we have examined the various effects of particular orientations individually, we would of course like to have some more exact idea of the nature of the relationship among all of these variables and the perception of violence as efficacious. In order to examine these points, we utilized the M.C.A. program described previously. We selected two behaviors to present the range of behaviors we had asked about. These two behaviors, voting and taking part in political violence, represent two ends of the political-behavior continuum. Each was run as the dependent variable utilizing the variables we have been discussing as independent variables. The results are presented in Table 26.

We can begin our comparison of the psychoexperiential origins of the perceived efficacy of violence and the vote by

TABLE 26. FACTORS ASSOCIATED WITH THE PERCEPTION OF THE EFFICACY OF VOTING AND VIOLENCE

	Voting		*Violence*	
	Eta	*Beta*	*Eta*	*Beta*
Percent of Past Rewards	.25	.11	.40	.55
Percent of Future Rewards	.29	.62	.49	.11
Satisfaction with Government Impact	.30	.33	.29	.64
Political Alienation	.25	.12	.24	.21
Faith in People	.52	.15	.63	.26
Faith in Government	.56	.14	.66	.70
Civic Duty	.53	.77	.64	.67
Political Impatience	.55	.44	.67	.88
Personal Control	.38	.11	.49	.65
Government Responsiveness	.86	.54	.66	.65
Taken Part in (Voting)	.58	.49		
(Violence)			.59	.15
Multiple R(Adjusted) = .66			Multiple R(Adjusted) = .74	
Multiple R(Squared) = .43			Multiple R(Squared) = .54	

looking at both the percentage of past rewards for participation and the expectation of future ones. For voting, the percentage of past rewards has a low beta (remember that beta gives an indication of the amount of variance explained by the particular variable with the effects of all of the others taken into account), while the expectation of future rewards has a very high one (.62). Exactly the opposite pattern can be discerned for the perception of violence as efficacious. In that case it is the percentage of past rewards (low) that has a high beta, while the impact of future expectations is rather low. This suggests a fundamental experiential difference between these two groups. Those who view voting as efficacious have not had great experience (this was before the advent of the 18-year-old vote) with voting, but they are positively orientated toward their expected future rewards. The violence group, however, has had low rewards in the past and is not expecting to fare better in the future. We shall return again to this difference in orientation to time.

The next two independent variables, the satisfaction with government impact and political alienation, are two ways of looking at similar phenomena. We would expect that those individuals with high political alienation would not be satisfied with the nature of the impact of the federal and local government and would evaluate this impact negatively. These variables appear to have little impact on voting efficacy, but they do for violence efficacy. The satisfaction with government impact has a strong relationship to violence efficacy, while political alienation has a moderately strong relationship. These two dimensions may be thought of as the attitudinal and behavioral components of political alienation. Political alienation is the psychic perception of self-polity separation, while impact satisfaction refers to the behavioral rather than attitudinal consequences of particular government policies and actions. Positive satisfaction with the impact of the government has a strong relationship with voting efficacy, while political alienation has a weak impact.

When we turn to an examination of the trust variables, faith in people and faith in government, we find that both have a rather weak impact on voting efficacy. Indeed, there is no reason why faith in people should have a strong impact, since our discussion in this area stressed its importance for undertaking some sort of collective social and/or political effort. Voting requires no such social effort. The political analogue of faith in people, faith in government, has only a moderate relation with voting efficacy. On the other hand, faith in people has a moderately strong relation to violence efficacy, such that less faith in people is more highly associated with higher violence efficacy. The same is true, but to a much larger extent, for the faith in government variable. The rather high beta (.70) suggests that lack of faith in government has an important impact on the perception of violence efficacy.

We can view this from a different perspective by examining the impact of perceived government responsiveness. In both cases, that is, for voting and violence, there is a strong relationship between responsiveness and perceiving these behaviors as efficacious. It will be remembered that we previously suggested that one could tell about the nature of the relationship (that is, whether it was positive, negative, or curvilinear) by examining the deviations from the mean. When we do this for the responsiveness variable, an interesting, but not unexpected, finding emerges. Voting efficacy and governmental responsiveness are positively associated, while violence efficacy and governmental responsiveness are negatively associated. That is, individuals who feel that the government is responsive are likely to support the efficacy of voting and perhaps other traditional behaviors, while those who believe that the government is unresponsive are willing to entertain the possibility that violence is efficacious.

We spoke before about the difference in time orientations for the two groups, regarding political-reward structures and expectations. When we turn to an examination of the other time-concern variable, political impatience, strong patterns again emerge. For both voting efficacy and violence efficacy, political impatience shows strong associations with the effects of the other variables held constant. There is a strong negative association between political impatience and voting efficacy (beta = .44), and an even stronger positive association between political impatience and violence efficacy (beta = .88). In fact, the relationship between political impatience and violence efficacy is the strongest in the entire table. This suggests that political impatience may play a large role in the etiology of political violence.

When we turn to the effects of personal control, we find that it has only a slight impact on voting efficacy (beta = .11). If it is true that for many of our respondents voting is largely civically motivated, then this result would be expected. That is, as we previously suggested, civic duty and voting are closely tied together; in fact the most powerful independent variable in predicting voting efficacy is civic duty (beta = .77). Since civic duty and personal control are different motivators (see the discussion in Chapters One and Ten), we would expect personal control to play a small part in the perception of voting efficacy. The same is not the case, however, for violence efficacy. Here the relationship is very strong (beta = .65) and in the negative direction. That is, the less personal control a respondent has, the more likely he is to perceive that violence is efficacious. We would expect this to be the case given the finding that the low personal control respondents actually participate more frequently, but have been rewarded less often than their high personal-control counterparts.

Finally, as part of the analysis of the origins of the perception of particular behaviors as efficacious, we examined the impact of past participation in a particular mode. That is, if one has voted before is he more or less likely to have perceived that behavior as efficacious. Conversely, does one have to have participated in violence in order to feel that it is efficacious. Each respondent was asked whether he had ever voted or taken part in political violence (along with a number of other behaviors) and this past participation was utilized as an independent variable. When we examine the results for past voting participation, we can see that there is a strong relationship (beta = .49) between past voting participation and the perception that voting is an efficacious behavior. When viewing these results, we must remember that most of our respondents were not old enough to vote, since at the time this survey was conducted, the 18-year-old vote was not yet a reality. When we turn to an examination of the perceived efficacy of violence and actual participation in political violence, we find that there is a very small relationship (beta = .15) in the controlled condition. That is, it appears that past participation in violent political acts has only a small impact on the perception that violence is efficacious.

At this point let us summarize those factors that have emerged as being strongly connected with the perception that voting and violence are efficacious behaviors. For voting, they are the expectation of future rewards from the political system, satisfaction with the nature of the impact of the government, a certain degree of political patience, and a belief in governmental responsiveness. By far, however, the single most powerful predictor for voting efficacy is the sense of civic obligation. In view of the fact that most of the respondents in our sample have never voted, it is possible to suggest that voting efficacy is in this case not based on concrete results arising out of the individuals' immediate personal experiences, but may be based on the social norm that voting in the United States should be considered an efficacious act.

Turning to the perception of violence as efficacious, we find that the strongest predictors are low amounts of perceived rewards for past participation, dissatisfaction with the nature of government, a high sense of citizen obligation, feelings of low personal control, and lack of faith in the government and its responsiveness. By far, however, the single most powerful predictor is political impatience, the feeling that rewards from the political system are not coming fast enough. At this point perhaps it would be well to emphasize that the word impatient is not meant to convey a judgment. The nature of the ratio between the optimal amount of change within a particular period of time has and will be the subject of continuing political debate. As an example one might think of ending segregation. Some people feel that to be impatient with what they consider a slow pace of change is to be positively valued, while others feel that the present rates are too fast. The question of political time emerges here as an important area and certainly one that offers potential advances in the explanation of political behavior.

Chapter Sixteen

THE POLITICAL RELEVANCE OF PERSONAL CONTROL

We began this book with some observations about the relationship between political theory and political participation. There were, we suggested, three sets of questions that traditionally have connected these two areas: (1) should the opportunity for widespread political participation for citizens be made available; (2) what is the nature of political participation in any given political system; and (3) what are the consequences for the political system given the answers to questions (1) and (2). To this point we have been mainly concerned with the answers to questions (2) and (3), but our work is not without implications for the first question.

We began our analysis by looking at the three major explanations of political participation; political utility, political obligation, and political efficacy. Each of these was suggested to provide a partial explanation for political participation, although each explanation had its problems. For example, the concept of political utility as a political motivator was shown to rest upon three assumptions: (1) maximization, (2) system allocation acceptance, and (3) fixed quantity, quality, and distribution. Examined in depth, each of these assumptions was suggested to be in need of substantial modification. Furthermore, the concept of reinforcement itself presented certain problems of prior and post-hoc operationalization.

Moving to civic obligation, we noted that it is a norm that one learns. That is, civic obligation is an "ought" rather than a motivation that springs from the nature of the individual. Insofar as civic obligation does motivate political behavior, we suggested that it would be only for a limited range of behaviors and in the absence of other motivating forces might not be very powerful. We then examined some data from a nationwide survey which suggested that 42 percent of the adult population defined the good-citizen role without reference to any political participation. Thus, one could have a high sense of civic duty, participate little, if at all, and still think of oneself as a good citizen.

Finally, we examined the concept of political efficacy and noted that it was generally put forward as a correlate of participation and not as an explanation for the motivation to participate. We hypothesized that efficacy could, under certain conditions, become intrinsically motivating. Before we went on to examine these conditions, we first examined the traditional concept of political efficacy in order to assess both its strengths and weaknesses.

The problem of conceptualization was suggested to arise from the lack of conceptual development of the political-efficacy concept. In part this has been a result of the empirical success of the scale which has been taken to be *the* measure of the concept. There has been more interest in the predictive and less interest in the theoretical aspects of the concept. Thus, recent developments in personality, theory, social psychology, child development, and developmental psychology which might have had some impact on the conceptual difficulties of the efficacy concept, have not been utilized.

Another problem has been operationalization. The measure, developed over two decades ago at the Survey Research Center, was suggested to have a number of problems including problems of content validity, and response set. In addition there have been problems of reliability. A recent examination of the long-term stabilizing of political efficacy scores has lead two authors to question whether there is in fact a stable attitude of political efficacy for most adults.[1]

[1] Shirley Welch and C. Clark, *op. cit.*

We also noted that there were problems of reliability in the few studies that attempted to deal with the socialization of political efficacy.

Lastly, we suggested that there were problems with the motivational implications of political efficacy. Why is it, we asked, that the more efficacious participate more? Using the current definition of political efficacy as, "a feeling of effectiveness and capacity in the public sphere,"[2] the assumption is that people participate in the political arena because they are effective there. This suggests that politics becomes salient as a result of their feelings that they can have an impact, rather than as the result of the impact of the political system upon their lives. Another definition suggests that political efficacy is the feeling that one can have an impact on the political process," in other words, that it is worthwhile to perform one's civic duties."[3] Here efficacy is considered rewarding because it allows one to do one's civic duties. Yet, we had already presented data to show that for many people the good-citizen role requires no participation!

We suggested that efficacy itself was, under certain specified conditions, intrinsically motivating. However, before moving to document that assertion, many of the points raised in the preceding criticisms had to be answered, in the form of presenting a need-based theory of political efficacy.

We began our theory building by attempting to establish a clear and conceptually distinct demarcation of the political-efficacy concept. We began with the hypothesis that political efficacy (and some amount of political participation) had its origin in *the basic need for people to obtain control over relevant aspects of their life-space,* which under specified conditions included the political system.

In order to examine the evidence for this need for per-

[2] D. Easton and J. Dennis, *Children in the Political System: Origins of Political Legitimacy* (New York: McGraw-Hill, 1969).

[3] A. Campbell *et al., The American Voter* (New York: Wiley & Sons, 1960).

sonal control, we examined a number of branches of psychological research, including comparative (animal) psychology, psychoanalytic theory, Neo-Freudian theory, developmental psychology, and "third force" psychology. In each we found evidence to support the existence of a need for personal control.

With the above as a base, we then turned to a fuller theoretical statement of a need theory of political efficacy. Political efficacy, as we defined it, was *the belief that one had sufficient personal control over political processes to satisfy the need for personal control.* The use of the word "belief" alerts us to the possibility that it is the subjective evaluation of personal control which is being utilized and not an outside objective evaluation of the amount of personal control. Unless these outside evaluations of social or political reality become part of the person's world, we must still deal with the "social fact" of his belief.

The word sufficient also points to another problem area. There are, no doubt, variations in the amount of personal control that will satisfy the need for personal control. This, in turn, we suggested, was a function of the strength of the need for the person. If we had an accurate scale of the degree of control necessary for satisfaction, arranged from one to ten for illustrative purposes, we would suggest that some people would be satisfied with a level of two, while others would be satisfied only with a level of eight. Clearly, the amount of satisfaction required before one feels that he has obtained personal control would be related to the possibility of obtaining satisfaction. To the extent that satisfaction demands were excessive or unrealistic, the potential of feelings of personal control and political efficacy would be decreased.

Lastly, the definition focused on an important link between the need for personal control and political efficacy; namely, it is only when politics becomes control relevant that feelings of political efficacy may emerge. Viewed from this perspective, personal control is a necessary but insufficient component of political efficacy.

We suggested that political salience might best be understood phenomenologically as the perceived impact of the political system on the individual's daily life. We then distinguished and explicated three major types of political salience. Political-punishment salience was defined as the perception that the government had an important impact on one's daily life and that this impact was perceived to be negative. Political-reward salience was that the outputs of the political system had an important impact, but that the impact was in the form of perceived rewards (either material or symbolic). Finally, political-obligation salience was defined as the perception that politics was salient, not because of its impact on the individual's life, but because the good-citizen role required a certain degree of political salience.

Viewed from this perspective then, political efficacy was suggested to be logically preceded by (1) the need for personal control, (2) the perception that politics is a control relevant sphere, and (3) a successful history of participation, at least to the extent that it brings the perception of the necessary degree of personal control. The idea of past participatory success is important, because it distinguishes political efficacy as a norm, from our definition of political efficacy. This is especially important in view of the research that has found that children as young as six-years-old have already internalized political efficacy as a norm.[4]

Several implications were suggested to flow from our need theory of political efficacy. One important consequence is the hypothesis that individuals with low personal control and high political salience would participate more frequently than those individuals with high personal control and high

[4] See the discussion in Easton and Dennis, *op. cit., passim.*

political salience. This would follow since the frustration of a need (the need for personal control) in a relevant arena (politics) might bring more attempts to gain the needed feelings of control. For individuals who had already obtained this feeling of control through participation, there would be less urgency for a new act of participation. At this point an important question arises. Our theory suggests that individuals with *low personal control and high salience might be more likely to participate in any given political event, yet most of the research done in the last decade has found that those with high political efficacy participate more. How do we explain this seeming incongruity?*

One difference between our formulation and past findings is that we posit the necessity of political salience. Very often survey research has simply assumed political salience and then gone on to present the results of cross-tabulations of attitudes and behaviors. Also, the way in which we have operationalized political efficacy (as the generalized expectancy of control over the outcomes in one's life) allows us to assess the degree to which the need for personal control has been satisfied. On the other hand, the traditional operationalization is confounded by identification with particular traditional political behaviors, such as voting, response sets, and social expectations centering around feelings of efficacy in American political culture.

Even if all of the above were not the case, however, we can resolve the apparent paradox by pointing out that insights from other research would suggest not a monotonic relationship between personal control and political participation, but rather a curvilinear relationship. That is, individuals with low personal control and high levels of political salience, we hypothesize, will participate in order to gain personal control. If after a certain period or amount of participation such feelings were not forthcoming, we would expect either a withdrawal from participation or an escalation of the participatory mode.

The often repeated finding that the least efficacious participate less suggests that withdrawal may be the dominant form of reaction to unsuccessful attempts to gain personal control. Here again our theory suggests an alternative explanation of frequently reported findings. The finding that people with low feelings of political efficacy participate less, leaves unexamined the developmental sequence by which people arrive at feelings of political inefficacy. Our theory suggests *that those with low political efficacy, did not always, nor may not at present, withdraw from political participation. Rather, political inefficacy is viewed as the consequence of unsuccessful attempts to gain personal control in the political arena.* Of course, there might also be a form of anticipatory inefficacy in which the individual never attempts to participate because of fear of failure. This kind of inefficacy might be associated with the defense mechanism of denying the salience of the political system.

These remarks are further complicated by the fact that most survey research has a snap-shot effect, because it obtains data at only one point in time. Because of this it would be extremely difficult, given the conventional operationalization of political efficacy, to assess whether or not someone with low personal control and high political salience was participating less frequently because of past nonrewards for participation.

Having found some evidence of a need for personal control, and having presented a need-based theory of political efficacy, we turned our attention to a reconceptualization of political efficacy. The reconceptualization proceeded along the lines suggested by our concept of a need for personal control. We focused on the work of Julian Rotter and his concept of Internal-External control, which relates to the generalized expectancies of rewards from individually initiated action. Individuals who feel their rewards are independent of their own efforts are said to have feelings of external control, while those who felt that their reward outcomes were directly related to their own actions are said to have internal control. Following Rotter's discussion, we suggested that an individual with external control, or what we would call low personal control, might attribute his outcomes to either luck, fate, the work of powerful others, or to great complexity. We reviewed each of these possibilities, suggesting where appropriate, their relation to political phenomena.

After the analysis of the suggested reconceptualization of political efficacy, we began to explore the socialization process associated with the acquisition of personal-control beliefs. We had suggested that the need for personal control grew out of the dependency of the early life experiences of the child. Given that early origin of the need, we attempted to demarcate some general parameters of the socialization of personal control beliefs. This in turn suggested the importance of tracing the ways in which human needs and personality development are shaped not only by life experiences, but also by proximate and remote social contexts. Our discussion of the latter focused on the impact of culture on the acquisition of personal control and the way in which the cultural assumptions about what constitutes control and control satisfaction shape the potentialities for the acquisition of that personal control.

Moving from the more remote to the more immediate, we examined the impact of socioeconomic status on the acquisition of personal control. We suggested that SES was in fact a summative variable, an indicator of the effects of transversing a certain life path. That is, SES was a shorthand way of describing the psychological effects of one's life experiences and the way in which what we think is shaped by the life experiences we have been through. Under this framework, we traced specific impacts of wealth, family occupational status, and family values on the acquisition of personal control.

With these broad social contexts as background we then proceeded to a more micro-level analysis of the acquisition of personal control. More specifically, we focused on those dimensions of family life associated with the acquisition of personal control.

We began with an examination of the impact of the authority structure on the acquisition of personal control. We hypothesized and found support for the proposition that individuals who are given the greatest amount of autonomy while growing up will have the highest levels of personal control. Further examination of this relationship revealed significant differences for males and females in the degree of autonomy allowed, suggesting one potential explanation of the lower feelings of efficacy traditionally found among women. We found no relation between the father being head of the family and level of personal control of the children.

We did hypothesize and find support for the proposition that consistency of rule enforcement was associated with high levels of personal control. This grew out of the recognition that environmental consistency is a prerequisite for the development of mastery skills which lead to personal control.

Turning to the emotional structure of family life and their impact on the acquisition of personal control, a number of important findings emerged. We found no significant association between personal control and taking a personal problem to a parent, but we did find a strong and statistically significant relationship between the perception of parental empathy and the degree of personal control. Respondents who reported that they felt that either or both of their parents understood the way they felt about things, were significantly more likely to have high personal control. Of related interest was the finding that respondents with parents who had high empathy were also significantly more likely to develop a greater degree of faith in people, an orientation associated with political trust and political participation.

We then turned to an examination of the impact of sequential arrival into the family and its impact on the socialization of personal control. We found no relation between family size and personal control. We did, however, find a significant association between ordinal position and personal control, such that only children were significantly more likely to have low personal control, while children in the later part of their family were more likely to have high personal control. These results were interpreted in the framework of Schachter's hypothesis about parental anxiousness and inconsistency with first children.

Lastly, we examined the impact of the parent's level of personal control on the level of personal control of their children. As hypothesized we found a significant association between these two variables. We then submitted all of the socialization variables to a multivariate procedure for ordinal level data in order to assess their relative impact. By far the strongest predictor to our adolescent respondent's level of personal control was the parent's level of personal control. After parent personal-control levels the two most powerful predictors were the degree of allowed autonomy while growing up, and consistent rule enforcement.

The nature of this analysis suggests the importance of the direct transmission of basic personality orientations in the study of political socialization. Rather than focus on parent-child correspondence in political attitudes and opinions, which have not yielded particularly high levels of association, our research suggests that the study of the direct transmission of more basic personality orientations might be a fruitful area for future research. Our study of the impact of the dimensions of family life should not be taken to suggest that each dimension of family life has equal impact for the acquisition of other basic personality orientations. For example, in another place I have compared and contrasted the nature of the impact of the dimensions of family life on both personal control and basic interpersonal trust.[5] Clearly future research might attempt to establish the impact of the dimensions of family life for a variety of basic orientations to the world that have political consequences.

Having explored in some detail the socialization experiences associated with the acquisition of personal control, we turned our attention in the following chapters to the attitudinal (both social and political) correlates of personal control. Turning first to the self and personal control we found a significant association between personal control and faith in people. As expected this generalized orientation also was significantly associated with political trust, such that the higher the personal control, the higher both the interpersonal and political trust. Respondents with personal control were also significantly more likely to report themselves as happy and satisfied, lending some support for the proposition that having personal control is intrinsically rewarding.

Turning to evaluations of the political system, we found that respondents with low personal control were more likely to attribute their lack of control to the nature of the system rather than to any personal failures. Given this association, how do respondents with low personal control evaluate a political system which they feel does not allow them to exercise the level of control they need? The answer is that they overwhelmingly evaluate it negatively. Respondents with low personal control perceive the government to be ineffective, and feel that governmental outputs are punishing and not rewarding. This suggests that a political system which is perceived to frustrate the fulfilling of basic needs is in some degree of trouble. If sufficient numbers of people are frustrated on one or another need, then the system may

[5] Stanley Renshon, "Personality and Family Dynamics in the Political Socialization Process," paper presented to the annual meeting of the American Political Science Association, New Orleans, La., 1973.

be in more substantial trouble. We have dealt here with only one need, but this should not be taken to suggest that it is the only need that can be frustrated by the nature of the political system.

If we adopt Maslow's need hierarchy as a reasonable theory of human needs, then it is clear that individuals can be frustrated not only on their control needs, but on their material needs, their love needs, and their self-esteem needs. Much political theory has concentrated on the material aspects of need deprivation, such as food or shelter (housing deprivation), but individuals and groups can also be deprived of self-esteem, which is as much a human need as food, indeed under some conditions a more salient one. Our work suggests that to the extent that basic needs are perceived to be frustrated by the political system, that system is at least potentially in trouble. It is not only in trouble because it will lose "diffuse support," but it also may mark the beginning of direct steps taken against the political system.

This perspective gives us another view of the onset of revolutionary behavior. That is, it appears unlikely that any revolution is the result of one need deprivation. Rather our analysis suggests that different groups may experience different need deprivations and when these deprivations become extensive and intense enough, a revolutionary situation is at least a potential. This may explain why revolutions are led by individuals with *higher* need deprivations and fed by individuals with *lower* need deprivations. In many developing countries people are concerned about the basic needs for food, but displaced or colonized intellectuals can feel equal levels of deprivation of their self-esteem and self-worth.

Further support of the deleterious political consequences of need deprivation was found in our examination of the political attitudinal correlates of personal control. We found that individuals with low personal control were significantly more likely to feel highly politically alienated, and were much more likely to rate the government as highly ineffective. Of related importance was the finding that those respondents with low personal control were more likely to be politically impatient. That is, they were more likely to desire immediate gratifications from the political system and less likely to be able to wait. Since politics is not a sphere in which immediate rewards are usually forthcoming, we expected that the level of past rewards from the political system would not be perceived to be significant. In fact there was a strong negative association between low personal control and past political reward satisfaction. This also held true for political impatience and level of past reward satisfaction.

Having examined some attitudinal correlates, we then went on to examine the important relationship between personal control and political participation. We found that for most of our respondents politics was a control relevant sphere. That is, most of the respondents did feel that the outputs of the political system did have an impact (negative) on their daily lives. From this we would expect from our theory a potential for greater participation from individuals who had still not satisfied their need for personal control in politics and who continued to have high political salience. In order to test this hypothesis we collected data on a range of political behaviors from voting to taking part in political violence. In 10 out of the 12 behaviors, respondents with low personal control were more likely to have participated than respondents with high personal control. In seven of these cases the results were statistically significant. We attempted to check these results by examining participation in two concrete political events that we collected data around; participation in an "unstructured period" during the off-year elections and participation in a mass demonstration held in Washington, D.C. In both cases respondents with low personal control were more likely to have participated than respondents with high personal control. The data allow some confidence in the need theory of political efficacy. Further research needs to be done, especially more longitudinal research, but our results do indicate that we may be on the right track.

Lastly, we examined the implications of the need for personal control on the selection of participation modes. As we discussed earlier, the frustration of the attempt to secure personal control in a control relevant sphere (like politics) might lead to either withdrawal or to escalation of the participatory mode. We suggested that for many people withdrawal might be the dominant response, but for some the search for personal control will entail the selection of more forceful modes of participation, including the possibility of political violence.

Besides these considerations, however, a need theory of political efficacy and political participation speaks to a number of fundamental issues in political theory and political life. One of the assumptions made by those who desired independence from England in the seventeen hundreds was that decisions could not be made for people but rather had to be made by people. Democratic theory has always assumed that people *ought* to have control over areas in which decisions that effect their lives are made. Our analysis and data have, we hoped, provided some support to the proposition that the "ought" of democratic theory need not rest solely on moral imperatives. If our theory proves in later trials to be valid, then the suggestion can be made that people do have a need to have control over areas of their lives which have important effects on them. We have already documented the negative effects that such lack of control might have for the political system in our own limited sample. Clearly more work is called for before we can have increased confidence in our theory. However, if the theory holds, then an excellent self-interest argument (from the point of view of the political system) for a government that encourages the widest possible participation and governmental responsiveness will have been made. For, if it is true that people need to have personal control, and are more personally and politically satisfied when they have it, then the implications for democratic and participatory theory are clear. In this sense the need for personal control that lies within each of us is the foundation of democratic theory; in both practice and theoretical justification.

Appendix A

STUDENT QUESTIONNAIRE FOR THE "UNSTRUCTURED PERIOD"

Instructional Period

1 - 3. Identification Number ______________________

4. Sex ______________________

5. Appearance Code ______________

Males: 1 = very long hair and/or hippy style clothes and/or beard or moustache and/or rimless glasses (ANY THREE OF THE PRECEDING)
2 = less than three of the above
3 = traditional dress, medium to short hair

Females: 1 = long or frizzy hair, hippy dress, rimless glasses (AT LEAST TWO OF THE PRECEDING)
2 = one of the preceding
3 = traditional dress (i.e., regular dresses, skirts, etc.)

6. Race ______________

---

7. ARE YOU AN AMERICAN <u>CITIZEN</u>? ____________

8. WHAT YEAR ARE YOU IN AT PENN?
FROSH
SOPH
<u>Class</u> JR
SENIOR

9. DO YOU HAVE A <u>MAJOR</u>? . . . IF SO WHAT IS IT? ______________

10. DO YOU HAVE ANY <u>RELIGIOUS</u> PREFERENCE? IF SO WHAT IS IT?
NONE
PROTESTANT
CATHOLIC
JEWISH
OTHER ______________

11. WHAT DOES YOUR FATHER DO FOR A LIVING? ______________

12. DO YOU HAPPEN TO REMEMBER THE LAST GRADE OF SCHOOL THAT HE COMPLETED? ______________

DO YOU EVER REMEMBER EITHER ONE OF YOUR PARENTS (read the following one at a time)

13. DISCUSSING POLITICS WITH YOU? YES NO

14. ATTENDING A POLITICAL MEETING OF ANY SORT? YES NO

15. WORKING FOR A POLITICAL YES NO

16. CONTRIBUTING MONEY TO A POLITICAL CAMPAIGN OR PARTY? YES NO

17. TAKING PART IN ANY POLITICAL DEMONSTRATION, LIKE A MARCH OR A SIT IN? YES NO

18. (Interviewer add up total of yes answers for 13, 14, 15, 16, 17) __________

19. HOW WOULD YOU DESCRIBE YOUR GENERAL STATE OF HEALTH RECENTLY? WOULD YOU SAY THAT IT HAS BEEN .....

EXTREMELY GOOD
GENERALLY GOOD
JUST FAIR

NOW I'D LIKE TO ASK YOU A FEW QUESTIONS ABOUT THE UNSTRUCTURED PERIOD AT PENN.

20. IN GENERAL DO YOU THINK IT WAS A GOOD IDEA FOR THE UNIVERSITY TO HAVE AN UNSTRUCTURED PERIOD, SO THAT STUDENTS COULD PARTICIPATE IN THE CAMPAIGN?

YES NO

21. (If answer above is yes) WHY DO YOU THINK SO?

22. (If answer to #20 is no) WHY DO YOU FEEL THAT WAY?

23. HOW ABOUT YOURSELF? . . . DID YOU PARTICIPATE AT ALL IN ANY OF THE CAMPAIGN ACTIVITIES DURING THE ELECTION?

YES NO

24. (If answer to #23 is no) WHY DID YOU DECIDE NOT TO PARTICIPATE? (Check one of the following, but <u>do not read</u> the list)

No interest in politics in general ______
No interest in this particular election campaign ______
Interested, but unavailable for some reasons ______
Personal . . . I couldn't have done anything anyway ______
General . . . decided that nothing would help or that it didn't make a difference ______

(Go directly on to question #39)

(If answer to #23 is yes) WHAT DID YOU DO DURING THE CAMPAIGN? DID YOU:

25. ENGAGE IN MORE POLITICAL DISCUSSIONS? YES NO
26. ATTEND CAMPAIGN MEETINGS? YES NO
27. DO ANY POLITICAL ORGANIZING? YES NO
28. ACTIVELY TRY TO GET PEOPLE TO VOTE FOR YOUR CANDIDATE OR PARTY? YES NO
29. DID YOU DO ANYTHING ELSE? IF SO, WHAT?

30. (Interviewer add up total of yes answers for 25, 26, 27, 28, 29) ______

31. HOW MANY HOURS DID YOU SPEND DURING THE UNSTRUCTURED PERIOD DOING THESE THINGS? DID YOU SPEND .....

LESS THAN 5 HOURS
BETWEEN 5 AND 10 HOURS
BETWEEN 10 AND 20 HOURS
MORE THAN 20 HOURS

32. HOW DID YOU GET INVOLVED IN THE CAMPAIGN? ..... WAS IT PRIMARILY A GROUP OF YOU THAT DECIDED TO WORK TOGETHER ..... OR SOME FRIENDS ASKING OR SUGGESTING THAT YOU HELP, OR DID YOU DECIDE BY YOURSELF TO DO IT?

GROUP OR FRIENDS

YOURSELF

33. LOOKING BACK ON THE EXPERIENCE, WHICH PART DID YOU ENJOY THE MOST? WAS IT THE CHANCE TO PUT YOUR BELIEFS INTO ACTION BY WORKING FOR THE CANDIDATE OR PARTY OR ..... WAS IT THE PERSONAL ASPECT OF THE EXPERIENCE ..... MEETING NEW PEOPLE, WORKING WITH FRIENDS ..... ?

PUTTING BELIEFS INTO ACTION
PERSONAL ASPECT

34. DID THE CANDIDATE OR PARTY THAT YOU WORKED FOR WIN OR LOSE?

WIN
LOSE

35. WHICH PARTY WAS THAT?

DEMOCRATIC
REPUBLICAN
SOCIALIST
OTHER ______________________

36. IN WHAT STATE DID YOU WORK?

PA.
OTHER ______________________

37. DID YOU FIND YOUR EFFORT A PERSONALLY VALUABLE EXPERIENCE?

YES NO

38. HOW ABOUT POLITICALLY? ..... DID YOU FIND THE EXPERIENCE POLITICALLY REWARDING?

YES NO

39. DO YOU THINK THAT YOU WOULD EVER WORK IN ANY FUTURE CAMPAIGN?

YES NO

40. DID YOU EVER PARTICIPATE IN CAMPAIGN ACTIVITIES OF ANY SORT BEFORE THIS ELECTION?

YES NO

41. IF YOU HAD TO PLACE YOURSELF ON A POLITICAL CHART, WOULD YOU SAY THAT YOU WERE A

RADICAL
LIBERAL
MIDDLE OF THE ROAD
CONSERVATIVE
VERY CONSERVATIVE
NON-POLITICAL

42. WHAT IS YOUR GRADE POINT AVERAGE?

(Check one of the following, but do not read list)

1. below 2.0
2. 2.0 - 2.49
3. 2.50- 2.99
4. 3.0 - 3.49
5. 3.5 or above

43. DO YOU BELIEVE THAT THE GOVERNMENT REPRESENTS PEOPLE WITH YOUR POLITICAL AND SOCIAL BELIEFS?

YES NO

44. SOME PEOPLE SAY THAT YOU CAN"T BE TOO CAREFUL IN DEALING WITH OTHER PEOPLE, OTHERS SAY THAT MOST PEOPLE CAN BE TRUSTED: HOW DO YOU FEEL?

OTHERS CAN BE TRUSTED
OTHERS CANNOT BE TRUSTED

45. HAVE YOU EVER TAKEN PART IN ANY FORM OF DIRECT POLITICAL PROTECT, SUCH AS A MASS MARCH OR OTHER MASS DEMONSTRATION, OR SIT IN?

YES NO

(If the answer to #45 was yes)

46. WHAT DO YOU REMEMBER AS THE MOST REWARDING ASPECT OF THE EXPERIENCE ..... WAS IT

THE PERSONAL INVOLVEMENT
THE SHARING OF AN EXPERIENCE WITH OTHERS OR
THE FEELING OF PUTTING YOUR PRINCIPLES INTO ACTION?

47. DOES THE GOVERNMENT SEEM UNABLE OR UNWILLING TO DO THE THINGS THAT YOU THINK NEED TO BE DONE?

(If the answer to #47 was yes)

48. HOW DOES THAT MAKE YOU FEEL?

49. SOME PEOPLE ALWAYS SEEM TO HAVE A LOT OF ENERGY, OTHERS HAVE LESS. IN GENERAL, WOULD YOU SAY THAT YOU HAD:

A GREAT DEAL OF ENERGY
AN AVERAGE AMOUNT OF ENERGY
LESS THAN AN AVERAGE AMOUNT OF ENERGY

50. DO YOU THINK THAT PUBLIC OFFICIALS CARE ABOUT WHAT PEOPLE LIKE YOU THINK?

YES NO

51. DO YOU FEEL THAT YOU COULD BE EFFECTIVE IN GETTING THE POLICIES THAT YOU FAVOR ADOPTED BY THE GOVERNMENT?

YES NO

52. WHICH OF THE FOLLOWING DO YOU FEEL WOULD BE MOST EFFECTIVE IN CHANGING GOVERNMENT POLICY:

TRADITIONAL POLITICAL BEHAVIOR SUCH AS VOTING
THE NEW POLITICS - MARCHES, DEMONSTRATIONS, ETC.

53. DO YOU BELIEVE THAT PEOPLE WILL TAKE ADVANTAGE OF YOU IF YOU ARE NOT CAREFUL?

YES NO

54. COULD YOU TELL ME WHO THE CANDIDATES FOR GOVERNOR IN PENNSYLVANIA WERE? AND DO YOU KNOW WHO WON?

REPUBLICAN CANDIDATE ______________________________
DEMOCRATIC CANDIDATE ______________________________
WINNER ____

55. WHEN YOU THINK OF YOUR OWN IDEAS AND THE IDEAS AND ACTION OF THE FEDERAL

GOVERNMENT IN GENERAL, DO YOU FEEL THERE IS:

NO GAP AT ALL
A SMALL GAP
A FAIRLY WIDE GAP
A VERY WIDE GAP

56. WHICH OF THE FOLLOWING WOULD YOU FIND MOST SATISFACTORY?

A. A CHANGE IN THE DECISION MAKING PROCESS OF GOVERNMENT, SO THAT YOU HAD MORE OF A VOICE, ASSUMING THAT YOUR POSITION WOULDN'T ALWAYS BE ADOPTED ..... OR

B. A CHANGE IN GOVERNMENT POLICIES IN THE DIRECTION THAT YOU DESIRED, EVEN IF YOU DIDN'T GET MORE OF A VOICE IN THE DECISION MAKING PROCESS.

57. WHAT WOULD YOU SAY IS THE DOMINANT POLITICAL ORIENTATION OF YOUR FRIENDS? WOULD YOU SAY THEY WERE:

RADICAL
LIBERAL
MIDDLE OF THE ROAD
CONSERVATIVE
VERY CONSERVATIVE
NOT POLITICAL AT ALL

58. IF YOU HAD TO GUESS, WHICH OF THE ABOVE WOULD YOU THINK IS GENERALLY THE CASE WITH PENN STUDENTS?

____

59. DO YOU BELONG TO ANY SOCIAL ORGANIZATIONS LOCALLY AND/OR ON CAMPUS? IF SO, COULD YOU GIVE ME THE NAMES OF SOME OF THEM:

60. DO YOU BELONG TO ANY CAMPUS OR LOCAL POLITICAL ORGANIZATIONS? COULD YOU GIVE THE NAMES OF SOME OF THEM:

61. HOW WOULD YOU DESCRIBE YOUR GENERAL STATE OF HEALTH WHILE GROWING UP. WOULD YOU SAY THAT IT WAS:

EXTREMELY GOOD
GENERALLY GOOD
JUST FAIR

WE ARE ALMOST AT THE END OF THE INTERVIEW NOW AND I'D LIKE TO ASK YOU SEVERAL PERSONAL QUESTIONS ..... YOU DON"T HAVE TO ANSWER IF YOU DON'T WANT TO ..... BUT JUST REMEMBER THAT THESE INTERVIEWS ARE COMPLETELY ANONYMOUS.

62. HAVE YOU EVER HAD PRE-MARITAL SEX?

NEVER
SELDOM
MORE THAN A FEW TIMES
FREQUENTLY

63. HAVE YOU EVER TRIED MARIJUANA OR HASHISH?

NEVER

ONCE IN A GREAT WHILE
FAIRLY OFTEN
A LOT

64. HAVE YOU EVER TRIED ANY OF THE MIND EXPANDING DRUGS, LIKE L.S.D., OR MESCALINE?

NEVER
ONCE OR TWICE
MORE THAN A FEW TIMES
MANY TIMES

Appendix B

STUDENT QUESTIONNAIRE FOR THE MARCH ON WASHINGTON

RESIDENTIAL LIFE QUESTIONNAIRE

PLEASE INDICATE YOUR ANSWER BY CIRCLING THE APPROPRIATE WORD OR NUMBER

1. We would like to begin by asking how you feel about several issues that have been in the news. Recently, the extent of U.S. involvement in other parts of the world has become a subject of debate. Some feel that it is inevitable that a powerful country like the U.S. should have worldwide involvements . . . others are not so sure. How do you feel?

IT'S INEVITABLE   IT ISN'T INEVITABLE

2. Some people have said that we would be better off if we stayed at home and did not concern ourselves with problems in other parts of the world. Do you . . .

STRONGLY AGREE   AGREE   DISAGREE   STRONGLY DISAGREE

3. Do you feel that world affairs have become so complex that even our elected officials have difficulty keeping control of events?

NEVER   SOMETIMES   OFTEN

4. How much of a role do you think "luck" or "chance" plays in world affairs?

NO EFFECT   SOME EFFECT   MUCH EFFECT   A GREAT DEAL OF EFFECT

5. It has been suggested that it is no longer necessary to keep our troops in Western Europe. How illing would you be to support an immediate substantial reduction of our troops there?

VERY WILLING   SOMEWHAT WILLING   SOMEWHAT UNWILLING   VERY UNWILLING

6. Turning now to domestic politics . . . we have noticed that people do a variety of things during political campaigns. Would you please indicate which of the following, if any, you have done . . . Have you ever . . .

...voted in a national election? YES NO About how many times? ____________
...worked for a political party? YES NO In how many campaigns? ____________
...worked for a particular candidate? YES NO Hoa many times? ____________
...run for public office? YES NO How many times? ____________
...worked for a community organization dealing with a social issue?
YES NO How many times? ____________
...served as an officer in any political groups? YES NO How many times? ______
...voted in a local election? ALWAYS OFTEN SOMETIMES NEVER
...contributed money to a candidate? YES NO
...tried to influence someone about an issue or a candidate? YES NO

7. Recently, there has been a great deal of talk about health care. Do you feel the federal government ought to do more to help people get doctors and hospital care at low cost?

YES   NO

8. Have you had a surgic al operation in the last ten years? YES NO
(IF YES) Were you satisfied with the care you received in the hospital? YES NO

9. In the last few years how often have you visited a doctor?

NOT AT ALL   RARELY   SEVERAL TIMES   FAIRLY REGULARLY
(IF YOU VISITED) Were you satisfied with the attention and care you received?
YES   NO

10. Returning to some foreign policy questions . . . Looking ahead several years after the war ends in Vietnam . . . how likely do you feel it is that U.S. troops will become involved in another shooting conflict?

VERY LIKELY   SOMEWHAT LIKELY   SOMEWHAT UNLIKELY   VERY UNLIKELY

11. Do you feel that the world has become so complicated today, that many people have lost control over a great deal of what happens to them?

STRONGLY AGREE   AGREE   DISAGREE   STRONGLY DISAGREE

12. Different groups are working to end our involvement in Vietnam, but there is disagreement over how quickly we should leave. How willing would you be to support a total withdrawal of U.S. troops by the end of 1971?

VERY WILLING   SOMEWHAT WILLING   SOMEWHAT UNWILLING   VERY UNWILLING

13. Turning once again to domestic politics . . . it has often been noted that some Americans do not limit their political involvement activity to election campaigns. Have you ever done any of the following? . . .

...written to a public official or newspaper to let them know how you feel?
YES   NO   How many times? ____________
...signed a petition for or against some issue?   YES   NO
...attended a protest rally of any sort?   YES   NO   How many times? ____________
...been on a picket line during a labor dispute?
YES   NO   How many times? ____________
...broken a law to dramatize your feelings about an issue?
YES   NO   How often? ________________
...taken part in a sit-in?   YES   NO   About how many times? ________________
...been involved in any physical confrontations (pushing, shoving, etc.) during any of the above?   YES   NO   How many times? ________________

14. Some people seem to follow what is going on in government all the time; others have less interest. How often do you follow what is going on in the government?

MOST OF THE TIME   SOME OF THE TIME   NOW AND THEN   HARDLY AT ALL

15. Thinking about the federal government, how much effect do you think its activities, the laws passed, and so on, have on your life?

A GREAT EFFECT   SOME EFFECT   A VERY SMALL EFFECT   NO EFFECT

16. Are you satisfied with that, or do you wish the federal government had . . .

MORE EFFECT   LESS EFFECT   on you?

17. Now think about your local government. How much effect do you think its activities have on your day-to-day life?

A GREAT EFFECT   SOME EFFECT   A VERY SMALL EFFECT   NO EFFECT

18. Are you satisfied with that, or do you wish your local government had

MORE EFFECT   LESS EFFECT   on you?

19. Thinking back to when you have become involved in politics . . . how often have things turned out the way you wanted them to?

0____20____30____40____50____60____70____80____90____100____percent of the time

20. Looking ahead five or six years, how often do you think things will turn out the way you want them to when you get involved in politics?

0____20____30____40____50____60____70____80____90____100____percent of the time

21. Some people are saying that the government is run by a few big interests looking out for themselves, and not for all the people. Do you . . .

STRONGLY AGREE   AGREE   DISAGREE   STRONGLY DISAGREE

There has been a lot of talk recently about the "quality of life" here in the United States. Some people are saying that everything is getting too complicated, that people are not as friendly as they used to be, and that generally things do not seem to work the way they used to . . . others say all of this is exaggerated. We would like to get your feelings on some of these issues/questions . . .

22. Some people have said that, given human nature, there will always be social problems like poverty and discrimination. How do you feel? Do you . . .

STRONGLY AGREE   AGREE   DISAGREE   STRONGLY DISAGREE

23. Would you agree that if you don't watch yourself today, people will take advantage of you?

STRONGLY AGREE   AGREE   DISAGREE   STRONGLY DISAGREE

24. Have you found in meeting people that it doesn't pay to try too hard to please people, because if they like you they like you, and if they don't, there isn't much you can do?

STRONGLY AGREE   AGREE   DISAGREE   STRONGLY DISAGREE

25. Would you say that today most people are inclined to look out for themselves, or more inclined to help others?

LOOK OUT FOR THEMSELVES   HELP OTHERS

26. Some people feel that getting ahead today depends more on knowing the right people than doing a good job. How do you feel? Do you . . .

STRONGLY AGREE   AGREE   DISAGREE   STRONGLY DISAGREE

27. With the current job market, some people feel that getting a good job is just/mostly a matter of being in the right place at the right time. Do you . . .

STRONGLY AGREE   AGREE   DISAGREE   STRONGLY DISAGREE

28. In your life, generally, do you ever find yourself wishing you could return to a less complicated, less demanding way of life?

OFTEN   SOMETIMES   NEVER

29. How much effect do you think "luck" or "chance" plays in your life?

A GREAT DEAL OF EFFECT   MUCH EFFECT   SOME EFFECT   NO EFFECT

(IF "MUCH," SOME," OR "GREAT DEAL") Do you feel it has generally been

GOOD or BAD luck?

30. Do you think that the government has become so large and powerful that it is almost impossible for an individual citizen to have much influence on what happens in government?

YES   NO

31. When you think of your own ideas and those of government officials, do you feel that there is . . .

A VERY WIDE GAP   A WIDE GAP   A SMALL GAP   NO GAP

32. There are many different ways to try to influence the government, but people

today are often in disagreement about which ones are effective. HOW EFFECTIVE WOULD YOU SAY THAT EACH OF THE FOLLOWING IS IN MAKING THE GOVERNMENT PAY ATTENTION TO WHAT PEOPLE THINK? (Please circle your answer)

...voting	EFFECTIVE	1 2 3 4 5	INEFFECTIVE
...trying to personally influence someone on an issue or a candidate	EFFECTIVE	1 2 3 4 5	INEFFECTIVE
...writing to public officials and newspapers to express your views	EFFECTIVE	1 2 3 4 5	INEFFECTIVE
...contributing money to a campaign	EFFECTIVE	1 2 3 4 5	INEFFECTIVE
...sit-ins	EFFECTIVE	1 2 3 4 5	INEFFECTIVE
...attending political meetings	EFFECTIVE	1 2 3 4 5	INEFFECTIVE
...political parties	EFFECTIVE	1 2 3 4 5	INEFFECTIVE
...mass demonstrations	EFFECTIVE	1 2 3 4 5	INEFFECTIVE
...breaking a law to dramatize opposition to a policy	EFFECTIVE	1 2 3 4 5	INEFFECTIVE
...taking part in some sort of violence during a protest	EFFECTIVE	1 2 3 4 5	INEFFECTIVE
...assassination of a government official	EFFECTIVE	1 2 3 4 5	INEFFECTIVE
...picketing	EFFECTIVE	1 2 3 4 5	INEFFECTIVE
...being an informed citizen	EFFECTIVE	1 2 3 4 5	INEFFECTIVE

33. Is there a political group that adequately represents your views?

YES NO NOT SURE

(IF YES) Which political group is that? ____________________

34. Do you feel that each citizen has the obligation to work for better government?

STRONGLY AGREE AGREE DISAGREE STRONGLY DISAGREE

35. Do you feel that citizens should always take the time to vote?

STRONGLY AGREE AGREE DISAGREE STRONGLY DISAGREE

Following are a number of pairs of words that might be used to describe the GOVERNMENT IN WASHINGTON. Note that the words describe opposites on a continuum, for example, ACTIVE versus PASSIVE. Please circle the number between each pair of words that you feel best describes the GOVERNMENT. As an example, using the first pair of words, a "1" is more ACTIVE (and therefore, less PASSIVE) than a "2," and a "6" is more PASSIVE (and less ACTIVE) than a "5."

1. ACTIVE	1	2	3	4	5	6	7	PASSIVE
2. RIGID	1	2	3	4	5	6	7	PLIABLE
3. INEFFECTIVE	1	2	3	4	5	6	7	EFFECTIVE

4. CONSISTENT	1	2	3	4	5	6	7	INCONSISTENT
5. REWARDING	1	2	3	4	5	6	7	PUNISHING
6. UNPREDICTABLE	1	2	3	4	5	6	7	PREDICTABLE
7. INITIATING	1	2	3	4	5	6	7	REACTING
8. COMPLEX	1	2	3	4	5	6	7	SIMPLE
9. IMPOTENT	1	2	3	4	5	6	7	POWERFUL
10. DECISIVE	1	2	3	4	5	6	7	INDECISIVE
11. WAR LIKE	1	2	3	4	5	6	7	PEACEFUL
12. HONEST	1	2	3	4	5	6	7	DISHONEST
13. OPEN	1	2	3	4	5	6	7	CLOSED
14. TRUSTWORTHY	1	2	3	4	5	6	7	UNTRUSTWORTHY

1. There has been a lot of talk recently about who is to blame for the deterioration in the "quality of life" in this country. Some people feel that each individual person is responsible, while others feel that the real responsibility lies with certain powerful groups in government and industry. What do you think?

EACH INDIVIDUAL GROUPS IN GOVERNMENT AND INDUSTRY

2. Now how about improving the "quality of life"; do you feel that the best way to improve it is to stress that each person must begin to take some responsibility for improvement, or do you feel that change is better brought about by pressure and social action?

INDIVIDUAL SOCIAL ACTION

3. There's been a lot of talk recently about racial discrimination in job hiring. Some people say that it is a lack of skills and abilities that keep blacks from getting jobs, while others say that even if he were qualified, a black would not get a job which a white person with the same training would get. Which do you feel is closer to the way things are?

LACK OF SKILLS WHITE PERSON GETS JOB

WE ARE ALMOST FINISHED WITH THE INTERVIEW . . . WE HAVE JUST A FEW MORE TOPICS WE WOULD LIKE TO ASK YOU ABOUT . . . LET'S BEGIN WITH YOUR HIGH SCHOOL DAYS.

4. Did you attend a PRIVATE or PUBLIC high school?

5. Did you play any sports while there? YES NO
   (IF YES) Which ones? ______________________________

6. Were you ever a class officer? YES NO

7. Did you belong to any school clubs or organizations? YES NO
   (IF YES) Which ones? ______________________________

8. How often were you given an opportunity to discuss and debate political issues in your school? Would you say it was . . .

VERY OFTEN OFTEN INFREQUENTLY RARELY, IF EVER

9. How much of a voice did students have about what went on at the school?

A GREAT DEAL A FAIR AMOUNT LITTLE ALMOST NONE

10. How often did you discuss politics with your best school friends then?

VERY OFTEN SOMETIMES INFREQUENTLY RARELY, IF EVER

11. How about now . . . how often would you say you discuss politics with your best school friends?

VERY OFTEN SOMETIMES INFREQUENTLY RARELY, IF EVER

12. How about with your parents . . . do you discuss politics with them?

VERY OFTEN SOMETIMES INFREQUENTLY RARELY, IF EVER

Appendix C

PARENT QUESTIONNAIRE

RESIDENTIAL LIFE QUESTIONNAIRE

PLEASE INDICATE YOUR ANSWER BY CIRCLING THE APPROPRIATE WORD OR NUMBER

1. We would like to begin by asking how you feel about several issues that have been in the news. Recently, the extent of U.S. involvement in other parts of the world has become a subject of debate. Some feel that it is inevitable that a powerful country like the U.S. should have worldwide involvements . . . others are not so sure. How do you feel?

IT'S INEVITABLE IT ISN'T INEVITABLE

2. Some people have said that we would be better off if we stayed at home and did not concern ourselves with problems in other parts of the world. Do you . . .

STRONGLY AGREE AGREE DISAGREE STRONGLY DISAGREE

3. Do you feel that world affairs have become so complex that even our elected officials have difficulty keeping control of events?

NEVER SOMETIMES OFTEN

4. How much of a role do you think "luck" or "chance" plays in world affairs?

NO EFFECT SOME EFFECT MUCH EFFECT A GREAT DEAL OF EFFECT

5. It has been suggested that it is no longer necessary to keep our troops in Western Europe. How willing would you be to support an immediate substantial reduction of our troops there?

VERY WILLING SOMEWHAT WILLING SOMEWHAT UNWILLING VERY UNWILLING

6. Turning now to domestic politics . . . we have noticed that people do a variety of things during political campaigns. Would you please indicate which of the following, if any, you have done . . . Have you ever . . .

...voted in a national election? YES NO About how many times? ______
...worked for a political party? YES NO In how many campaigns? ______
...worked for a particular candidate? YES NO How many times? ______
...run for public office? YES NO How many times? ______
...worked for a community organization dealing with a social issue?
YES NO How many times? ______
...served as an officer in any political group?
YES NO How many times? ______
...voted in a local election? ALWAYS OFTEN SOMETIMES NEVER
...contributed money to a candidate? YES NO
...tried to influence someone about an issue or a candidate? YES NO

7. Recently, there has been a great deal of talk about health care. Do you feel the federal government ought to do more to help people get doctors and hospital care at low cost? YES NO

8. Have you had a surgical operation in the last ten years? YES NO
(IF YES) Were you satisfied with the care you received in the hospital? YES NO

9. In the last few years how often have you visited a doctor?

NOT AT ALL RARELY SEVERAL TIMES FAIRLY REGULARLY
(IF YOU VISITED) Were you satisfied with the attention and care you received?
YES NO

10. Returning to some foreign policy questions . . . Looking ahead several years after the war ends in Vietnam . . . how likely do you feel it is that U.S. troops will become involved in another shooting conflict?

VERY LIKELY SOMEWHAT LIKELY SOMEWHAT UNLIKELY VERY UNLIKELY

11. Do you feel that the world has become so complicated today, that many people have lost control over a great deal of what happens to them?

STRONGLY AGREE AGREE DISAGREE STRONGLY DISAGREE

12. Different groups are working to end our involvement in Vietnam, but there is disagreement over how quickly we should leave. How willing would you be to support a total withdrawal of U.S. troops by the end of 1971?

VERY WILLING SOMEWHAT WILLING SOMEWHAT UNWILLING VERY UNWILLING

13. Turning once again to domestic politics . . . it has often been noted that some Americans do not limit their political involvement activity to election campaigns. Have you ever done any of the following? . . .

...written to a public official or newspaper to let them know how you feel? YES NO
How many times? ____________
...signed a petition for or against some issue? YES NO
...attended a protest rally of any sort? YES NO How many times? ________
...been on a picket line during a labor dispute? YES NO How many times? _______
...broken a law to dramatize your feelings about an issue? YES NO How often? ______
...taken part in a sit-in? YES NO About how many times? __________
...been involved in any physical confrontations (pushing, shoving, etc.) during any of the above? YES NO How many times? ________

14. Some people seem to follow what is going on in government all the time; others have less interest. How often do you follow what is going on in the government?

MOST OF THE TIME SOME OF THE TIME NOW AND THEN HARDLY AT ALL

15. Thinking about the federal government, how much effect do you think its activities, the laws passed, and so on, have on your life?

A GREAT EFFECT SOME EFFECT A VERY SMALL EFFECT NO EFFECT

16. Are you satisfied with that, or do you wish the federal government had . . .

MORE EFFECT LESS EFFECT on you?

17. Now think about your local government. How much effect do you think its activities have on your day-to-day life?

A GREAT EFFECT SOME EFFECT A VERY SMALL EFFECT NO EFFECT

18. Are you satisfied with that, or do you wish your local government had

MORE EFFECT LESS EFFECT on you?

19. Thinking back to when you have become involved in politics . . . how often have things turned out the way you wanted them to?

0___20___30___40___50___60___70___80___90___100___percent of the time

20. Looking ahead five or six years, how often do you think things will turn out the way you want them to when you get involved in politics?

0___20___30___40___50___60___70___80___90___100___percent of the time.

21. Some people are saying that the government is run by a few big interests looking out for themselves, and not for all the people. Do you . . .

STRONGLY AGREE AGREE DISAGREE STRONGLY DISAGREE

There as been a lot of talk recently about the "quality of life" here in the United States. Some people are saying that everything is getting too complicated, that people are not as friendly as they used to be, and that generally things do not seem to work the way they used to . . . others say all of this is exaggerated. We would like to get your feelings on some of these issues/questions . . .

22. Some people have said that, given human nature, there will always be social problems like poverty and discrimination. How do you feel? Do you . . .

STRONGLY AGREE   AGREE   DISAGREE   STRONGLY DISAGREE

23. Would you agree that if you don't watch yourself today, people will take advantage of you?

STRONGLY AGREE   AGREE   DISAGREE   STRONGLY DISAGREE

24. Have you found in meeting people that it doesn't pay to try too hard to please people, because if they like you they like you, and if they don't, there isn't much you can do?

STRONGLY AGREE   AGREE   DISAGREE   STRONGLY DISAGREE

25. Would you say that today most people are inclined to look out for themselves, or more inclined to help others?

LOOK OUT FOR THEMSELVES   HELP OTHERS

26. Some people feel that getting ahead today depends more on knowing the right people than doing a good job. How do you feel? Do you . . .

STRONGLY AGREE   AGREE   DISAGREE   STRONGLY DISAGREE

27. With the current job market, some people feel that getting a good job is just/mostly a matter of being in the right place at the right time. Do you . . .

STRONGLY AGREE   AGREE   DISAGREE   STRONGLY DISAGREE

28. In your life, generally, do you ever find yourself wishing you could return to a less complicated, less demanding way of life?

OFTEN   SOMETIMES   NEVER

29. How much effect lo you think "luck" or "chance" plays in your life?

A GREAT DEAL OF EFFECT   MUCH EFFECT   SOME EFFECT   NO EFFECT

(IF "MUCH," "SOME," OR "GREAT DEAL") Do you feel it has generally been
GOOD   or   BAD   luck.

30. Do you think that the government has become so large and powerful that it is almost impossible for an individual citizen to have much influence on what happens in government?

YES   NO

31. When you think of your own ideas and those of government officials, do you feel that there is . . .

A VERY WIDE GAP   A WIDE GAP   A SMALL GAP   NO GAP

32. There are many different ways to try to influence the government, but people today are often in disagreement about which ones are effective. HOW EFFECTIVE WOULD YOU SAY THAT EACH OF THE FOLLOWING IS IN MAKING THE GOVERNMENT PAY ATTENTION TO WHAT PEOPLE THINK? (Please circle your answer)

...voting   EFFECTIVE   1 2 3 4 5   INEFFECTIVE

...trying to personally influence someone on an issue or a candidate
EFFECTIVE 1 2 3 4 5 INEFFECTIVE

...writing to public officials and newspapers to express your views
EFFECTIVE 1 2 3 4 5 INEFFECTIVE

...contributing money to a campaign	EFFECTIVE	1 2 3 4 5	INEFFECTIVE
...sit-ins	EFFECTIVE	1 2 3 4 5	INEFFECTIVE
...attending political meetings	EFFECTIVE	1 2 3 4 5	INEFFECTIVE
...political parties	EFFECTIVE	1 2 3 4 5	INEFFECTIVE
...mass demonstrations	EFFECTIVE	1 2 3 4 5	INEFFECTIVE

...breaking a law to dramatize opposition to a policy
EFFECTIVE 1 2 3 4 5 INEFFECTIVE

...taking part in some sort of violence during a protest
EFFECTIVE 1 2 3 4 5 INEFFECTIVE

...assassination of a government official
EFFECTIVE 1 2 3 4 5 INEFFECTIVE

...picketing	EFFECTIVE	1 2 3 4 5	INEFFECTIVE
...being an informed citizen	EFFECTIVE	1 2 3 4 5	INEFFECTIVE

33. Is there a political group that adequately represents your views?

YES NO NOT SURE

(IF YES) Which political group is that? ____________________

34. Do you feel that each citizen has the obligation to work for better government?

STRONGLY AGREE AGREE DISAGREE STRONGLY DISAGREE

35. Do you feel that citizens should always take the time to vote?

STRONGLY AGREE AGREE DISAGREE STRONGLY DISAGREE

Following are a number of pairs of words that might be used to describe the <u>GOVERNMENT IN WASHINGTON</u>. Note that the words describe opposites on a continuum, for example, ACTIVE versus PASSIVE. Please circle the number between the pair of words that best describes the <u>GOVERNMENT</u>. As an example, using the first pair of words, a "1" is more ACTIVE (and therefore, less PASSIVE) than a "2," and a "6" is more PASSIVE (and less ACTIVE) than a "5."

36a.	ACTIVE	1	2	3	4	5	6	7	PASSIVE
b.	RIGID	1	2	3	4	5	6	7	PLIABLE
c.	INEFFECTIVE	1	2	3	4	5	6	7	EFFECTIVE
d.	CONSISTENT	1	2	3	4	5	6	7	INCONSISTENT
e.	REWARDING	1	2	3	4	5	6	7	PUNISHING
f.	UNPREDICTABLE	1	2	3	4	5	6	7	PREDICTABLE
g.	INITIATING	1	2	3	4	5	6	7	REACTING

h.	COMPLEX	1	2	3	4	5	6	7	SIMPLE
i.	IMPOTENT	1	2	3	4	5	6	7	POWERFUL

NOW . . . USING THE SAME DIRECTION AS ABOVE, CIRCLE THE NUMBER BETWEEN THE PAIRS OF WORDS THAT BEST DESCRIBES YOURSELF.

37a.	PAST ORIENTED	1	2	3	4	5	6	7	FUTURE ORIENTED
b.	ACTIVE	1	2	3	4	5	6	7	PASSIVE
c.	DECISIVE	1	2	3	4	5	6	7	HESITANT
d.	REACTING	1	2	3	4	5	6	7	INITIATING
e.	EFFECTIVE	1	2	3	4	5	6	7	INEFFECTIVE
f.	IMPOTENT	1	2	3	4	5	6	7	POWERFUL
g.	LUCKY	1	2	3	4	5	6	7	UNLUCKY
h.	DOER	1	2	3	4	5	6	7	THINKER
i.	COMMITTED	1	2	3	4	5	6	7	APATHETIC

38. Please indicate all Brothers and Sisters in their age order by listing them as B's and S's. Below each B and S, write in the year of birth. Be sure to include yourself in this list by placing an X in the appropriate place within the list.

____

____

____

Appendix D

SCALE AND INDEX ITEMS

Internal-External Control Items for Parents and Students

1. Do you feel that world affairs have become so complex that even our elected officials have difficulty keeping control of events?

2. Looking ahead several years after the war ends in Vietnam how likely do you feel it is that U.S. troops will become involved in another shooting conflict?

3. Do you feel that the world has become so complicated that many people have lost control over a great deal of what happens to them?

4. Some people say the government is run by a few big interests looking out for themselves, and not for all the people. How do you feel?

5. Some people feel that getting ahead today depends more on knowing the right people than on doing a good job. How do you feel?

6. With the current job market some people feel that getting a good job is mostly a matter of being in the right place at the right time. How do you feel?

7. In your life generally, do you ever find yourself wishing that you could return to a less complicated, less demanding way of life?

8. How much of an effect do you think luck or chance plays in your life?

9. Do you think that the government has become so large and powerful that it is almost impossible for an individual citizen to have much influence?

10. Have you found that in meeting people it doesn't pay to try too hard to make them like you, because if they like you they like you and if they don't there isn't much you can do?

Faith in People Index

1. Would you agree that if you don't watch yourself today, people will take advantage of you?

2. Would you say today that most people are inclined to look out for themselves or to help others?

Individual versus System Blame Index

1. There has been a lot of talk recently about the deterioration of the quality of life in this country. Some people feel that each individual person is responsible while others feel that the real responsibility lies with certain powerful groups in government and industry. How do you feel?

2. Do you feel that the best way to improve the way things are is to stress that each person must begin to take responsibility for the way things are, or do you feel that change is better brought about by pressure and collective social action?

3. There's been a lot of talk recently about racial discrimination. Some

Note: All scale and index items correlate at .01 or better with each other.

people say that it is lack of skills and ability that keep people from getting jobs, while others say that even if a black were qualified, a white person with the same training would get the job. Which do you feel is closer to the way things are?

Political Alienation Index

1. When you think of your own ideas and those of the government do you feel there is a wide gap . . . a very wide gap . . . a small gap . . . or no gap at all?

2. Do you believe that the government represents people with your social and political beliefs?

3. Does the government seem unable or unwilling to do the things that you feel should be done?

Civic Obligation Index

1. Do you feel that every citizen has the obligation to work for a better government?

2. Do you feel that every citizen should always take the time to vote?

Faith in Government Index

1. Honest- __ __ __ __ __ __ __ __ Dishonest

2. Open - __ __ __ __ __ __ __ __ Closed

3. Trustworthy- __ __ __ __ __ __ Untrustworthy

Government Accessability Index

1. Active __ __ __ __ __ __ __ __ Passive

2. Initiating __ __ __ __ __ __ __ Reacting

3. Decisive __ __ __ __ __ __ __ Indecisive

Political Time Orientation Index

1. It has been suggested that it is no longer necessary to keep our troops stationed in Western Europe. How willing would you be to support an <u>immediate</u> substantial withdrawal of troops there?

2. Different groups are working to end our involvement in Vietnam, but there is disagreement about how quickly we should leave. How willing would you be to support a total withdrawal of U.S. troops within the next two months?

Political Participation Behaviors

1. Working for a political party

2. Working for a particular political candidate

3. Working for a community organization dealing with social issues

4. Being an officer in a political group

5. Contributed money to a political party

6. Tried to influence someone on an issue of candidate

7. Written to a public official

8. Signed a petition

9. Attended a mass demonstration

10. Broken a law to dramatize opposition to a law or policy

11. Taken part in a sit-in

12. Taken part in a physical confrontation (pushing, shoving, etc.) during any of the above

BIBLIOGRAPHY

Aberbach, Joel, "Alienation and Political Behavior," *American Political Science Review*, 1969, *62*

Adler, Alfred, "Individual Psychology," in C. Murchison (ed.), *Psychologies of 1930* (Worcester, Mass.: Clark University Press, 1930)

Adler, Alfred, *What Life Should Mean to You* (Boston: Little, Brown, 1931)

Adorno, Theodore, *et al.*, *The Authoritarian Personality* (New York: Harper, 1950)

Agger, Robert, *et al.*, "Political Cynicism: Measurement and Meaning," *Journal of Politics*, 1961, *23*

Agger, Robert, *et al.*, *The Ruler and the Ruled: Political Power and Impotence in an American Community* (New York: Wiley & Sons, 1964)

Agnello, T., "Aging and the Sense of Political Powerlessness," *Public Opinion Quarterly*, 1973, *37*

Allardt, Erik and Personen, Pertti, "Citizen Participation in Political Life in Finland," *International Social Science Journal*, 1960, *12*

Allport, Gordon, "Attitudes," in M. Fishbein (ed.), *Readings in Attitude Theory and Measurement* (New York: Wiley & Sons, 1967)

Almond, Gabriel and Verba, Sidney, *The Civic Culture* (Princeton: Princeton University Press, 1963)

Andrain, Charles, *Children and Civic Awareness* (Columbus, Ohio: Charles E. Merrill, 1971)

Andrew, Frank, *et al.*, *Multiple Classification Analysis* (Ann Arbor: Institute for Survey Research, 1968)

Andry, R. G., *Delinquency and Parental Pathology* (London: Methuen, 1960)

Angyal, A., *Foundations for a Science of Personality* (New York: Commonwealth Fund, 1941)

Balch, George, "Multiple Indicators in Survey Research: The Concept Sense of Political Efficacy," paper presented to the American Political Science Association Meeting, Chicago, 1971

Banfield, E., *The Moral Basis of a Backward Society* (New York: The Free Press, 1958)

Barber, James, *Citizen Politics* (Chicago: Markham, 1961)

Becker, Wesley, "Consequences of Different Kinds of Parental Discipline," in M. Hoffman and L. Hoffman (eds.), *Review of Child Development Research* (New York: Russell Sage Foundation, 1964)

Becker, W. C., "The Matching of Behavior Ratings and Questionnaire Personality Factors," *Psychological Bulletin*, 1960, 57

Bell, Daniel (ed.), *Towards the Year 2000* (Boston: Houghton Mifflin, 1968)

Berelson, Bernard, *et al.*, *Voting* (Chicago: University of Chicago Press, 1954)

Bert, C., *The Young Delinquent* (New York: Appleton, 1929)

Bettleheim, Bruno, "Individual and Mass Behavior in Extreme Situations," *Journal of Abnormal and Social Psychology*, 1943, 38

Blau, Peter, *Exchange and Power in Social Life* (New York: Wiley & Sons, 1967)

Bossard, J. H. S., and Boll, E. S., *The Large Family System* (Philadelphia: University of Pennsylvania Press, 1956)

Boulding, Kenneth, *The Meaning of the 20th Century* (New York: Harper & Row, 1964)

Bowlby, John, *Attachment* (New York: Basic Books, 1966)

Boynton, G. R. *et al.*, "The Structure of Public Support for Legislative Institutions," *Midwest Journal of Political Science*, 1968, *12*

Brown, N. O., *Life Against Death* (New York: Random House, 1959)

Buckley, Walter, *Sociology and Modern Systems Theory* (Englewood Cliffs, N.J.: Prentice-Hall, 1967)

Buhler, Charlotte, "The Reality Principle," *American Journal of Psychotherapy*, 1954, 8

Butler, R. A., "Exploratory and Related Behavior: A New Trend in Animal Research," *Journal of Individual Psychology*, 1958, *14*

Campbell, A., *et al.*, *The American Voter* (New York: Wiley & Sons, 1960)

Campbell, Angus, Eurin, Gerald, and Miller, Warren, *The Voter Decides* (Evanston, Ill.: Row, Peterson, 1954)

Clausen, John, "Family Structure Socialization and Personality," in M. Hoffman and L. Hoffman (eds.), *Review of Child Development Research* (New York: Russell Sage Foundation, 1966)

Converse, Philip E., "The Nature of Belief Systems in Mass Publics," in David Apter (ed.), *Ideology and Discontent* (New York: Free Press, 1965)

Crandall, M. J., "Achievement," in H. Stevenson (ed.), *Child Psychology* (Chicago: University of Chicago Press, 1964)

Crandall, V. C., *et al.*, "Children's Beliefs in Their Own Control of Reinforcements in Intellectual-Academic Achievement Situations," *Child Development*, 1965, *36*

Cutler, Neal, "Generation Maturation and Party Affiliation: A Cohort Analysis," *Public Opinion Quarterly*, 1970, *33*

Curry, R. L., Jr., and Wade, L. L., *A Theory of Political Exchange* (Englewood Cliffs, N.J.: Prentice-Hall, 1966)

Dahl, Robert, *A Preface to Democratic Theory* (Chicago: University of Chicago Press, 1956)

Dahl, Robert, *Who Governs?* (New Haven: Yale University Press, 1961)

Dashiell, J. F., "A Quantitative Demonstration of Animal Drive," *Journal of Comparative Psychology*, 1925, *5*

Davies, James, *Human Nature and Politics* (New York: Wiley & Sons, 1964)

Davis, K., "Final Note on a Case of Extreme Isolation," *American Sociological Review*, 1956, *4*

Davis, Lane, "The Cost of Realism: Contemporary Restatements of Democracy," *Western Political Quarterly*, 1964, *17*

Dean, D., "Alienation, Its Meaning and Measurement," *American Sociological Review*, 1959, *26*

de Charms, Richard, *Personal Causation* (New York: Academic Press, 1968)

de Charms, R., Capender, V., and Kuperman, A., "The 'Origin-Pawn' Variable in Personal Perception," *Sociometry*, 1965, *4* de Charms, R., and Dave, P. N., "Hope of Success, Fear of Failure, Subjective Probability and Risk-Taking Behavior," *Journal of Personality and Social Psychology*, 1965

Dennis, Jack, "Support for the Institution of Elections by the Mass Public," *American Political Science Review*, 1970, 64

Dennis, Jack, "Support for the Party System by the Mass Public," *American Political Science Review*, 1966, 60

Distler, L. S., "Patterns of Parental Identification," unpublished doctoral dissertation, University of California, 1965

Douglass, J. W. B., and Bloom, J. M., *Children Under Five* (London: Allen and Unwin, 1968)

Douvan, E., "Employment and the Adolescent," in F. Nye and L. Hoffman (eds.), *The Employed Mother in America* (Chicago: Rand McNally, 1963)

Easton, David, *A Framework for Political Analysis* (Englewood Cliffs, N.J.: Prentice-Hall, 1965)

Easton, David, *A Systems Analysis of Political Life* (New York: Wiley & Sons, 1965)

Easton, David, and Dennis, Jack, *Children in the Political System: Origins of Political Legitimacy* (New York: McGraw-Hill, 1969)

Easton, David, and Dennis, Jack, "The Child's Acquisition of Regime Norms: Political Efficacy," *The American Political Science Review*, 1967, 61

Edelman, Murray, *The Symbolic Uses of Politics* (Urbana, Ill.: University of Illinois Press, 1967)

Erikson, Erik, *Childhood and Society* (New York: Norton, 1952)

Erikson, Erik, "A Healthy Personality for Every Child: A Fact Finding Report: A Digest," in J. Seidman (ed.), *The Adolescent: A Book of Readings* (New York: Holt, Rinehart & Winston, 1953)

Escalona, S. and Heider, G. M., *Prediction and Outcome* (New York: Basic Books, 1959)

Feather, N. T., "Acceptance and Rejection of Arguments in Relation to Attitude Strength, Critical Ability, and Intolerance of Inconsistency," *Journal of Abnormal and Social Psychology*, 1964, 69

Feifel, H., "Death Relevant Variable in Psychology," in Rollo May (ed.), *Existential Psychology* (New York: Random House, 1960)

Fenichel, O., *The Psychoanalytic Theory of Neurosis* (New York: Norton, 1945)

Finifster, A., "Dimensions of Political Alienation," *The American Political Science Review*, 1970, *64*

Firth, Raymond, *Primitive Polynesian Economy* (London: Routledge, 1939)

Fishman, J. and Solomon, F., "Youth and Social Action," *Journal of Social Issues*, 1964, 2

Forward, John and Williams, Jay, "Internal-External Control and Black Militancy," *Journal of Social Issues*, 1970, *26*

Fraser, John, "The Mistrustful-Efficacious Hypothesis and Political Participation," *Journal of Politics*, 1970, 32

Freud, S., *Beyond the Pleasure Principle* (London: Hogarth Press, 1955)

Freud, S., *New Introductory Lectures on Psychoanalysis* (New York: Norton, 1933)

Freud, S., *An Outline of Psychoanalysis* (New York: Norton, 1949)

Gamson, William, "Stable Unrepresentation in American Society," *American Behavioral Scientist*, 1968, *12*

George, Alexander, "Some Uses of Dynamic Psychology in Political Biography: Case Materials on Woodrow Wilson," in F. Greenstein and M. Lerner (eds.), *A Source Book for the Study of Personality and Politics* (Chicago: Markham, 1971)

George, A. L., and George, J. L., *Woodrow Wilson and Colonel House: A Personality Study* (New York: Dover, 1964)

Glass, David, "Theories of Consistency and the Study of Personality," in E. Borgatta and W. Lambert (eds.), *Handbook of Personality Theory and Research* (Chicago: Rand McNally, 1968)

Goffman, Erving, *The Presentation of Self in Everyday Life* (New York: Anchor, 1959)

Gold, M., *Status Forces in Delinquent Boys* (Ann Arbor: Institute for Social Research, 1963)

Goldstein, Kurt, *The Organism* (New York: American Press, 1939)

Gore, P., and Rotter, J., "A Personality Correlate of Social Action," *Journal of Social Issues*, 1963, 31

Greenstein, Fred, *Children and Politics* (New Haven: Yale University Press, 1965)

Greenstein, Fred, *Personality and Politics* (Chicago: Markham, 1969)

Greenstein, Fred, "Political Psychology: A Pluralistic Universe," in J. Knutson (ed.), *Handbook of Political Psychology* (San Francisco: Jossey-Bass, 1973)

Gurin, Patricia, *et al.*, "Internal-External Control in the Motivational Dynamics of Negro Youth," *Journal of Social Issues*, 1969, 55

Harlow, H. F., *et al.*, "Learning Motivated by a Manipulation Drive," *Journal of Experimental Psychology*, 1950, 40

Harlow, H. F., *et al.*, "Manipulatory Motivation in the Infant Rhesus Monkey," *Journal of Comparative Physiological Psychology*, 1956, 49

Hartman, Harry, "Comments on the Psychoanalytic Theory of the Ego," *Psychoanalytic Study of the Child*, 1943, 314

Heider, Franz, *The Psychology of Interpersonal Relations* (New York: Wiley & Sons, 1958)

Hendrick, I., "The Discussion of the Instinct to Master," *Psychoanalytic Quarterly*, 1943, 12

Hess, Robert, "The Acquisition of Feelings of Political Efficacy in Pre-Adults," in G. Abcarian and J. Soule (eds.), *Social Psychology and Political Behavior* (Columbus, O.: Charles E. Merrill, 1971)

Hess, Robert and Tourney, Judith, *The Development of Political Attitudes in Children* (New York: Doubleday, 1967)

Hetherington, E. M., "A Developmental Study of the Effects of Sex of the Dominant Parent on Sex-Role Preference, Identification, and Imitation in Children," *Journal of Personality and Social Psychology*, 1965, 2

Hinkley, D., *Village in Vietnam* (New Haven, Yale University Press, 1966)

Hoffman, R. W., "The Father's Role in the Family and in the Child's Peer Group Adjustment," *Merrit-Palmer Quarterly*, 1961, 7

Hollander, Steve, "Idiosyncratic Credit," in I. David Singer (ed.), *Human Behavior and International Politics* (Chicago: Rand McNally, 1966)

Horney, Karen, *Neurotic Personality of Our Times* (New York: Norton, 1937)

Horney, Karen, *Our Inner Conflicts* (New York: Norton, 1945)

Horton, J. E., and Thompson, W. "Powerlessness and Political Negativism," *American Journal of Sociology*, 1962, 67

Itamsher, J. H., *et al.*, "Interpersonal Trust, Internal-External Control and the Warren Commission Report," *Journal of Personality and Social Psychology*, 1968, 9

Jennings, Kent M., and Niemi, Richard, "The Division of Political Labor Between Mothers and Fathers," *American Political Science Review*, 1971, 65

Jennings, Kent M., and Niemi, Richard, "The Transmission of Political Values from Parent to Child," *The American Political Science Review*, 1968, 62

Kagen, J, and Moss, H., *Birth to Maturity* (New York: Wiley & Sons, 1962)

Kardiner, A. and Spiegel, H., *War Stress and Neurotic Illness* (New York: Hoeber, 1947)

Kauffman, Arnold, *Existentialism* (New York: Bantam, 1967)

Kavanau, J. L., "Behavior of Captive White-footed Mice," *Science*, 1967, *155*

Keniston, Kenneth, "The Sources of Student Dissent," *Journal of Social Issues*, 1967, 4

Keniston, Kenneth, *The Uncommitted* (New York: Basic Books, 1965)

Key, V. O., *Public Opinion and American Democracy* (New York: Alfred A. Knopf, 1961)

Klecka, William, "Identifying Political Generations," mimeo., Northwestern University, Department of Political Science

Knutson, Jeanne, *The Human Basis of the Polity* (Chicago: Aldine, 1972)

Kohn, M. L., "Social Class and Parent-Child Relationships: An Interpretation," *American Journal of Sociology,* 1963, *68*

Kohn, M. L., "Social Class and Parental Values," *American Journal of Sociology,* 1959, *64*

Kroeber, A. L., and Kluckhohn, Clyde, *Culture: A Critical Review of Concepts and Definitions* (Cambridge, Mass., Harvard University Press, 1952)

Lane, Robert, *Political Ideology* (New York: Free Press, 1962)

Lane, Robert, *Political Life* (New York: Free Press, 1959)

Lane, Robert, *Political Man* (New York: Free Press, 1973)

LaPiere, "Attitudes vs. Actions," *Social Forces,* 1934, *13*

Leftwich, Richard, *The Price System and Resource Allocation* (New York: Holt, Rinehart, & Winston, 1966)

Leventhal, H., *et al.,* "Authoritarianism, Ideology, and Political Candidate Choice," *Journal of Abnormal and Social Psychology,* 1964, *69*

Levy, D. M., *Maternal Overprotection* (New York: Columbia University Press, 1954)

Linsky, Arnold, "A Factorial Experiment in Inducing Responses to a Mail Questionnaire," *Sociology and Social Research,* 1965, *49*

Lipset, Seymour Martin, *Political Man* (Garden City, N.Y.: Doubleday, 1960)

Lipsky, S., "Protest as a Social Resource," *American Political Science Review,* 1967, *3*

Liverant, S., and Scodel, A., "Internal-External Control Dimensions as Determinants of Decision Making Under Conditions of Risk," *Psychological Reports,* 1960, *7*

Longworth, Donald, "Use of a Mail Questionnaire," *American Sociological Review,* 1953, *18*

Lyons, Schley, "The Political Socialization of Ghetto Children: Efficacy and Cynicism," *Journal of Politics,* Spring, 1970, *32*

McDill, Edward and Ridley, Jeanne, "Status, Anomie, Political Alienation, and Political Participation," *American Journal of Sociology,* 1962, *67*

McGever, Pat, "The Sources of Impatient Demands," unpublished Ph.D. dissertation, University of Pennsylvania, 1971

McKeon, Richard (ed.), *The Basic Works of Aristotle* (New York: Oxford University Press, 1941)

Malcolm X., *The Autobiography of Malcolm X* (New York: Grove Press, 1964)

Malinowski, Bronislaw, *Argonauts of the Western Pacific* (London: Routledge, 1922)

Marquis, D. P., "Learning in the Neonate: The Modification of Behavior Under Three Feeding Schedules," *Journal of Experimental Psychology*, 1941, 29

Maslow, A., *Motivation and Personality* (New York: Harper, 1954)

Maslow, A., "A Theory of Human Motivation," *Psychological Review*, 1943, 50

May, Rollo, *et al.* (eds.), *Existence* (*A New Dimension in Psychiatry and Psychology*) (New York: Basic Books, 1958)

Mead, Margaret, *New Lives for Old: Cultural Transformations —1928–1953* (New York: Morrow, 1957)

Merriam, Charles, *The Making of Citizens* (Chicago: University of Chicago Press, 1930)

Merriam, Charles, and Gosnell, H., *Non-Voting* (Chicago: University of Chicago Press, 1924)

Milbrath, Lester, *Political Participation* (Chicago: Rand McNally, 1965)

Mittlemann, B., "Motility in Infants, Children, and Adults," *Psychoanalytic Study of the Child*, 1954, 9

Montgomery, K. C., "The Role of the Exploratory Drive in Learning," *Journal of Comparative Physiological Psychology*, 1954, 47

Mussen, Paul, *et al.*, *Child Development and Personality* (New York: Harper and Row, 1969)

Neal, A. and Rettig, S., "On the Multidimensionality of Alienation," *American Sociological Review*, 1967, 31

Neubauer, Deane, "Some Conditions of Democracy," *American Political Science Review*, 1967, 3

Niemi, Richard, "Review of Children in the Political System," *American Political Science Review*, 1970, 64

Ogborn, William, *On Culture and Social Change* (Chicago: University of Chicago Press, 1964)

Olsen, Marvin, "Alienation and Political Opinions," *Public Opinion Quarterly*, 1965, 29

Osgood, C., *et al.*, *The Measurement of Meaning* (Urbana: University of Illinois Press, 1967)

Piaget, Jean, *The Origins of Intelligence in Children* (New York: International University Press, 1952)

Phares, E. G., "Perceptual Threshold Decrements as a Function of Skill and Chance Expectancies," *Journal of Psychology*, 1961, 53

Pierce, Bessie, *Civic Attitudes in American School Textbooks* (Chicago: University of Chicago Press, 1930)

Pinner, G., "Parental Overprotection and Political Distrust," *Annals of the American Academy of Political and Social Science*, 1965, 361

Posner, M., "Components of Skilled Performance," *Science*, 1966, 21

Ranney, Austin, and Kendally, Willmoore, *Democracy and the American Party System* (New York: Harcourt, Brace & World, 1956)

Renshon, Stanley, "Birth Order, Personality Development and Political Socialization," in D. Schwartz and S. Schwartz (eds.), *New Directions in Political Socialization Research* (New York: Free Press, 1974)

Renshon, Stanley, "Personality and Family Dynamics in the Political Socialization Process," paper presented to the annual meeting of the American Political Science Association, New Orleans, La., 1973

Renshon, Stanley, "The Role of Personality Development in the Political Socialization Process," in D. Schwartz and S. Schwartz (eds.), *New Directions in the Study of Political Socialization* (New York: Free Press, 1974)

Renshon, Stanley, *Personality Theories and Political Analysis* (New York: Free Press, forthcoming)

Robinson, John, *et al.*, *Measures of Political Attitudes* (Ann Arbor: Institute of Social Research, 1968)

Rocher, G. Alan, "Effective Techniques in Increasing Responses to Mailed Questionnaires," *Public Opinion Quarterly*, 1963, 27

Rogers, Carl, *On Becoming a Person* (New York: Mifflin, 1955)

Rokeach, Milton, *The Open and Closed Mind* (New York: Basic Books, 1960)

Rokkan, Stein, "Cross-National Studies in Political Participation," *International Social Science Journal*, 1950, *44*

Rosen, B., "The Achievement Syndrome, " *American Sociological Review*, 1956, *21*

Rosen, B. C., "Family Structure and Achievement Motivation," *American Sociological Review*, 1961, *26*

Rosenberg, M., "Misanthropy and Political Ideology," *American Sociological Review*, 1956, *21*

Rosenberg, Morris, "Some Determinants of Political Apathy," *Public Opinion Quarterly*, 1954, *26*

Rotter, J. B., "Generalized Expectancies for Internal versus External Control of Reinforcement," *Psychological Monographs: General and Applied*, 1966, *80*

Rotter, J. B., *Social Learning and Clinical Psychology* (Englewood Cliffs, N.J.: Prentice-Hall, 1954)

Rotter, Julian, "External Control and Internal Control," *Psychology Today*, 1971, *5*

Rotter, J. B., *et al.*, "The Growth and Extinction of Expectancies in Chance Controlled and Skilled Tests," *Journal of Psychology*, 1961, *52*

Rotter, J., *et al.*, "Internal versus External Control of Reinforcement: A Major Variable in Behavior Theory," in N. E. Washburne (ed.), *Decisions, Values and Groups* (New York: Pergamon, 1962)

Sampson, E. E., "Birth Order, Need Achievement, and Conformity," *Journal of Abnormal and Social Psychology*, 1962, *64*

Sampson, E. E., "The Study of Ordinal Position," in B. Mayer (ed.), *Advances in Experimental Personality Research* (New York: Academic Press, 1965)

Samuelson, Paul, *Economics* (New York: McGraw-Hill, 1967)

Schachtel, E. G., *Metamorphosis* (New York: Basic Books, 1959)

Schachter, S. *The Psychology of Affiliation* (Stanford, University of California Press, 1959)

Schaefer, E. S., "A Circumplex Model for Maternal Behavior," *Journal of Abnormal and Social Psychology*, 1959, *59*

Schattschneider, E. E., *The Semi-Sovereign People* (New York: Holt, Rhinehart, & Winston, 1960)

Schwartz, David and Renshon, Stanley, "Social Orientations and Political Alienation in Confrontation Politics," in David Schwartz, *Political Alienation and Political Behavior* (Chicago: Aldine, 1973)

Sears, P., "Doll Play Aggression in Normal Young Children: Influence of Sex, Age, Sibling Status, Father's Absence," *Psychological Monographs*, 1951, 65

Sears, *et al.*, *Patterns of Child Rearing* (Evanston, Ill.: Row, Peterson, 1957)

Seeman, Melvin, "Alienation, Membership, and Political Knowledge," *Public Opinion Quarterly*, 1966, 30

Seeman, M., "On the Meaning of Alienation," *American Sociological Review*, 1959, 24

Seeman, M., "Powerlessness and Knowledge: A Comparative Study of Alienation and Learning," *Sociometry*, 1967, 30

Seeman, M., and Evans, J., "Alienation and Learning in a Hospital Setting," *American Sociological Review*, 1962, 27

Shirley, M., "Children's Adjustment to a Strange Situation," *Journal of Abnormal and Social Psychology*, 1942, 37

Sigel, Roberta, "Bases of Political and Civic Involvement Among Rural High School Youths—Internal-External Control and Involvement," paper presented to the annual meeting of the American Political Science Association, Chicago, 1971

Simmons, J. L., "Liberalism, Alienation, and Personal Disturbance," *Sociology and Social Research*, 1965, 49

Simmons, J. L., "Some Intercorrelations Among Alienation Measures," *Social Forces*, 1966, 44

Simon, H., *Models of Man* (New York: Wiley & Sons, 1957)

Skolnick, Jerome, *The Politics of Protest* (New York: Simon & Schuster, 1970)

Smelser, W., "Adolescent and Adult Occupational Choice as a Function of Family Socio-economic History," *Sociometry*, 1963, 26

Sorensen, Theodore, *Kennedy* (New York: Harper & Row, 1965)

Srole, Leo, "Social Integration and Certain Corollaries," *American Sociological Review*, 1956, 21

Staler, Phillip, "Parental Role Differential," *American Journal of Sociology*, 1961, 67

Steinstrager, James, "Political Socialization and Political Theory," *Social Research*, Spring, 1968, 35

Struening, E. and Richardson, A., "A Factor Analysis of the Alienation, Anomie, and Authoritarian Domain," *American Sociological Review*, 1965, 30

Teger, Allan I., and Renshon, Stanley, "Alienation and Motivation: New Directions in Student Political Behavior," paper presented to the Eastern Psychological Association Meeting, Boston, 1972

Thomas, E. L., "The I-E Scale, Ideological Bias and Political Participation," *Journal of Personality*, 1970, 38

Thomson, Wayne and Horton, John, "Political Alienation as a Force in Political Action," *Social Forces*, 1960, 38

Toffler, Alvin, *Future Shock* (New York: Bantam, 1970)

Torney, Judith V., "Structural Dimensions of Children's Political Attitude-concept Systems: A Study of Developmental and Measurement Aspects," unpublished Ph.D. dissertation, University of Chicago, 1965

Troop, W., and MacDonald, A. P., "Internal-External Laws of Control: A Bibliography," *Psychological Reports*, 1971, 28

Vaillancourt, Pauline, *The Political Socialization of Young People: A Panel Survey of Youngsters in the San Francisco Bay Area*, unpublished Ph.D. dissertation, Berkeley, University of California, 1970

Vaillancourt, Pauline, "The Stability of Children's Political Orientations: A Panel Study," paper presented to the American Political Science Association, Los Angeles, 1970

Waldman, Sidney, *Foundations of Political Action: An Exchange Theory of Politics* (Boston: Little, Brown, 1973).

Walker, Jack, "A Critique of the Elitist Theory of Democracy," *American Political Science Review*, 1966, 60

Welch, S., and Clark, C., "Political Efficacy as an Underlying Political Orientation: The Problem of Attitudinal Instability," unpublished manuscript, 1973

White, Elliot, "Intelligence and the Sense of Political Efficacy in Children," *Journal of Politics*, 1968, 30

Williams, C. B. and Nickels, J. B., "Internal-External Control Dimensions as Related to Accident and Suicide Proneness," *Journal of Consulting and Clinical Psychology*, 1969, 33

Wilson, James and Banfield, Edward, "Political Ethos Revisited," *American Political Science Review*, 1971, 4

Winterbottom, Marion, "The Relation of Need for Achievement to Learning Experiences in Independence and Mastery," in J. W. Atkinson (ed.), *Motives in Fantasy, Action, and Society*, (Princeton: Van Nostrand, 1958)

Wolfenstein, Martha and Mead, Margaret (eds.), *Child-Rearing in Six Cultures* (New York: Morrow, 1966)

Wolin, Sheldon S., *Politics and Vision* (Boston: Little, Brown, 1960)

Wollis, Robert, *Time: Fourth Dimension of the Mind* (New York: Harcourt, Brace & World, 1966)

Woodward, Julian L. and Roper, Elmo, "Political Activity of American Citizens," *American Political Science Review*, 1950, *44*

Yuo, S., *The Burmese Way* (London: Nortlidge, 1937)

Zelditch, Morris, "Role Differentiation in the Nuclear Family," in Talcott Parsons, *et al.*, *Family, Socialization and Interaction Process* (Glencoe: Free Press, 1955)

Zimbardo, P. G. and Miller, N. E., "Facilitation of Exploration by Hunger in Rats," *Journal of Comparative Physiological Psychology*, 1958, *51*

INDEXES

AUTHOR INDEX

SUBJECT INDEX